# Reaching Potentials:
## Appropriate Curriculum and Assessment for Young Children

### Volume
# 1

# Reaching Potentials:
## Appropriate Curriculum and Assessment for Young Children

### Volume 1

**Sue Bredekamp and Teresa Rosegrant, Editors**

**National Association for the Education of Young Children**
**Washington, DC**

**National Association for the Education of Young Children (NAEYC)**
**1509 16th Street, N.W.**
**Washington, DC 20036–1426**
**202–232–8777 or 1–800–424–2460**

The National Association for the Education of Young Children attempts through its publications programs to provide a forum for discussion of major issues and ideas in our field. We hope to provoke thought and promote professional growth. Chapter 2 of this volume represents an official position statement of NAEYC and the National Association of Early Childhood Specialists in State Departments of Education. The views expressed or implied in the other chapters are the opinions of the authors and are not necessarily those of NAEYC nor of NAECS/SDE. NAEYC wishes to thank the editors, contributors, and authors, who donated much time and effort to develop this book as a contribution to our profession.

*Library of Congress Catalog Card Number:* 92–085332

*ISBN Catalog Number:* 0–935989–53–6

NAEYC #225

*Book design and production:* Jack Zibulsky; *Copyediting:* Penny Atkins and Betty Nylund Barr

**Printed in the United States of America**

# Contributors

## Editors

**Sue Bredekamp** is the director of professional development for NAEYC and editor of NAEYC's position statements on accreditation, developmentally appropriate practice, and standardized testing. She represented NAEYC on the steering committee that guided the development of the Curriculum and Assessment Guidelines.

**Teresa Rosegrant** is a kindergarten teacher in Arlington County Public Schools in Virginia. She is a former faculty member of George Washington University, State University of New York at Buffalo, and Arizona State University.

## Contributors

**Mary Asper** is a principal of a K–8 school in Alaska and was formerly an early childhood specialist with the Alaska State Department of Education. She represented NAECS/SDE on the steering committee that guided the development of the Curriculum and Assessment Guidelines.

**Donald B. Bailey, Jr.,** is the director of the Frank Porter Graham Child Development Center at the University of North Carolina at Chapel Hill, North Carolina. His primary interests are in issues related to families of infants and young children with disabilities, preschool mainstreaming, and personnel preparation.

**Barbara Bowman** is the director of graduate studies at Erikson Institute, Loyola University of Chicago. She is a past president of NAEYC. Among her current projects is working with the Chicago Public Schools to establish appropriate assessment strategies and parent education.

**Bonnie C. Burchfield** is a teacher of primary-age children at Brownsville Elementary School in Albemarle County, Virginia. She leads workshops and seminars on developmentally appropriate practice and related instructional methods.

**David W. Burchfield** is a teacher of primary-age children at Brownsville Elementary School in Albemarle County, Virginia, and an educational consultant. He works with schools and conducts workshops and seminars on the implementation of developmentally appropriate practice and related instructional methods and strategies.

**Louise Derman-Sparks,** a faculty member of Pacific Oaks College in Pasadena, California, has worked for 25 years with the many-faceted issues of diversity and social justice as a teacher of children and adults, child care center director, researcher, parent, and activitist. She is the author of NAEYC's best-selling *Anti-Bias Curriculum: Tools for Empowering Young Children.*

**Harriet A. Egertson** is the administrator in the Office of Child Development, Nebraska Department of Education. She is a past president of NAECS/SDE and the Nebraska AEYC, and she contributed to the development of the Curriculum and Assessment Guidelines.

**Linda Espinosa** is the director of primary education and child development services for the Redwood City School District in Redwood City, California. She is a member of the NAEYC Governing Board and represented NAEYC on the steering committee that guided the development of the Curriculum and Assessment Guidelines.

**Victoria R. Fu** is a professor in the Department of Family and Child Development at Virginia Polytechnic Institute and State University in Blacksburg, Virginia. She is a former member of the NAEYC Governing Board and represented NAEYC on the Curriculum and Assessment Guidelines steering committee.

**Tynette W. Hills** is the coordinator of early childhood education for the New Jersey State Department of Education. She represented NAECS/SDE on the steering committee for the Curriculum and Assessment Guidelines and is currently serving as president of NAECS/SDE.

**Chalmer Moore, Jr.,** is retired from the Early Childhood Unit of the Illinois State Board of Education. He served as president of NAECS/SDE during the development of the Curriculum and Assessment Guidelines and served on the steering committee.

**Alice Paul** is an associate professor in the Division of Teaching and Teacher Education at the University of Arizona in Tucson. She is a former member of the NAEYC Governing Board and represented NAEYC on the steering committee that guided the development of the Curriculum and Assessment Guidelines.

**Joseph Showell** is an early childhood specialist with the Maryland State Department of Education. He represented NAECS/SDE on the steering committee that guided the development of the Curriculum and Assessment Guidelines.

**Phillip S. Strain** is the director of the early childhood intervention program at the Allegheny-Singer Research Institute in Pittsburgh, Pennsylvania. His primary interests are in the development and evaluation of integrated services for children with autism and children's social development within those arrangements.

**Mark Wolery** is senior research scientist at the Allegheny-Singer Research Institute in Pittsburgh, Pennsylvania. His primary interests are in issues related to preschool mainstreaming and the development and evaluation of instructional methodologies for young children with special needs.

**Liz Wolfe** is the director of bilingual education in the Redwood City School District, Redwood City, California. Her program serves approximately 45% of the total student population of 8,400 students, from kindergarten through Grade 8.

# Contents

## Section I
### REACHING POTENTIALS THROUGH APPROPRIATE CURRICULUM AND ASSESSMENT
1

# Section III
## REACHING POTENTIALS OF ALL CHILDREN
### 113

# Reaching Potentials Through Appropriate Curriculum and Assessment

# Reaching Potentials: Introduction

*Sue Bredekamp and Teresa Rosegrant*

## Curriculum and Assessment Guidelines: Some historical perspective

As with so many things in life, this book and its companion volume are the result of a developmental process. The purpose of this book is to operationalize—that is, make meaningful—the Guidelines for Appropriate Curriculum Content and Assessment, developed jointly by NAEYC and the National Association of Early Childhood Specialists in State Departments of Education (NAECS/SDE) (1991; see pp. 9–27, this volume). Those guidelines are the culmination of more than a decade of work defining best practice for early childhood programs. Much of this activity has been guided by NAEYC, beginning with the development of criteria for accreditation of early childhood programs (NAEYC, 1984, 1991), which led to the development of position statements defining developmentally appropriate practice (Bredekamp, 1987), which in turn led to position statements on testing and other relevant policies (NAECS/SDE, 1987; NAEYC, 1988). Each of these activities met one need while identifying a subsequent one; such is the nature of all developmental processes, and standard setting is also developmental.

By tracing the evolution of the Curriculum and Assessment Guidelines back one decade, we do not mean to oversimplify the lengthy history of early childhood education that includes many initiatives to define best practices (e.g., Davis, Johnson, & Richardson, 1930). It is important to put this work in more complete historical perspective. To do so, we include here an excerpt from a history of standard setting for early childhood education programs in the United States by Dorothy Hewes (1991):

When the International Kindergarten Union (IKU) was established at the National Education Association annual conference in 1892, one of its stated purposes was to elevate the standard of professional training for kindergarten teachers (Hill, 1942). Between 1903 and 1909, during the early years of scientific research studies, the IKU Committee of Nineteen explored diverse ideas about early childhood curriculum and methods. The Committee of Nineteen evolved into 3 subcommittees with overlapping memberships. The Committee maintained a tenuous but amicable debate between groups identified as liberal and conservative. The eventual report (Wheelock, 1913) consisted of three parts: the lengthy conservative statement authored by Susan Blow, an explanation by Patty Smith Hill of what was called the liberal point of view reflecting the influence of progressive education, and a third section by Lucy Wheelock representing a compromise position. To add to the confusion, many committee members signed more than one position statement, and some of those who signed included objections to certain points. Maria Krause-Boelte, for example, one of the few remaining immigrant Froebelians, signed the conservative report but objected to advance scheduling for the year because it interfered with the teacher's ability to respond to children's interests, so she also signed the compromise report which incorporated a more spontaneous program. While much has been made of the differences between liberal and conservative factions within the IKU, all remained Froebelian in their basic philosophy. However, the Committee of Nineteen failed to accomplish the assigned goals of setting standards or establishing clear curriculum guidelines for early childhood education.

We relate this particular event in history because we find it so relevant to our current work. Like the Committee of Nineteen, NAEYC and NAECS/SDE also struggled with the challenge of setting standards for curriculum. The original goal of the curriculum guidelines was to more specifically address the questions of what and when to teach that had not previously been tackled. In fact, the idea for the project originated at a Wingspread Conference on the content of the kindergarten curriculum. NAEYC and NAECS/SDE agreed to work on curriculum and assessment guidelines because each group had identified the need to be more specific about curriculum through attempting to implement developmentally appropriate practice.

When NAEYC produced its position statements on developmentally appropriate practice, they did so in response to specific, identified needs. First, the shorthand phrase *developmentally appropriate* was used throughout the NAEYC accreditation standards. When the accreditation system became operational, it was clear that a more specific definition of developmentally appropriate was needed. A second converging trend that necessitated defining developmentally appropriate was the trend toward more formal, academic instruction of younger and younger children—what has come to be called *downward escalation of curriculum* (Shepard & Smith, 1988). The call for developmentally appropriate practice was in many ways a call for kindergarten and primary grade practices that better reflect what is known about how children develop and learn (what is age appropriate) and practices that are more sensitive to individual and cultural variation (what is individually appropriate). In short, those position statements were designed to meet a specific purpose—to define developmentally appropriate practice, the "how" of teaching young children.

The guidelines for developmentally appropriate practice were not intended to address all aspects of early childhood education programs, and they are relatively silent on what to teach and how to assess. NAEYC realized that the field of early childhood education needed to pay more attention to curriculum and assessment. Through the accreditation experience NAEYC had observed all sorts of curriculum in preschool and child care programs described as "developmentally appropriate" simply because it involved hands-on activity or child choice. At the same time, NAEYC and NAECS/SDE observed kindergarten and primary grade classrooms in which the curriculum objectives were very clear but not appropriate for the age or experience of the children. The Curriculum and Assessment Guidelines were designed to address two basic problems: the "early childhood error" (inadequate attention to the content of the curriculum) and the "elementary error" (overattention to curriculum objectives, with less attention to the individual child).

Standards grow and change in response to new knowledge, the result of learning from the shared experiences of and interaction among professionals. The process that NAEYC uses to develop guidelines and position statements is a consensus-building, peer-review process. Literally thousands of early childhood professionals have had the opportunity to review and provide input into the development of the documents listed above. The results do not necessarily reflect the views of every early childhood practitioner (Walsh, 1991), but the documents result from a consensus-building process and reflect the views of the leadership of the Association at the time of the documents' adoption. Because knowledge expands and changes over time, the Association's positions are reviewed and revised periodically to ensure their currency and accuracy. For example, the accreditation criteria were reviewed and revised in 1991, and the positions on developmentally appropriate practice are currently undergoing review. Throughout all this work, NAEYC has tried to heed the caution of our predecessors regarding standard setting: "It is undesirable . . . that details and practices should become crystalized or even that objectives and standards should be fixed" (Davis, Johnson, & Richardson, 1930, p. 1; quoted in Hewes, 1991).

This brief look at our history demonstrates that the development of the Curriculum and Assessment Guidelines is only part of a long history of discussion within our profession about issues of content and practice. Exploration of the history of curriculum theory in the larger field of education is of equal interest and relevance to this discussion and is well presented elsewhere (Kessler, 1991). To be accurate, we would also need to relate our indebtedness to John Dewey and many others (Greenberg, 1987, 1992). The guidelines certainly reflect this broad historical perspective, but they were also influenced by more recent history—observations of interpretations and misinterpretations of the position statements on developmentally appropriate practice (Bredekamp, 1987), a discussion of which follows.

---

*THE CURRICULUM AND ASSESSMENT GUIDELINES WERE DESIGNED TO ADDRESS TWO BASIC PROBLEMS: THE "EARLY CHILDHOOD ERROR" (INADEQUATE ATTENTION TO THE CONTENT OF THE CURRICULUM) AND THE "ELEMENTARY ERROR" (OVERATTENTION TO CURRICULUM OBJECTIVES, WITH LESS ATTENTION TO THE INDIVIDUAL CHILD).*

---

# Correcting misinterpretations of developmentally appropriate practice (DAP)

NAEYC's purpose in defining developmentally appropriate practice is described above. Response to the document was both overwhelming and surprising. The document was met with considerable interest within and beyond our profession; more than 300,000 copies have been distributed. The construct that early childhood educators have owned for more than a century has been widely adopted (although sometimes misunderstood) by curriculum developers, equipment manufacturers, and even test publishers. While, on the one hand, we celebrate NAEYC's successes in raising public awareness about good programs for young children and advocating for change, we also recognize that misunderstandings are common and myths about developmentally appropriate practice perpetuate (Kostelnik, 1992). Developmentally appropriate practice has also been the subject of thoughtful criticism within the field (Swadener & Kessler, 1991). A few of the issues raised as well as the most common misinterpretations are presented and discussed here because these issues provide some of the context in which the Curriculum and Assessment Guidelines were developed.

© Nancy P. Alexander

## 1. *DAP is not a curriculum, nor is it a rigid set of expectations.*

Developmentally appropriate practice is not a curriculum; it is not a rigid set of standards that dictate practice. Rather, it is a framework, a philosophy, or an approach to working with young children that requires that the adult pay attention to at least two important pieces of information—*what we know* about how children develop and learn and *what we learn* about the individual needs and interests of each child in the group.

Some of the misinterpretations of developmentally appropriate practice result from attending to only one dimension of the definition. For example, some people think that NAEYC advocates one right way to structure a program and wishes to move toward a rigid view of practice in which all programs look alike. This interpretation of the position overemphasizes age appropriateness as a source of the program, an error that might lead to more uniformity than most educators find comfortable; however, good early childhood programs must adapt for individual diversity of all kinds, including the identified special needs of children; the cultural values of children's families and communities; children's varied interests; and the individual variation in growth, development, and learning (in both rate and style) among different children. Because developmentally appropriate classrooms are not only

age appropriate but also individually appropriate, they cannot all look alike, nor will the children within those classrooms all have the same experience. Some children will need more structure and adult guidance than others. Some will enter school as quite able decision makers, while others will need teachers to help them learn to make choices. Any teaching approach that is applied to all of the children in the same way without any adjustment for individual differences will fail for at least some of the children.

Part of the concern about the potential rigidity of interpretation may be a by-product of the format of the statements. Positioning inappropriate and appropriate practices as though these were polar opposites with no mid-points (of which there are many) on a continuum may have contributed to the either/or interpretation of developmentally appropriate practice and the concern of some people that the documents tend to narrow the standards of good practice (Spodek, 1991). Narrowing options was not NAEYC's intent. In fact, the goal was to "open up" the curriculum and teaching practices and move away from the narrow emphasis on isolated academic skills and the drill-and-practice approach to instruction. NAEYC chose to use both negative and positive exemplars as a strategy for enhancing concept development among a diverse audience and for protecting children from negative experiences.

## 2. DAP does not mean that teachers don't teach and that children control the classroom.

Another frequently heard misinterpretation of developmentally appropriate practice is that the children control the classroom and that teachers don't teach. This view equates child-initiated learning with chaos. It would be naive to pretend that there are not some classrooms that claim to be developmentally appropriate in which teachers abdicate responsibility and chaos does ensue, but these classrooms are *not* developmentally appropriate. The truth is that good early childhood programs are, of necessity, highly organized and structured environments that teachers have carefully prepared and in which teachers are in control. The difference is that children are also actively involved and assume some responsibility for their own learning (the teachers' perspective on this issue is presented in Chapters 11 and 12 of this book).

## 3. DAP does not reject goals and objectives; curriculum does not emerge only from children.

An aspect of the chaos argument is the notion that early childhood educators reject goals and objectives and let the curriculum emerge solely from the child's interests. Because NAEYC rejects narrow drill-and-practice on academic skills does not mean that they reject goals and objectives. All effective educational programs have clearly stated objectives (or outcomes) toward which the teacher plans and works with children to achieve. The difference in developmentally appropriate classrooms is that those goals are appropriate for children's age levels and individual patterns of learning and development; respectful of their needs and interests; and address all areas of human functioning, not just narrowly defined basic skills. The worst misinterpretation of developmentally appropriate practice is that if teachers just let children play, at Grade 3 they will emerge literate. Yes, play is important; it is essential for children to develop high-level social strategies and other important learnings. However, teachers must know why, when, and how they can help play become an enriching, meaningful learning experience, and they must also know what experiences and specific strategies children need to become literate.

## 4. DAP is for all children.

One of the most frequent and disturbing misinterpretations of DAP is that the position statements apply only to certain types of children, usually assumed to be typically developing, White, middle-class children. This issue is more thoroughly addressed in the third section of this book and is obviously an area in which much more work is needed, but in the meantime some clarifying statements can be made. By definition, to be individually appropriate requires that programs attend to individual and cultural variation among the children they serve. It is clear that more work needs to be done to ensure that programs are culturally as well as developmentally appropriate (these issues are discussed by Barbara Bowman and Liz Wolfe in Chapters 9 and 10). Perhaps the most potentially destructive iteration of this interpretation is that rejecting inappropriately formal instruction with very young children equates to rejecting intervention strategies for children with identified special needs (this issue is addressed in greater detail in Chapter 7 by representatives of the Division for Early Childhood of the Council for Exceptional Children). Again, this misinterpretation ignores the critical dimension of individual appropriateness in the definition. A developmentally appropriate program must attend to the individual needs of all of the children. NAEYC and NAECS/SDE believe that good early childhood programs derive from children's *needs* and interests; neither aspect can be neglected in a good program.

## 5. Curriculum is not child development.

Among the criticisms of DAP has been that it implies that child development is the curriculum or is the only determinant of curriculum or the only justification for appropriate practice (Kessler, 1991; Spodek, 1991). Emphasis on child development knowledge in determining appropriate teaching practice may have overshadowed the other principles that need to be considered in curriculum decisions. The Curriculum and Assessment Guidelines address many more considerations in addition to child development knowledge. Just knowing child development does not enable teachers to help children reach their potentials as individuals or as citizens of a democracy (Greenberg, 1990, 1992; Kessler, 1991). At the same time, child development knowledge and curriculum must be integrally linked, as illustrated in the analogy that follows.

## The relationship of child development knowledge and curriculum theory: An analogy

Child development knowledge and curriculum theory are two important and, it is hoped, intersecting strands of work within the field of early childhood education. The goal is to bring these disciplines more closely together through implementation of the guidelines; this effort is essential if children and schools are to reach their potentials. The following analogy illustrates the potential of this intersection between curriculum and child development knowledge.

Children's clothing is an entire industry that successfully applies child development knowledge. The construction of clothing is based on its own knowledge base, the intricacies of tailoring, that is analogous to curriculum theory; but when the product of the tailor is a piece of clothing for a child, knowledge of child development must be activated. First, the tailor must know what is age appropriate. The basic size dimensions of the typical client are determined by typical growth patterns. Similarly, the tailor must be aware of the client's other developmental needs. For example, the fine-motor development of toddlers prohibits zippers, just as their diapering needs dictate snaps along the legs. The range of options in children's clothing, similar to the breadth and depth of curriculum, is influenced by children's development in general. Occasionally a designer applies child development knowledge with brilliant results, such as using Velcro™ to fasten preschoolers' shoes.

For clothing to actually sell and be functional, it must also be individually appropriate. Some children, despite the growth charts, are much larger or smaller than average. It is not sufficient to know a child's age to purchase appropriate clothing; one must also know the individual child's size, cultural background, and preferences. While overalls may be the most developmentally appropriate clothing design for active 3-year-olds, an individual 3-year-old may prefer dresses—and only dresses in lavender. Knowledge of clothing construction and design as well as knowledge of child development are essential, but still inadequate. Knowledge of individual and cultural differences must be activated by the responsible person (usually the parent) if the clothing is to be worn, appreciated, and practical. Similar connections must be made between child development knowledge and curriculum if programs for young children are to reach their potential. The link between child development and curriculum is described in much greater detail in Chapters 5 and 6.

# Where we want to go: Reaching potentials

Having seen where we've been, we turn to the question of where we want to go. That question drove the development of the Curriculum and Assessment Guidelines and eventually led to this book—*Reaching Potentials*. What does it mean to reach potential, much less to reach multiple potentials? The title of this book, like much of its content, has several layers of interpretation and implication. First and foremost, the potentials addressed here are the virtually unlimited potentials of young children. Unless they suffer serious abuse or neglect or are severely disabled, children under the age

*CHILDREN UNDER THE AGE OF 8 HAVE ALMOST UNLIMITED POTENTIAL TO BECOME. PERHAPS MORE IMPORTANTLY, EACH OF THESE INDIVIDUALS HAS THE POTENTIAL TO BECOME A HEALTHY, SENSITIVE, CARING, AND FULLY CONTRIBUTING MEMBER OF SOCIETY.*

of 8 have almost unlimited potential to become. Every preschool and kindergarten class contains future artists, writers, musicians, mathematicians, scientists, and athletes. Perhaps more importantly, each of these individuals has the potential to become a healthy, sensitive, caring, and fully contributing member of society. Even in most cases of individuals with identified disabilities, given appropriate intervention and support, damage can be alleviated and greater potential can be achieved than is sometimes predicted. The goal, then, of early education is to ensure that children acquire the foundation of healthy development and learning necessary to achieve their potential in the future—and to prevent the all-too-common situation in which early school experiences serve to limit and restrict future accomplishments.

But the potentials of children are only one of the potentials we wish to address in this book. All teachers of young children have the potential to be caring, creative, professional decision makers; too many teachers, however, find themselves to be technicians or taskmasters. Whether teachers achieve their full potential is the result of many factors, including their own commitment and motivation, but the curriculum and assessment practices of the program or school in which they are employed can help or hinder the potential professional and personal development of teachers.

The curriculum itself has many potentials; it is not static and predetermined, but rather a dynamic, developing entity that changes as we acquire new knowledge and apply it differently to individual children and groups. Early childhood curriculum has the potential to be challenging, engaging, and interesting; but curriculum for young children can also be boring, trivial, and meaningless. Curriculum potentials are almost as unlimited as the potentials of children and teachers; whether curriculum achieves these potentials depends on the vision and motives of curriculum developers and implementors.

Like curriculum, assessment tools and procedures also have potentials. Assessment can be used to ensure that individual children's needs are met and that each child benefits from educational experiences; unfortunately, assessment can also be used to harm children—to label, track, or deny children opportunities. Similarly, assessment can be used to inform and enhance curriculum or to narrow and limit curriculum. Assessment has the potential to improve teaching or to impoverish it.

The many potentials of children, teachers, curriculum, and assessment are interrelated. When curriculum and assessment practices are optimum, then children and teachers will more likely reach their potentials. This book is designed as a tool to help reach all of these many potentials.

The guidelines presented in this book (pp. 9–27) are principles to guide decisions, both theoretical and practical, about what should be included in curriculum for young children and how their learning should be assessed. Development of the guidelines was a challenging task involving the input of literally hundreds of people. A few of the critics pointed out that the guidelines are not specific enough to help curriculum developers determine what content is appropriate and when; to make optimum use of the guidelines, it is necessary to possess a level of expertise in child development and current views of best practice in early childhood education. In developing the guidelines NAEYC and NAECS/SDE hesitated to be more specific because it would not have been appropriate to be prescriptive, but we do want the guidelines to reach their potential of influencing curriculum and assessment decisions; hence, we offer this two-volume book in which various authors offer their perspectives on applying the guidelines.

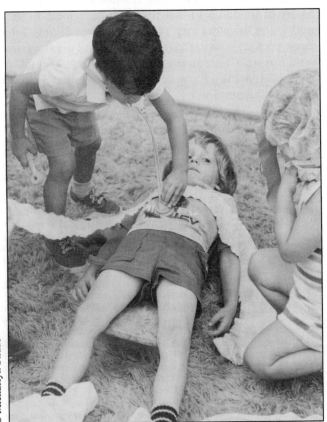

© Michaelyn Straub

# Overview of the book

This book is published in two volumes. The foundation for both volumes is the Guidelines for Appropriate Curriculum Content and Assessment in Programs Serving Children Ages 3 through 8, a joint position statement of the National Association for the Education of Young Children (NAEYC) and the National Association of Early Childhood Specialists in State Departments of Education (NAECS/SDE). Volume 1 has four parts:

## 1. *Reaching Potentials Through Appropriate Curriculum and Assessment*

Section I includes the complete list of guidelines and includes background information and a brief description of the theoretical framework on which the guidelines are based. Although the guidelines can stand alone, implicit in the position statement is a large body of knowledge and experience; to fully and effectively implement the guidelines requires access to additional information. Sue Bredekamp and Teresa Rosegrant discuss the guidelines in more detail, offering conceptual frameworks for interpreting and applying them with different age groups. Tynette Hills describes the exciting potential of improving assessment by elaborating on the assessment guidelines and illustrating their potential with concrete examples.

## 2. *Reaching Individual Potentials*

These chapters address the child in the curriculum, defining and clarifying what child-centered curriculum really is and offering a new paradigm for conceptualizing curriculum derived from the guidelines—transformational curriculum. This model addresses the relationship of child development and curriculum, providing examples of age-appropriate and individually appropriate curriculum decisions. In developing their vision of appropriate curriculum and teaching, NAEYC and NAECS/SDE assumed that the same guidelines apply to programs serving all children, including children with special abilities and children with disabilities. This assumption is discussed for the population of children with special needs by Mark Wolery, Phillip Strain, and Donald Bailey.

## 3. *Reaching Potentials of All Children*

These chapters address the culturally appropriate dimension of appropriate curriculum and teaching. Louise Derman-Sparks applies the guidelines to antibias, multicultural curriculum in general; Barbara Bowman addresses the issue of developmentally and culturally appropriate programs for minority children; Liz Wolfe applies the guidelines to programs serving children who speak languages other than English; and

Teresa Rosegrant provides commentary from the perspective of a teacher in a multilingual classroom.

## 4. *Reaching Potentials of Teachers and Administrators*

Implementation of the guidelines implies that change will be necessary in curriculum, assessment, and teaching practices in many schools and programs throughout this country. David and Bonnie Burchfield describe their own growth as teachers and the insights they have developed in implementing more appropriate classroom practices in primary classrooms. Linda Espinosa describes the process of change in one school district and describes the principles of change that must be addressed if the early childhood profession and children are to reach their full potentials.

Volume 2 "cuts" the curriculum vertically by addressing the content of the curriculum across the age span by subject matter. The early childhood profession's guidelines are only one of many converging efforts to reform curriculum and assessment in this nation. The subject matter disciplines have been active in recent years, with several national organizations issuing standards for curriculum and evaluation that are more or less congruent with these guidelines. In Volume 2, noted experts apply the NAEYC and NAECS/SDE Guidelines to the curriculum standards of national organizations, where relevant, and in most cases expand on that work by discussing its implications for preschool-age children. Each of the chapters in Volume 2 takes the current thinking about goals and expectations of a specific content area and places it in developmental perspective. Volume 2 further operationalizes several of the guidelines by describing what content is of most worth, what content goals are accepted by the disciplines and are of greatest intellectual integrity, and what content goals are realistic and attainable for children of different ages.

Of course, whenever a decision is made to address an aspect of curriculum, a potential error is made. Dividing the curriculum by subject matter area raises the question of how to meet another of the guidelines—integrated curriculum. Volume 2 also addresses the issue of integrated curriculum but acknowledges the distinctiveness of the disciplines. Successful integrated curriculum is based on initial understanding of the commonalities and differences among the disciplines on the part of curriculum developers and teachers. Finally, Volume 2 tackles the interesting question of "curriculum" for infants and toddlers.

# Now to begin

The Curriculum and Assessment Guidelines and this book represent an ending as well as a beginning. These issues are not new, as any examination of the history of schooling and of early childhood education reminds us. While it is important to remember our past and place current developments in historical context, it is also important to realize that we are still a relatively new profession and much remains to be learned. **With the exception of the guidelines themselves, these chapters do *not* present official positions of national organizations; they are the opinions of the authors.** Many of the ideas in this book are described by their authors as "exploratory"; therefore, the editors of this book present it with the expectation and the hope that it will begin a dialogue rather than end one. We will go right on reaching for potentials as long as we remain humans developing.

## *References*

Bredekamp, S. (Ed.). (1987). *Developmentally appropriate practice in early childhood programs serving children from birth through age 8* (exp. ed.). Washington, DC: NAEYC.

Bredekamp, S. (1991). Redeveloping early childhood education: A response to Kessler. *Early Childhood Research Quarterly, 6*(2), 199–209.

Davis, M.D., Johnson, H., and Richardson, A. (Eds.). (1930). *Minimum essentials for nursery school education.* New York: National Association for Nursery Education (forerunner of NAEYC).

Greenberg, P. (1987). Lucy Sprague Mitchell: A major missing link between early childhood education in the 1980's and progressive education in the 1890s–1930s. *Young Children, 42*(5), 70–84.

Greenberg, P. (1990). Ideas that work with young children. Why not academic preschool? Part 1. *Young Children, 45*(2), 70–80.

Greenberg, P. (1992). Ideas that work with young children. Why not academic preschool? Part 2. Autocracy or democracy in the classroom? *Young Children, 47*(3), 54–64.

Hewes, D. (1991). *On the road to appropriate curriculum and assessment.* Unpublished paper.

Hill, P.S. (1942). *Kindergarten.* Washington, DC: ACEI.

Kessler, S. (1991). Alternative perspectives on early childhood education. *Early Childhood Research Quarterly, 6*(2), 183–197.

Kostelnik, M.J. (1992). Myths associated with developmentally appropriate programs. *Young Children, 47*(4), 17–23.

National Association for the Education of Young Children. (1984; rev. ed., 1991). *Accreditation criteria and procedures of the National Academy of Early Childhood Programs.* Washington, DC: Author.

National Association for the Education of Young Children. (1988). Position statement on standardized testing of young children 3 through 8 years of age. *Young Children, 43*(3), 42–47.

National Association for the Education of Young Children and National Association of Early Childhood Specialists in State Departments of Education. (1991). Guidelines for appropriate curriculum content and assessment in programs serving children ages 3 through 8. *Young Children, 46*(3), 21–38.

National Association of Early Childhood Specialists in State Departments of Education. (1987). *Unacceptable trends in kindergarten entry and placement.* Unpublished position paper.

Shepard, L., & Smith, M. (1988). Escalating academic demand in kindergarten: Some nonsolutions. *Elementary School Journal, 89*(2), 135–146.

Spodek, B. (1991). Early childhood curriculum and cultural definitions of knowledge. In Spodek, B., & Saracho, O. (Eds.), *Issues in early childhood curriculum* (pp. 1–20). New York: Teachers College Press.

Swadener, B.B., & Kessler, S. (Eds.). (1991). Reconceptualizing early childhood education: Special issue. *Early Education and Development, 2*(2).

Walsh, D. (1991). Extending the discourse on developmental appropriateness: A developmental perspective. *Early Education and Development, 2*(2), 109–119.

Wheelock, L. (Ed.). (1913). *The kindergarten: Reports of the Committee of Nineteen on the theory and practice of the kindergarten.* New York: Houghton Mifflin.

# Guidelines for Appropriate Curriculum Content and Assessment in Programs Serving Children Ages 3 Through 8

*A position statement of*
*the National Association for the Education of Young Children and*
*the National Association of Early Childhood Specialists in State Departments of Education*
*Adopted November 1990*

## Endorsers

*The following organizations join with the National Association for the Education of Young Children and the National Association of Early Childhood Specialists in State Departments of Education in endorsing the Guidelines for Appropriate Curriculum Content and Assessment:*

*Association for Childhood Education International*

*Association for Supervision and Curriculum Development*

*National Association of State Boards of Education*

*National Council for the Social Studies*

*National Council of Teachers of Mathematics*

*Southern Early Childhood Association (formerly Southern Association on Children Under Six)*

## Supporters

*The following organizations support the concepts contained in the Guidelines for Appropriate Curriculum Content and Assessment:*

*American Association of Physical Education, Health, Recreation, and Dance*

*International Reading Association (for U.S. programs only)*

*National Black Child Development Institute*

*National Science Teachers Association*

# Background information

The National Association for the Education of Young Children (NAEYC) and the National Association of Early Childhood Specialists in State Departments of Education (NAECS/SDE) jointly developed these guidelines to inform decisions about curriculum content and assessment in programs serving children 3 through 8 years of age.* The purpose of this document is to guide teachers and supervisors to (1) make informed decisions about appropriate curriculum content and assessment, (2) evaluate existing curriculum and assessment practices, and (3) advocate for more appropriate approaches. This document is designed to assist teachers and administrators with only one part of their complex jobs—their important roles as curriculum decision makers and evaluators.

Curriculum decisions not only involve questions about *how* children learn but also *what* learning is appropriate and *when* it is best learned (Katz, 1991). In addition, the way learning is assessed directly influences what is taught and when it is expected to be learned. Therefore, these guidelines address both curriculum and assessment. The early childhood profession believes that curriculum and assessment should be planned based on the best knowledge of theory and research about how children develop and learn, with attention given to individual children's needs and interests in relation to program goals.

**Curriculum** is an organized framework that delineates the content that children are to learn, the processes through which children achieve the identified curricular goals, what teachers do to help children achieve these goals, and the context in which teaching and learning occur. The early childhood profession defines curriculum in its broadest sense, encompassing prevailing theories, approaches, and models. As-

sessment is the process of observing, recording, and otherwise documenting the work children do and how they do it, as a basis for a variety of educational decisions that affect the child, including planning for groups and individual children and communicating with parents. Assessment encompasses the many forms of evaluation available to educational decision makers. Assessment in the service of curriculum and learning requires teachers to observe and analyze regularly what the children are doing in light of the content goals and the learning processes.

## The need for guidelines

The decade of the 1980s saw numerous calls for widespread school reform, with changes recommended in teacher education, graduation requirements, school structure, and accountability measures. With the advent of the 1990s, school reform finally took on the essential question: what to teach (Rothman, 1989). Critiques of prevailing curriculum content and methods and calls for sweeping change were issued by national organizations representing the subject-matter disciplines and administrators, including the National Council of Teachers of Mathematics (1989), the American Association for the Advancement of Science (1989), the International Reading Association (1989), the National Council of Teachers of English (Lloyd-Jones & Lunsford, 1988), the National Commission on Social Studies in the Schools (1989), the National Association of Elementary School Principals (1990), the National Association of State Boards of Education (1988), and the Association for Supervision and Curriculum Development (1989), among others. The early childhood profession, represented by the National Association for the Education of Young Children (NAEYC), entered the educational reform debate by issuing influential position statements defining developmentally appropriate practices for young children (Bredekamp, 1987).

These reports reflect a growing consensus that the traditional scope and sequence approach to curriculum, with its emphasis on drill and practice of isolated academic skills, does not reflect current knowledge of human learning and fails to produce students who possess the kind of higher order thinking and problem-solving abilities that will be needed in the 21st century. Past success in improving basic skills in the three Rs has not been matched by success in improving reading comprehension, writing fluency, or math problem-solving ability. In addition, it is evident that our schools are failing to produce future generations with even a working knowledge of the natural, physical, and social sciences, much less the kinds of minds that will create new knowledge in these areas. Specifically, these

---

*It is important to explain how the scope of these guidelines for 3- through 8-year-olds was determined. NAEYC defines early childhood as birth through age 8. NAEYC has not changed its position that education begins at birth; however, curriculum and assessment for infants and toddlers looks different from what is described here. In fact, many infant specialists object to the use of the word* curriculum *with infants. Because this document is a joint position statement of NAEYC and NAECS/SDE, one of its primary audiences will be public school personnel; the document was originally conceived to address the age range of 4- through 8-year-olds, to be compatible with the early childhood unit concept recommended by the National Association of State Boards of Education (1988). NAEYC and NAECS/SDE expanded the scope to address 3-year-olds, in anticipation of future trends toward increased educational services for this age group in public schools, Head Start, and child care programs.*

national organizations call for schooling to place greater emphasis on active, hands-on learning; conceptual learning that leads to understanding, along with acquisition of basic skills; meaningful, relevant learning experiences; interactive teaching and cooperative learning; and a broad range of relevant content, integrated across traditional subject-matter divisions. At the same time, these organizations unanimously criticize rote memorization, drill and practice on isolated academic skills, teacher lecture, and repetitive seatwork.

Along with calling for change in curriculum, major national organizations have raised concerns about the negative effects of traditional methods of evaluation, particularly standardized paper-and-pencil, multiple-choice achievement tests. There is increasing recognition that curriculum reform must be accompanied by testing reform. National organizations are now calling for more performance-based assessments that align with current views of curriculum and more accurately reflect children's learning (NAECS/SDE, 1987; NAEYC, 1988; NCTM, 1989; Fair-Test, 1990; Kamii, 1990; National Commission on Testing and Public Policy, 1990).

The emerging consensus about needed curriculum and assessment reform is very encouraging but has been slow to result in real change in curriculum and assessment practices in the early grades. The basic problem is that in some ways current curriculum does not demand enough of children, and in other ways it demands too much of the wrong thing. On one hand, the accountability movement with its emphasis on standardized test scores has narrowed the curriculum to those basic skills that can be easily measured on multiple choice tests, thus diminishing the intellectual challenge for many children. This narrow focus also leads to children's being drilled on content that is devoid of meaning for many children. On the other hand, current curriculum expectations in the early years of schooling often are *not* appropriate for the age groups served. Overemphasis on standardized test scores has contributed to a curriculum in which next-grade expectations of mastery of basic skills are routinely pushed down to the previous grade (Shepard & Smith, 1988). As a result, what used to be taught in first grade is now routinely taught in kindergarten, and what used to be taught in kindergarten appears on the entrance test for admittance to school. The trend toward drill and practice on isolated academic skills in kindergarten and first grade has trickled down further to programs for 3- and 4-year-olds. As a result, the early school experiences of many children are marred by unnecessary struggle and failure.

The most common solutions to the problem of early school failure—testing children for kindergarten entry and placement; raising the entrance age for kindergarten; adding an extra, "transitional" year between kindergarten and first grade; or retaining children in preschool, kindergarten, or first grade (as many as 20 to 30% in some districts)—are all veiled attempts to obtain an older, more capable cohort of children at each grade level. These strategies reveal the fact that current curriculum expectations do not match the developmental level of the children for whom the grade is intended. In effect, these strategies blame the victims—the children—rather than confronting the real problem—an inappropriate curriculum.

Since major national organizations have issued position statements on curriculum and evaluation that are congruent with the early childhood profession's positions, what is the rationale for developing this set of guidelines for early childhood curriculum and assessment? NAEYC's previously published positions (Bredekamp, 1987) provide clear guidance about *how* to teach young children, but are less specific about content, *what* to teach. In implementing developmentally appropriate practice, teachers and administrators must make decisions about what to teach and when, and how to best assess that learning has taken place. This document is designed to help guide those important decisions about curriculum content and assessment.

The development of guidelines for curriculum content and assessment is a challenging task. As professionals, we place great value on individualization. Justifiably, we refuse to dictate curriculum because good curriculum must be individually appropriate to the needs and interests of the children in a program. In addition, it must be culturally salient and locally relevant and meaningful in the context of a specific community. Historically, early childhood educators have hesitated to officially address the issue of curriculum because we place great value on emergent curriculum, what successful teachers do in conjunction with and in response to children. Others, however, have not hesitated to fill the void (Hirsch, 1987; Bennett, 1988). Most often, curriculum decisions are abdicated to commercial textbook publishers, distributors of packaged curricula, and developers of standardized tests. These practices have been disastrous for children and can no longer go unchallenged. When policies and practices are necessary to "protect" children from school, and when kindergarten and first grade are routinely described as "aversive environments," something is seriously wrong with the curriculum.

Curriculum development should take into account the many sources of curriculum: child development knowledge, individual characteristics of children, the knowledge base of various disciplines, the values of our culture, parents' desires, and the knowledge children need to function competently in our society (Spodek, 1977, 1988). The task of developing curriculum is made more difficult by the fact that these diverse sources of curriculum may be in conflict with one another. For example, the values and priorities of parents and the community are significant factors to be considered in determining what should be learned; however, parents and the community will not necessarily agree on all goals. The expertise of early childhood professionals should also influence decisions about appropriate goals for children (Katz, 1991). To some extent, curriculum decisions represent a negotiation process, with parent and community expectations about what is taught influenced by professional expertise about how to teach and when content is appropriate.

## Content versus process: The curriculum debate

In establishing guidelines for curriculum, it is advisable to heed the warnings of Eisner and Vallance (1974) against the three most common fallacies that mark curriculum debate. One fallacy is to emphasize process to the exclusion of content, placing utmost importance on how children learn rather than what they learn. The opposite error is to emphasize content over process, assuming that there is a body of content that all students should master and that emphasizing content is necessary to ensure academic rigor. A logical extension of this argument leads to the third fallacy—that there is a universal curriculum that is "best" for all children.

Early childhood education covers a broad age-span. For example, programs for 3- and 4-year-olds tend to emphasize process rather than content. As a result, in evaluating early childhood programs, it quickly becomes apparent that the "curriculum" may vary from the intellectually important to the trivial. At the other end of the early childhood continuum, many primary grade schools have stressed the acquisition of content, primarily basic academic skills, and only recently have some begun to emphasize the development of learning processes such as writing, thinking, and problem solving. Finally, early childhood professional organizations are so opposed to the specter of one best curriculum that in the past we have avoided the task of defining appropriate curriculum.

The fact remains that the question of which is more important, content or process, is really a moot point. To write, think, or solve problems, learners must have something to write about, something to think about, or some real problem to solve. In short, these important learning processes require content. Similarly, content cannot be learned without learning processes being engaged; the question is more one of the effectiveness or value of the learning processes. The content-versus-process debate should be put to rest since "any form of

learning can deal with the intellectually trivial as well as the intellectually significant" (Eisner & Vallance, 1974, p. 14) and "no matter how well something is taught, if it is not worth teaching, it is not worth teaching well" (Eisner, 1990, p. 524).

In developing these guidelines NAEYC and NAECS/SDE acknowledge the importance of rich, meaningful content in a program of developmentally appropriate teaching practices. We draw on prevailing theories of development and learning to guide process, and we look to well-established traditions in curriculum theory to support decisions about appropriate content. We do not advocate any one model curriculum. Instead, we offer guidelines—a framework for decision making—about appropriate curriculum content and assessment.

# Theoretical framework

What does it mean to approach children developmentally? It means that we recognize the child's changing capacities, and that we recognize that a child has the capacity for change. (Garbarino, 1989, p. 30)

Decisions about appropriate curriculum and assessment inevitably derive from a particular perspective or theoretical framework. These guidelines are based on specific assumptions about how children learn and develop and also on relevant theories of curriculum that guide decisions about what is important to learn and when. The purpose of this section is to make explicit the theoretical framework or belief system that underlies the guidelines.

## How children learn: Theoretical perspectives on development and learning

All educators have a belief system, whether explicit or implicit, about how children learn and what they should be learning, that guides and influences their practice. Theories are useful because they help teachers understand why they do what they do and explain why something happens. There are many theories of learning and development that explain various phenomena. Many early childhood professionals have found some theories, such as those developed by Piaget (1952), Vygotsky (1978), and Erikson (1963) more comprehensive and explanatory, and therefore more useful, than others. It is these theories that inform this document.

Learning is such a complex human activity that no one theory entirely explains it. To some extent, the complexity of learning results in part from the fact that there are different kinds of knowledge that have been variously described by different theorists. One framework for categorizing knowledge is provided by Piaget (1952). He differentiates physical, logical-mathematical, and

## CURRICULUM PLANNING: A METAPHOR

There are many legitimate approaches to curriculum planning, just as there are many ways to plan a menu. For example, in meal planning, one can be guided by knowledge of nutrition derived from theory and research. Meals planned from this perspective will undoubtedly be nourishing. Without attention given to the interests and preferences of the diner, however, the nourishing meal may go uneaten. Some menus are based simply on what the eaters like. Again, without attention to the nutritional needs, the meal may be consumed but provide less value. Some menus are planned by flipping through the cookbook and picking what sounds interesting or fun. Again, this random approach may or may not result in healthy outcomes. Lastly, many meals are planned by going to the cupboard and seeing what is there. If the food on hand is fresh and nutritious, the outcome may by chance be positive. If only junk food is available, however, the meal will be composed of empty calories.

As in menu planning, curriculum can be derived from many sources, and the outcomes can vary enormously. Curriculum should be based on sound theoretical principles of how children develop and learn, but it must also be derived from the needs and interests of individual children if it is to be fully effective. For example, if food is served that is very different from children's experiences at home, they may reject it and fail to obtain its nutritional benefits. The same result may occur when curriculum is not relevant to children's family backgrounds and cultures.

Overemphasis on preferences and interests, however, in the absence of clear goals and objectives, can lead to haphazard curriculum planning that may or may not achieve worthwhile outcomes. Too often, early childhood programs have been criticized as ineffective learning environments because they have emphasized children's play without articulating the goals for children, the value of play for learning, or the essential role of the teacher in planning the environment and facilitating learning through play. A fine balance must be achieved in planning curriculum for young children. On one hand, teachers may err by not doing enough planning to stimulate children's learning (the milling-around model), but if their activity is dictated by the plans, the teacher may fail to adapt to individual differences and interests (Jones, 1989).

Unfortunately, the cookbook approach is all too common in early childhood programs. In fact, activity books abound that frequently serve as the only curriculum guide. As in menu planning, the individual recipes may be appropriate and valuable, but without a framework and organization, they may fail to provide the opportunity for rich conceptual development that is likely with a more coherent, thoughtful approach.

Lastly, curriculum may be implemented using the cupboard approach. This approach is totally dependent on the appropriateness of the available materials and activities. If they are basically age appropriate, then the result is not harmful but not optimal. If they are inappropriate and even trivial, as is much of available commercial curricula, then they are a waste of children's and teachers' time.

Curriculum should be planned based on the best knowledge of theory, research, and practice about how children develop and learn, with attention given to the individual needs and interests in a group in relation to program goals.

---

social-conventional knowledge as determined by the source of the knowledge. The source of physical knowledge is external observable reality, such as when a ball rolls down an incline; the source of logical-mathematical knowledge is the relationships mentally constructed inside the individual, as in classifying or sequencing where the system originates in the classifier's head, not in the objects themselves; finally, the source of social-conventional knowledge is the agreed-upon conventions of society, such as the days of the week,

holidays, and names given to numerals and the alphabet (Kamii, 1990).

Vygotsky (1978) also provides a useful framework for categorizing, and therefore understanding, the nature of knowledge. He distinguishes spontaneous concepts from school-learned concepts. Spontaneous concepts are those that the child discovers through direct experience, such as that adding ice cubes to water makes it colder; these are concepts that the child constructs mentally without need of instruction from adults. On the other hand, school-related or scientific concepts originate in the culture and represent the body of knowledge from past generations; for example, the Fahrenheit scale informs us that ice freezes at 32 degrees, while the Celsius scale names the freezing point at 0. It would be virtually impossible for each generation of learners to construct this type of knowledge from direct, personal experience; instead, its origin is in the social experience that occurs in school (Strauss, 1987).

Vygotsky's school-learned concepts are analogous to Piaget's social-conventional knowledge, just as Vygotsky's notion of spontaneous concepts parallels Piaget's view of construction of knowledge. These frameworks are useful in helping educators conceptualize the nature of learning, but it is important to emphasize that in real life these types of learning are interrelated. For instance, in becoming literate, children do not construct their own language system; even their most inventive writing reflects principles of the language of their culture. What they personally construct is their understanding of the relationships that constitute the reading or writing process. Perhaps this is why a major contributor to early school failure is submersion of non-English-speaking children into classrooms where the children's own culture and language background are neither incorporated nor valued.

The theories of Piaget and Vygotsky do not explain everything that educators need to know about learning, but they are very useful in helping to overcome the artificial dichotomies that too often arise within the field of early childhood education. The curriculum debate over content versus process, described earlier, is really symptomatic of the fact that early childhood educators tend to emphasize spontaneous, constructed knowledge, while traditional public education tends to consider only school-learned, social-conventional knowledge as legitimate learning. The content emphasis identifies a variety of content and tends to assume the process of teacher-directed instruction; the process emphasis identifies a variety of processes, including child-initiated learning, and mostly assumes the content. Each of these positions can inform the other so that ideally, curriculum incorporates both rich, meaningful content and interactive child-centered learning processes.

The nature of learning should inform the practice of teaching. Again, the artificial dichotomy between spontaneous, constructed learning and school-related learning is reflected in arguments over child-initiated versus teacher-directed instruction. The fact is that children construct important learning, particularly physical and logical-mathematical knowledge, through child-initiated, spontaneous activity. But they also learn a great deal from adults. For example, language learning begins in the parent-child relationship, and language is

the essential prerequisite for communication (Smith-Burke, 1985). Rather than dichotomizing aspects of learning and/or teaching, the teaching-learning process is better characterized as an *interactive* process. Following is a summary of the basic assumptions about learning and teaching as an interactive process that inform this document.

• **Children learn best when their physical needs are met and they feel psychologically safe and secure.**

Appropriate curriculum does not violate but rather respects children's biological needs. For example, in appropriate programs children are not required to sit and attend to paperwork or listen to adult lectures for extended periods of time because such activity is at odds with children's biological needs. Likewise, the curriculum provides for active physical play and periods of more restful, quiet activity since this pattern is compatible with children's physical needs.

In addition to meeting children's physical needs, adults ensure an environment in which children feel safe, secure, and accepted. The social and economic conditions in which many American children live today intensify the need for programs to support children's social and emotional development. Children need to know that school is a safe place where adults will protect and support them and where they can be happy, comfortable, and relaxed. If children experience stress-related symptoms, such as stomachaches, headaches, or sleeping disruptions, or simply do not want to go to school, then the school may not be meeting their need for psychological safety. Additionally, the degree to which children perceive continuity between their school and home experiences, a connectedness between the culture of the school and the culture of their family, influences the degree to which children feel psychologically safe in out-of-home environments. When parents are meaningfully involved in the program, the program is more likely to provide an effective learning environment for all children.

• **Children construct knowledge.**

A child's mind is not a miniature model of an adult's, nor is it an empty vessel that gradually fills with information. From infancy, children are mentally and physically active, struggling to make sense of the world. Children are continually acting on and organizing experiences mentally, whether they are social experiences with adults and other children or physical experiences with objects. In short, children construct their own knowledge through repeated experiences involving interaction with people and materials (Piaget, 1952). Knowledge is constructed as a result of dynamic interactions between the individual and the physical and social environments.

The child's active experimentation is analogous to spontaneous research; in a sense, the child discovers knowledge. Central to experimentation is making "constructive errors" that are necessary to mental development. We know that children construct knowledge because they possess so many ideas that adults do not teach them (DeVries & Kohlberg, 1990). These "errors" or "incorrect" ideas—from the adults's viewpoint—reflect children's developing attempts to understand relationships and form concepts based on their own experiences. When a 3-year-old inquires about a neighbor woman's husband, "What's your daddy's name?," she demonstrates her construction of knowledge. No one has told her that the man is the woman's father. From her limited experience, she defines men we live with as daddies. For all children ideas, objects, relationships, and experiences become meaningful because of the interpretation the child gives them.

Studies of children's emerging literacy clearly demonstrate that children actively construct their understanding of written language (Ferreiro & Teberosky, 1982; Teale & Sulzby, 1986). When a 4-year-old makes four scribbles on the page and rereads, "This is my house"; when a 5-year-old writes VESAB and reads, "This is a birthday"; or when a 6-year-old puts a dash between each word she writes in her journal, they display evidence of their internal construction of writing. They are not reproducing writing behaviors they have seen because adults do not write this way; these "errors" reflect their active construction of the writing process.

Children need to form their own hypotheses and keep trying them out through mental actions and physical manipulations—observing what happens, comparing their findings, asking questions, and discovering answers. When objects and events resist the working model that the child has mentally constructed, the child is forced to adjust the model or alter the mental structures to account for the new information. Throughout childhood these mental structures are continually being reshaped, expanded, and reorganized by new experiences. In the example above, the 3-year-old girl gradually comes to understand that there are many categories of males in families, including fathers, brothers, husbands, uncles, and grandfathers, as she hears about and experiences different family structures. Similarly, our budding writers will change their writing strategies over time as their literacy learning develops. Children's understanding of concepts is facilitated by providing repeated experiences and real problems to solve so they can see contradictions between their thinking and the reality of the world.

• **Children learn through social interaction with adults and other children.**

The healthy development of young children begins in a relationship with another human being, the parent-child relationship being the primary example of social interaction through which very young children develop and learn. It is well recognized that disruptions in early attachment relationships often lead to general social and emotional difficulties (Garbarino, 1989); however, the importance of social relationships to cognitive development should not be underestimated. For example, language development is fundamental to learning, and language development requires social interaction.

According to Vygotsky (1978), the development of higher order mental functions, such as conceptualization, begins in social interaction and then is internalized psychologically. Most adults can think of situations where they did not really understand something until after they had discussed it with several people. At other times, we find that we really do not own a concept until we have articulated it to someone else. This kind of learning through social interaction is important throughout life but essential for children who need to test the mental hypotheses they construct against the thinking of other people.

The vital role of teachers and other adults is to support children's development in terms of both their actual development and their potential. Vygotsky (1978) uses the term *zone of proximal development* to describe the level of development at which the child can function with the assistance of adults or more capable peers, the level beyond which the child is able to function independently. The principle of learning is that children can do things first in a supportive context and then later independently and in a variety of contexts. The support of adults and more competent peers provides the necessary assistance or "scaffold" that enables the child to move to the next level of independent functioning. The teacher's role is one of supporting, guiding, and facilitating development and learning, as opposed to the traditional view of teaching as transmission of knowledge.

Social interaction is necessary for intellectual development, but it is also necessary for children to develop social competence and self-esteem. Social interaction calls for reciprocity, mutual respect, and cooperation, that is, the adjustment of individual differences in beliefs, ideas, perspectives, and intentions to create mutually acceptable rules and conventions (Piaget, 1952; Erikson, 1963). All of these capabilities are related to school success and are required of full participants in a democracy.

• **Children's learning reflects a recurring cycle that begins in awareness and moves to exploration, to inquiry, and finally, to utilization.** (Rosegrant, 1989; see also Chapter 3, this volume)

Any new learning by children (or adults) follows a relatively predictable pattern or cycle. To learn anything new, we must first become aware of the phenomenon. *Awareness* is generated from experience. Children can only become interested in objects, events, or people if they are aware that these things exist and have had some experience with them. The next step in the cycle of learning is *exploration*. If children are really to know about and understand something, they must explore it. Exploration is the process of figuring out the components of what is being learned, by whatever means possible, usually employing the various senses (seeing, hearing, touching, smelling, and tasting). Children must have direct, hands-on experience with the content in order to make it personally meaningful. This meaning will be governed by their own rules and views of the world but is an important step toward true understanding. Awareness and exploration are essential to the learning process, but more is needed for complete understanding. Children's own rule systems must eventually be adapted to conform to the conventional rule systems of society. *Inquiry* is the process whereby children analyze and compare their own behaviors or concepts to what is observed in society and make closer approximations to the conventional patterns of the culture. The final aspect of the cycle of learning is *utilization*, when children are able to use what they have learned for multiple purposes and apply their learning to new situations. When children have opportunities to become aware and develop interest, explore and inquire, the learning becomes functional for them; in short, they own it.

The cycle of learning from awareness, to exploration, to inquiry, to utilization is not linear; for example, children may be exploring and inquiring simultaneously. Furthermore, this cycle of learning recurs as children's (and adults') learnings become more elaborated and refined. Children learn by doing—touching, experimenting, choosing, talking, and negotiating (Dewey, 1916; Jones, 1989). Active manipulation of the environment is essential for children to construct knowledge. Children's actions related to objects, events, and people—and their thinking about the consequences of their actions—inevitably change their knowledge, reasoning, and understanding about their experiences. As Elkind (1976) states, "Not only are the child's thought and action changed by experience, but experience itself is changed as a direct result of the child's maturing mental operations. In short, there is inevitably an interaction, and what a child learns is always a product of experience that is itself conditioned by his or her level of cognitive development" (p.112).

• **Children learn through play.**

The various kinds of play by young children are effective vehicles for promoting learning. Children's spontaneous play provides opportunities for exploration, experimentation, and manipulation that are essential for constructing knowledge. Play contributes to the development of representational thought. A child expresses and represents his or her ideas, thoughts, and feelings when engaged in symbolic play. During play a child learns to deal with feelings, to interact with others, to resolve conflicts, and to gain a sense of competence. Perhaps most important, it is through play that children develop their imaginations and creativity.

Children's play also provides opportunities for children to practice spontaneously in a variety of situations the newly acquired skill or knowledge. This self-initiated practice is part of the process of inquiry; during play, children examine and refine their learning in light of the feedback they receive from the environment and other people. Children are naturally interested in participating in activities that strengthen their skills and deepen their understanding of concepts.

During the primary grades children's play becomes more rule oriented. As their learning moves toward utilization, they naturally desire that it conform to more conventional rule systems. Playing board and card games and group games with rules promotes the development of autonomy and cooperation that contributes to social, emotional, and intellectual development (Kamii & DeVries, 1980; Kamii, 1982; DeVries & Kohlberg, 1990). Throughout primary grades children need to continue to explore, experiment, imagine, and create, and play naturally promotes these processes.

• **Children's interests and "need to know" motivate learning.**

Children have an inherent need or "inner push" to exercise their emerging mental abilities and to make sense of their experiences. Teachers need to "identify content that intrigues children and arouses in them a need and desire to figure something out" (DeVries & Kohlberg, 1990, p. 25). In short, teachers create awareness and foster interest in children by planning the environment and introducing new and stimulating objects, people, and experiences. Activities that are based on children's interests provide intrinsic motivation for learning. Children then demonstrate initiative, "the quality of undertaking, planning, and attacking a task" (Erikson, 1963, p. 255). Curriculum that is based on children's interests and internal motivation to understand fosters desirable dispositions and feelings, such as initiative, curiosity, attention, self-direction, industry, competence, and love of learning.

• **Human development and learning are characterized by individual variation.**

Each of the foregoing assumptions about learning begins with the word "children," as though generalizations about children apply equally to all. No discussion, however brief, of human development and learning is complete without attention to the principle of human variation. The fact is that every generalization about development and learning carries a caveat: A wide range of individual variation is normal and to be expected. Each human being has an individual pattern and timing of growth and development as well as individual styles of learning. Personal family experiences and cultural backgrounds also vary. Recognition that individual variation is not only normal but also valuable requires that decisions about curriculum and assessment be as individualized as possible.

## *What should children learn: Curriculum theory*

Curriculum has many sources in addition to child development knowledge, including the knowledge base of various disciplines and the values of the culture and community. Just as curriculum decisions draw on these many sources, principles or guidelines about curriculum content must take into consideration these diverse theoretical foundations. Spodek (Spodek, 1988; Spodek & Saracho, 1990) cautions that we cannot justify the content of what we teach solely on how children learn because the "how" is more concerned with method; decisions about what to teach, the content of the curriculum, are heavily influenced by curriculum theory. Curriculum theories address questions about which knowledge is most important or worthy of inclusion.

A complete discussion of conflicting conceptions of curriculum and their historical influence is beyond the scope of this document and has been well articulated elsewhere (Eisner & Vallance, 1974; Kliebard, 1986). Eisner and Vallance identify five disparate conceptions of curriculum—the development of cognitive processes, self-actualization, social reconstruction-relevance, academic rationalism, and technology—that have had varying degrees of influence on American schools. The influence of curriculum theorists cannot be understated. Examination of curriculum debates over the last century (Kessler, 1991) reveals that it was the theory of curriculum as technology, most often associated with the "Tyler Rationale," that limited curriculum goals to observable, measurable, behavioral objectives as much as or more than behaviorist learning theory.

The foundation for "developmentally appropriate practice" advocated here and elsewhere relates to at least two of Eisner's conceptions of curriculum; it promotes the development of cognitive processes, and it also emphasizes the role of personal relevance in curriculum decisions. The dominant rationale for the kind of child-centered, experiential learning we advocate, however, is its consistency with democratic values. NAEYC clearly acknowledges that the principles of practice it espouses have their roots in John Dewey's vision of school and society (Bredekamp, 1987, p. 66). Similarly, these guidelines for curriculum and assessment reflect the theoretical perspective that the proper role of the schools is to prepare citizens for democracy and that such a goal dictates that schools emulate democratic communities.

An important American value is personal autonomy, possessing the inner resources to function as a contributing member of a free society. The long-term goal of American education is not only to help children develop personal integrity and fulfillment but also to enable them to think, reason, and make decisions necessary to participate fully as citizens of a democracy (Dewey, 1916). If producing such citizens is the long-term goal of education, then early childhood education programs need to establish goals that are congruent and that contribute to achieving this objective for all children. The box on page 18 is a *sample* statement of goals for programs serving children from 3 through 8 years of age. A program designed to meet these goals would not only be developmentally appropriate for children now but would also develop the kind of citizens that our country will need in the 21st century—individuals who are able to think critically, work cooperatively, and solve problems creatively. The sample statement of goals is derived from many sources, primarily the Missouri Department of Elementary and Secondary Education's *Project Construct: Curriculum and Assessment Specifications* (1989), the Connecticut Department of Education's *Guide to Program Development for Kindergarten* (1988), and the Report of NAEYC's Commission on Appropriate Education for 4- and 5-Year-Olds (Spodek, 1985).

This introduction briefly described the practical and theoretical perspectives about curriculum and learning that inform this document. In short, early childhood educators view learning as a developmental, interactive process; learning occurs in children's minds as a result of an interaction—an interaction between thought and experience, an interaction with a physical object, or an interaction between a child and an adult or between children and their peers. The guidelines that follow were derived from this theoretical perspective of how children learn and what learnings are important.

# Guidelines for curriculum content and assessment for 3- through 8-year-olds

The National Association for the Education of Young Children (NAEYC) and the National Association of Early Childhood Specialists in State Departments of Education (NAECS/SDE) jointly developed the following guidelines to inform decisions about what constitutes appropriate curriculum content and assessment procedures in programs serving children ages 3 through 8. Decisions about curriculum and assessment are among the most important decisions that educators make. Curriculum and assessment decisions usually reflect a compromise of sorts among the many parties who have an interest in what is taught and learned in schools: parents, community leaders, subject-matter experts, as well as professional educators. NAEYC and NAECS/SDE believe that early childhood educators bear a responsibility to ensure that such decisions are based on current knowledge about child development and learning, as well as knowledge of individual children.

The purpose of these guidelines is to ensure that the knowledge base of early childhood education is applied when decisions are made about curriculum and assessment for young children 3 through 8 years old. Curriculum and assessment decisions must be based on knowledge of what is age appropriate as well as what is individually appropriate if we truly want all children to learn and succeed in school and in life. Similarly, curriculum content and assessment procedures in a free society such as ours should reflect the ideals of a participatory democracy, such as personal autonomy, decision making, equality, and social justice. Schools should not only teach about democratic values but should provide opportunities for children "to live democratically in the microcosm of the classroom" (Kessler, 1991).

---

## SAMPLE*
## EARLY CHILDHOOD PROGRAM GOALS

Each individual early childhood program should establish its own goals for children as the result of a consensual process. Those goals should address all domains—emotional, social, cognitive, and physical—and should attend to the development of desirable attitudes and dispositions, skills and processes, knowledge and understanding. Following is a *sample* goal statement for a program serving children 3 through 8 years of age.

## Responsible adults want children to

• develop a positive self-concept and attitude toward learning, self-control, and a sense of belonging;

• develop curiosity about the world, confidence as a learner, creativity and imagination, and personal initiative;

• develop relationships of mutual trust and respect with adults and peers, understand perspectives of other people, and negotiate and apply rules of group living;

• understand and respect social and cultural diversity;

• know about the community and social roles;

• use language to communicate effectively and to facilitate thinking and learning;

• become literate individuals who gain satisfaction, as well as information, from reading and writing;

• represent ideas and feelings through pretend play, drama, dance and movement, music, art, and construction;

• think critically, reason, and solve problems;

• construct understanding of relationships among objects, people, and events, such as classifying, ordering, number, space, and time;

• construct knowledge of the physical world, manipulate objects for desired effects, and understand cause-and-effect relationships;

• acquire knowledge of and appreciation for the fine arts, humanities, and sciences;

• become competent in management of their bodies and acquire basic physical skills, both gross motor and fine motor; and

• gain knowledge about the care of their bodies and maintain a desirable level of health and fitness.

---

*\* For illustrative purposes only—not an official position*

Curriculum content (what children are to learn), learning processes (how children learn), instructional strategies (how to teach), environment (the learning context), and assessment strategies (how to know that learning has occurred and what curriculum adjustments are needed) are all interrelated and constitute the educational program. A complete discussion of these topics is beyond the scope of this document. For more information on NAEYC's positions on appropriate instructional strategies and learning processes, see *Developmentally Appropriate Practice in Early Childhood Programs Serving Children From Birth Through Age 8*, edited by S. Bredekamp (1987).

# Guidelines for curriculum content

## *Who the guidelines are for*

The guidelines in this document apply to educational programs for *all* children ages 3 through 8. Recently many specialized programs—such as those for children identified as at-risk for school failure, gifted, developmentally delayed, learning disabled, or physically or emotionally disabled—have been developed primarily because traditional curriculum and classroom practice have not been responsive to a wide range of individual differences. Developmentally appropriate curriculum and practices, such as those described in this document, are more likely to accommodate to a broader range of individual differences. When a child requires specialized services that go beyond what can be provided within regular classroom experiences, then those services should be provided in programs that also meet these guidelines.

## *How to use the guidelines*

Guidelines are standards or principles by which to make a judgment or determine a course of action. The following statements are guidelines to use in making decisions about developing and/or selecting curriculum content for young children (what children are expected to know and be able to do). Guidelines are followed by elaborating paragraphs. To judge curriculum appropriate and acceptable, positive evidence should exist that *all* guidelines are met. Curriculum should be evaluated at the level of implementation, as well as at previous points in time when curriculum decisions are made. For instance, a curriculum decision made at a district or agency level may appear to conform to the guidelines, but when implemented at the classroom level, it may not. Likewise, if curriculum appears to be weak in meeting one or more guidelines, it may be possible to compensate for the weakness during implementation by teachers in classrooms.

**1. The curriculum has an articulated description of its theoretical base that is consistent with prevailing professional opinion and research on how children learn.**

Curriculum should be grounded in the most current knowledge of child development and learning. The prevailing world view reflects a developmental, interactive, constructivist approach to learning that is not limited to the almost exclusively behaviorist approach that has permeated curriculum and assessment in this country for the past several decades.

**2. Curriculum content is designed to achieve long-range goals for children in all domains—social, emotional, cognitive, and physical—and to prepare children to function as fully contributing members of a democratic society.**

Curriculum should address the development and learning of the whole child. This means that curriculum in primary grade schools must attend to social, emotional, and physical goals as well as cognitive goals. Likewise, programs for 3- and 4-year-olds need to address cognition as well as social, emotional, and physical development. In addition, curriculum content and processes should reflect democratic ideals of community involvement, liberty, freedom of choice, equality, fairness, and justice.

**3. Curriculum addresses the development of knowledge and understanding, processes and skills, dispositions and attitudes.**

The acquisition of knowledge and the mastery of skills is accomplished so as to ensure that children will be disposed to apply the knowledge or skill and so that children associate positive feelings with the learning (Katz & Chard, 1989). For example, if reading instruction is limited to drill and practice on phonics and word-attack skills, children may choose to not read because they find no pleasure or satisfaction in reading or do not understand what they decode. On the other hand, if children are motivated to get meaning from reading, they are more likely to respond to instruction in use of phonetic cues.

**4. Curriculum addresses a broad range of content that is relevant, engaging, and meaningful to children.**

The human mind is a pattern detector; the child naturally attempts to make meaning out of every experience. As a result, what is meaningful is always more easily learned, understood, and remembered. Effective curriculum develops knowledge and skills in a meaningful context, not in isolation. For example, children learn numerals and number concepts by counting real objects, not by filling in workbook pages. Children learn letters and their sounds from using them in their name, signs, or stories that are meaningful to them rather than by tracing them on a page or reciting the alphabet repeatedly. The younger the child, the more important it is to provide curriculum content that is close to the child's experience and therefore more likely to be meaningful.

**5.** **Curriculum goals are realistic and attainable for most children in the designated age range for which they were designed.**

Curriculum planning should adjust for normative differences in children's development and learning. Children should not be expected to comprehend abstract/symbolic concepts or master skills or content that can be acquired much more easily later on. To some extent, this guideline addresses the issue of efficiency in teaching and learning. For instance, first, second, and third grade teachers all report that children cannot comprehend place value; teachers spend hours trying to teach this abstract concept, and children either become frustrated or resort to memorizing meaningless tricks. This is an example of an unrealistic objective that could be attained much more easily later on.

Curriculum decisions about when children are expected to acquire knowledge and skills are based on age-group, individual, and cultural expectations. Curriculum expectations of young children are flexible and dynamic rather than deterministic and lock-step since there is no universal sequence of skills development. The curriculum allows for children to work at different levels on different activities and does not require all of the children to do the same thing at the same time. Decisions about when knowledge and skills are introduced and/or expected to be accomplished are based on knowledge of the prior experiences of individual children in a group, knowledge of prerequisite intellectual structures, and knowledge about typical patterns of development and learning.

**6.** **Curriculum content reflects and is generated by the needs and interests of individual children within the group. Curriculum incorporates a wide variety of learning experiences, materials and equipment, and instructional strategies, to accommodate a broad range of children's individual differences in prior experience, maturation rates, styles of learning, needs, and interests.**

Curriculum planning should anticipate the interests that are typical of children of different ages and should also emerge from the interests that children demonstrate. Interest can also be generated by exposing children to events, materials, and people that children

would not experience otherwise. Educators must choose which of children's interests to support and which to ignore. In addition, educators have a responsibility to nurture certain interests, particularly those that are tied to cultural values, such as the value of children's autonomy and creative experience.

**7.** **Curriculum respects and supports individual, cultural, and linguistic diversity. Curriculum supports and encourages positive relationships with children's families.**

The curriculum embraces the reality of multiculturalism in American society by providing a balance between learning the common core of dominant cultural knowledge (for example, the English language, democratic values) and knowledge of minority cultures. Curriculum accommodates children who have limited English proficiency. All of the cultures and primary languages of the children are respectfully reflected in the curriculum.

**8.** **Curriculum builds upon what children already know and are able to do (activating prior knowledge) to consolidate their learning and to foster their acquisition of new concepts and skills.**

For example, there is no body of knowledge possessed by all children of the same age, just as there is no universal sequence of learning. Because children bring meaning to learning experiences based on their past experiences and individual development, different children acquire different learnings from the same experience. As a result, curriculum for young children should not be based on a rigid scope and sequence but should help children connect new learning to what they already know and are able to do.

**9.** **The curriculum provides conceptual frameworks for children so that their mental constructions based on prior knowledge and experience become more complex over time.**

Conceptual organizers such as themes, units, or projects give children something meaningful and substantive to engage their minds. It is difficult for children to make sense of abstract concepts such as colors, mathematical symbols, or letter sounds when they are presented at random or devoid of any meaningful context.

**10.** **Curriculum allows for focus on a particular topic or content while allowing for integration across traditional subject-matter divisions by planning around themes and/or learning experiences that provide opportunities for rich conceptual development.**

Children's learning is not compartmentalized or divided into artificial subject-matter distinctions. The purpose of integrating curriculum is to reflect the natural way children learn and also to help children make connections between what they learn at home and in the program, between what they learn in school and in the real world, and between different disciplines or subject-matter areas (British Columbia Ministry of Education, 1990). The curriculum provides for long blocks of time to bring naturally related subjects together and does not require minimal time allotments for instruction in discrete subject matter. For example, children read and write about a science experiment they have done or measure and estimate the number of blocks they will need to build a store.

**11.** **The curriculum content has intellectual integrity; content meets the recognized standards of the relevant subject-matter disciplines.**

Regardless of the age of the child, educators have a responsibility to respect the knowledge base of the appropriate disciplines when formulating curriculum. In an attempt to simplify content, curriculum developers sometimes present inaccurate, misleading, or potentially confusing information. If the specific content is related to a particular discipline, then it should be as accurate as possible (although children's constructions of knowledge will not mirror adult conceptions). For example, science curriculum should be factual and not promote magical thinking in children; likewise, children should be exposed to literature, poetry, and the works of art and music of recognized quality.

**12.** **The content of the curriculum is worth knowing; curriculum respects children's intelligence and does not waste their time.**

Content should be included in curriculum for specific age groups because it is important for children to learn to function capably in their world. Content goals should include what children can learn efficiently and effectively at this time. Children and teachers should not have to waste time trying to address content that is meaningless or could be learned much more easily when the child is older.

**13.** **Curriculum engages children actively, not passively, in the learning process. Children have opportunities to make meaningful choices.**

The curriculum provides for children's direct experience before moving to more abstract levels of understanding. The curriculum or learning experience builds on children's prior learning and previous knowledge, thus sensory experience is not prerequisite in every situation but is vital when introducing new concepts or information. Encouraging and permitting children to make real choices fosters interest and engagement. For instance, children should have opportunities to express their own ideas in writing and to read books of their choosing as well as those that the entire group will address.

**14.** **Curriculum values children's constructive errors and does not prematurely limit exploration and experimentation for the sake of ensuring "right" answers.**

Overemphasis on standardized test scores and the acquisition of basic skills has made teachers and parents uncomfortable with the natural process of the child's construction of knowledge. The fact is that teachers can learn a great deal about children' thinking and reasoning and level of cognitive development by attending to their "wrong" answers.

**15.** **Curriculum emphasizes the development of children's thinking, reasoning, decision-making, and problem-solving abilities.**

Curriculum emphasizes both content and process, what children need to know and be able to do. Curriculum content gives meaning to process, rather than focusing on isolated facts. Skills are taught in the context of activities that are meaningful to the child, rather than teaching skills in isolation (Lloyd-Jones & Lunsford, 1988).

**16.** **Curriculum emphasizes the value of social interaction to learning in all domains and provides opportunities to learn from peers.**

Social interaction with peers and adults is essential for children to develop real understanding. Social interaction also provides opportunities for children to learn cooperation and other kinds of positive social behavior. Multiage grouping is one strategy to promote social interaction among individual children and their more capable peers, an effective way of enhancing language competence and generally assisting children's progress to the next level of development and understanding.

**17.** **Curriculum is supportive of children's physiological needs for activity, sensory stimulation, fresh air, rest, hygiene, and nourishment/elimination.**

Curriculum should respect and meet children's physical needs while also promoting children's independent functioning and ability to meet their own needs. Children should not be required to sit still for long periods without a break. Under no circumstances should children who need regular opportunities to move their bodies be kept indoors to complete tasks or be deprived of food as punishment.

**18.** Curriculum protects children's psychological safety, that is, children feel happy, relaxed, and comfortable rather than disengaged, frightened, worried, or stressed.

Decisions about curriculum should respect children's psychological safety. For instance, the content itself should not generate fear or confusion, nor should the premature expectation of mastery of skills generate stress.

**19.** The curriculum strengthens children's sense of competence and enjoyment of learning by providing experiences for children to succeed from their point of view.

Sometimes teachers seem to use as their primary criterion for selecting curriculum, "But the children just love it!" Enjoying the curriculum is an important but insufficient criterion for curriculum selection. Worthwhile curriculum does not have to entertain children; instead, children's enjoyment can derive from positive feelings about self and meaningful learning as they realize their own progress and growing competence.

**20.** The curriculum is flexible so that teachers can adapt to individual children or groups.

The curriculum suggests alternatives as well as assumes that teachers will use their own professional judgment.

# Suggestions for using the curriculum guidelines

Developing curriculum or deciding whether a particular curriculum is appropriate for a specific group of children is a complex task that requires consideration of many variables. To facilitate the task of using the curriculum guidelines, we have phrased each of the guidelines as a question. We suggest that a curriculum committee, composed of six to eight teachers, review a proposed curriculum by subjecting it to these questions. An approved curriculum would be one for which a group of early childhood professionals could consensually agree in the affirmative to each of the following questions:

**1.** Does it promote interactive learning and encourage the child's construction of knowledge?

**2.** Does it help achieve social, emotional, physical, and cognitive goals and promote democratic values?

**3.** Does it encourage development of positive feelings and dispositions toward learning while leading to acquisition of knowledge and skills?

**4.** Is it meaningful for these children? Is it relevant to the children's lives? Can it be made more relevant by relating it to a personal experience children have had, or can they easily gain direct experience with it?

**5.** Are the expectations realistic and attainable at this time, or could the children more easily and efficiently acquire the knowledge or skills later on?

**6.** Is it of interest to children and to the teacher?

**7.** Is it sensitive to and respectful of cultural and linguistic diversity? Does it expect, allow, and appreciate individual differences? Does it promote positive relationships with families?

**8.** Does it build on and elaborate children's current knowledge and abilities?

**9.** Does it lead to conceptual understanding by helping children construct their own understanding in meaningful contexts?

**10.** Does it facilitate integration of content across traditional subject-matter areas?

**11.** Is the information presented accurate and credible according to the recognized standards of the relevant discipline?

**12.** Is this content worth knowing? Can it be learned by these children efficiently and effectively now?

**13.** Does it encourage active learning and allow children to make meaningful choices?

**14.** Does it foster children's exploration and inquiry, rather than focusing on "right" answers or "right" ways to complete a task?

**15.** Does it promote the development of higher order abilities, such as thinking, reasoning, problem solving, and decision making?

**16.** Does it promote and encourage social interaction among children and adults?

**17.** Does it respect children's physiological needs for activity, sensory stimulation, fresh air, rest, hygiene, and nourishment/elimination?

**18.** Does it promote feelings of psychological safety, security, and belonging?

**19.** Does it provide experiences that promote feelings of success, competence, and enjoyment of learning?

**20.** Does it permit flexibility for children and teachers?

# Guidelines for appropriate assessment

Assessment is the process of observing, recording, and otherwise documenting the work children do and how they do it, as a basis for a variety of educational decisions that affect the child. Assessment is integral to curriculum and instruction. In early childhood programs, assessment serves several different purposes: (1) to plan instruction for individuals and groups and for communicating with parents, (2) to identify children who may be in need of specialized services or intervention, and (3) to evaluate how well the program is meeting its goals.

The following guidelines first address the primary use of assessment: for planning instruction and communicating with parents. Guidelines for screening and program evaluation follow. (For additional information on the topic of assessment, see NAEYC's Position Statement on Standardized Testing of Young Children [NAEYC, 1988], Unacceptable Trends in Kindergarten Entry and Placement [NAECS/SDE, 1987], and *Achievement Testing In Early Childhood Education: The Games Grown-Ups Play* [Kamii, 1990].)

## Guidelines for planning instruction and communicating with parents

Assessment of children's development and learning is absolutely necessary if teachers are to provide curriculum and instruction that is both age appropriate and individually appropriate. An initial assessment is necessary for teachers to get to know children and to adjust the planned curriculum. The appropriate use of initial assessment is to find out what children already know and are able to do and to use this information to adjust the curriculum to the individual children. Too often, initial assessment takes the form of "readiness testing" with young children or "achievement testing" with older children, the results of which are used to exclude children from the program, track them by ability, or otherwise label them. How the initial assessment is conducted will determine the accuracy and usefulness of the findings. To provide an accurate picture of children's capabilities, teachers must observe children over time; information obtained on one brief encounter may be incomplete or distorted. Likewise, initial assessment information must be used to adjust curriculum and instruction. If assessment data are ignored and no adjustments are made, then the data should not be collected. Moreover, assessment data should be used to bring about benefits for children, such as more individualized instruction; it should not be used to recommend that children stay out of a program, be retained in grade, or be assigned to a segregated group based on ability or developmental maturity.

The following principles should guide assessment procedures for children ages 3 through 8:

**1.** Curriculum and assessment are integrated throughout the program; assessment is congruent with and relevant to the goals, objectives, and content of the program.

**2.** Assessment results in benefits to the child, such as needed adjustments in the curriculum or more individualized instruction and improvements in the program.

**3.** Children's development and learning in all domains— physical, social, emotional, and cognitive—and their dispositions and feelings are informally and routinely assessed by teachers' observing children's activities and interactions, listening to them as they talk, and using their constructive errors to understand their learning.

**4.** Assessment provides teachers with useful information to successfully fulfill their responsibilities: to support children's learning and development, to plan for individuals and groups, and to communicate with parents.

**5.** Assessment involves regular and periodic observation of the child in a wide variety of circumstances that are representative of the child's behavior in the program over time.

**6.** Assessment relies primarily on procedures that reflect the ongoing life of the classroom and typical activities of the children. Assessment avoids approaches that place children in artificial situations, impede the usual learning and developmental experiences in the classroom, or divert children from their natural learning processes.

**7.** Assessment relies on demonstrated performance during real, not contrived, activities, for example, real reading and writing activities rather than only skills testing (Teale, 1988; Engel, 1990).

**8.** Assessment utilizes an array of tools and a variety of processes, including, but not limited to, collections of representative work by children (artwork, stories they write, tape recordings of their reading), records of systematic observations by teachers, records of conversations and interviews with children, and teachers' summaries of children's progress as individuals and as groups (Chittenden & Courtney, 1989; Goodman, Goodman, & Hood, 1989).

**9.** Assessment recognizes individual diversity of learners and allows for differences in styles and rates of learning. Assessment takes into consideration children's ability in English, their stage of language acquisition, and whether they have been given the time and opportunity to develop proficiency in their native language as well as in English.

**10.** Assessment supports children's development and learning; it does *not* threaten children's psychological safety or feelings of self-esteem.

**11.** Assessment supports parents' relationships with their children and does not undermine parents' confidence in their children's or their own ability, nor does it devalue the language and culture of the family.

**12.** Assessment demonstrates children's overall strengths and progress, what children *can* do, not just their wrong answers and what they cannot do or do not know.

**13.** Assessment is an essential component of the teacher's role. Since teachers can make maximal use of assessment results, the teacher is the *primary* assessor.

**14.** Assessment is a collaborative process involving children and teachers, teachers and parents, school and community. Information from parents about each child's experiences at home is used in planning instruction and evaluating children's learning. Information obtained from assessment is shared with parents in language they can understand.

**15.** Assessment encourages children to participate in self-evaluation.

**16.** Assessment addresses what children can do independently and what they can demonstrate with assistance since the latter shows the direction of their growth.

**17.** Information about each child's growth, development, and learning is systematically collected and recorded at regular intervals. Information such as samples of children's work, descriptions of their performance, and anecdotal records is used for planning instruction and communicating with parents.

**18.** A regular process exists for periodic information sharing between teachers and parents about children's growth and development and performance. The method of reporting to parents does not rely on letter or numerical grades but rather provides more meaningful, descriptive information in narrative form.

### Guidelines for identifying children with special needs.

Another major purpose of assessing children is to identify children with special needs in order to ensure that they receive appropriate services and/or intervention. The identification process involves at least two steps: screening and diagnosis. Screening is a brief assessment procedure designed to identify children who *may* have a learning problem or handicapping condition that requires more intensive diagnosis based on many sources of information, including that obtained from parents and expert diagnosticians (Meisels, 1985). Formal screening is warranted when parents, teachers, or other professionals suspect that a child may have such a problem. Screening should never be used to identify second-language learners as "handicapped" solely on the basis of their limited abilities in English. The word *screening* is sometimes used erroneously to refer to the administration of formal or informal readiness tests by which teachers get to know children so that they can begin the process of tailoring the curriculum that they planned for all of the children to the individual children in their group. This process is more accurately described as assessment for planning instruction, and therefore the guidelines above apply to these situations.

Components of the screening process (ILASCD, 1989) typically include a range of activities that allow the screener to observe and record children's physical health, fine-/ gross-motor skills, social interactions, emotional expressions, communications competence, concept development, and adaptive skills. A parent interview obtains the following information, at a minimum: medical history, general health, family health concerns, serious or chronic illness, family composition, and parent perception of child's socioemotional and cognitive development.

The following principles (ILASCD, 1989; Maryland State Department of Education, 1989) should guide assessment procedures used to identify children's special needs:

**1.** Results of screening tests are *not* used to make decisions about entrance to school or as the single criterion for placement in a special program but rather are used as part of a thorough process of diagnosis designed to ensure that children receive the individual services they need.

**2.** Any standardized screening or diagnostic test that is administered to a child is valid and reliable in terms of the background characteristics of the child being tested and the test's intended purposes. This is determined by a careful review of the reliability and validity information that is provided in the technical manual that accompanies the test and of independent reviews of tests, such as those available in Buros' Mental Measurements yearbooks (Kramer & Conoley, 1992).

**3.** When a child is formally tested, the procedures conform with all regulations contained in P.L. 94–142. Parents are informed in advance, and information about the test and test results are shared with the child's parents. Any interpretation of test scores describes, in nontechnical language, what the test covered, what the scores do and do not mean (common misinterpretations of the test scores), and how the results will be used. Allowances are made for parents to remain with the child during screening, if desired.

**4.** The screener approaches all interactions with children in a positive manner. The screener has knowledge of and prior experience with young children in order to score the measure accurately and support the validity of the results.

**5.** The younger the child, the more critical it is that the screening activities involve the manipulation of toys and materials rather than pictures and paper-and-pencil tasks.

**6.** If the results of the screening indicate that a child has not performed within an average developmental range, the child is seen individually by an experienced diagnostician who is also an expert in child development.

**7.** If a comprehensive diagnostic process is recommended after screening, key conditions warranting the implementation of this process should be delineated and documented for the parents in writing in nontechnical language that they can understand. Throughout the assessment process parents must be informed in writing about diagnostic resources, parent rights, and reasons for referral, as well as rights of refusal.

## Guidelines for program evaluation and accountability

Whenever children are served in a program, it is essential that the program be evaluated regularly to ensure that it is meeting its goals and that children and families are benefiting from participation. In recent years standardized test scores have become the primary vehicle for demonstrating that schools and teachers are accountable. Too often, this practice has led to blaming children who are ill served by the program or to punishing districts that do not measure up to expectations without examining all components of the program. Overreliance on standardized achievement test scores as the only indicator of program effectiveness has had a detrimental effect on curriculum; therefore, any effort to reform curriculum must be matched by testing reform. Data obtained through program evaluation should be used to identify areas in need of staff development or other support.

The following guidelines are designed to guide program evaluation efforts:

**1.** In constructing assessment procedures related to evaluating programs or determining program accountability, no other stated principles of curriculum or assessment are violated.

**2.** Performance data of children collected by teachers to plan instruction are summarized and quantified by teachers and administrators to use in evaluating how well the program is meeting its goals for children and families.

**3.** The program uses multiple indicators of progress in all developmental domains to evaluate the effect of the program on children's development and learning. Group-administered, standardized, multiple-choice achievement tests are prohibited before third grade, preferably before fourth grade (see Kamii, 1990).

**4.** All components of the program are evaluated to judge program effectiveness within the overall context of opportunities provided for children and families, including staff development and evaluation, parent satisfaction and feelings about how well the program serves their children and their opportunities for involvement, administration, physical environment, and health and safety. Results of outside, independent evaluation, such as that obtained from program accreditation, is useful in program evaluation.

**5.** Programs that are mandated to use a standardized test of children's progress for program evaluation or accountability purposes employ a sampling method

whenever feasible. This approach eliminates the need to subject all children to a testing procedure that can consume large blocks of time, cause undue stress, and produce results that are used for unwarranted decisions about individual children.

# Applying the assessment guidelines

As with curriculum decisions, assessment decisions should reflect the consensual opinion of early childhood professionals as well as assessment experts. To facilitate this process we have phrased the foregoing guidelines as questions. Evaluation of current or proposed assessment procedures and/or instruments should result in affirmative responses to *all* of these questions.

## Questions to ask in evaluating a program's assessment procedures

**1.** Is the assessment procedure based on the goals and objectives of the specific curriculum used in the program?

**2.** Are the results of assessment used to benefit children, i.e., to plan for individual children, improve instruction, identify children's interests and needs, and individualize instruction, rather than label, track, or fail children?

**3.** Does the assessment procedure address all domains of learning and development—social, emotional, physical, and cognitive—as well as children's feelings and dispositions toward learning?

**4.** Does assessment provide useful information to teachers to help them do a better job?

**5.** Does the assessment procedure rely on teachers' regular and periodic observations and record keeping of children's everyday activities and performance so that results reflect children's behavior over time?

**6.** Does the assessment procedure occur as part of the ongoing life of the classroom rather than in an artificial, contrived context?

**7.** Does the assessment procedure evaluate performance rather than only testing skills in isolation?

**8.** Does the assessment rely on multiple sources of information about children, such as collections of their work, results of teacher interviews and dialogues, as well as observations?

**9.** Does the assessment procedure reflect individual, cultural, and linguistic diversity? Is it free of cultural, language, and gender biases?

**10.** Do children appear comfortable and relaxed during assessment rather than tense or anxious?

**11.** Does the assessment procedure support parents' confidence in their children and their ability as parents rather than threaten or undermine parents' confidence?

**12.** Does the assessment examine children's strengths and capabilities rather than just their weaknesses or what they do not know?

**13.** Is the teacher the primary assessor, and are teachers adequately trained for this role?

**14.** Does the assessment procedure involve collaboration among teachers, children, administrators, and parents? Is information from parents used in planning instruction and evaluating children's learning? Are parents informed about assessment information?

**15.** Do children have an opportunity to reflect on and evaluate their own learning?

**16.** Are children assessed in supportive contexts to determine what they are capable of doing with assistance as well as what they can do independently?

**17.** Is there a systematic procedure for collecting assessment data that facilitates its use in planning instruction and communicating with parents?

**18.** Is there a regular procedure for communicating the results of assessment to parents in meaningful language, rather than letter or number grades, that reports children's individual progress?

## Questions to ask in evaluating screening/diagnostic procedures

**1.** Are screening test results used only as a first step in a systematic diagnostic procedure for identifying children with special needs? Are screening test results *never* used to deny children entrance to a program or as the sole criterion for assignment to a special program?

**2.** Are the screening tests used reliable and valid for the purpose for which they are used? Are the technical adequacies of standardized measures carefully evaluated by knowledgeable professionals?

**3.** Are parents informed in advance when children are screened? Is the purpose and procedure carefully explained to parents, and are parents permitted to stay with their child if desired?

**4.** Is the screener knowledgeable about young children and able to relate to them in a positive manner?

**5.** Does the screening procedure involve concrete, hands-on activities rather than paper-and-pencil tasks?

**6.** Does the screening procedure lead to systematic diagnosis of potential handicapping conditions or health problems for the children for which this step is warranted?

**7.** Are parents informed of the procedures and of their rights throughout the screening and diagnosis procedure?

## Questions to ask in evaluating program evaluation procedures

**1.** Is the program evaluation procedure congruent with all other stated principles of curriculum and assessment?

**2.** Does the program evaluation summarize and quantify the results of performance-based assessments of children's progress conducted by classroom teachers?

**3.** Does the program evaluation incorporate many indicators of children's progress rather than standardized, group-administered achievement test scores?

**4.** Does the program evaluation address all components of the delivery of the program instead of being limited to measuring outcomes for children?

**5.** Is sampling used in situations where the administration of a standardized achievement test is mandated?

## References

American Association for the Advancement of Science. (1989). *Science for all Americans: A project 2061 report on literacy goals in science, mathematics, and technology.* Washington, DC: Author.

Association for Supervision and Curriculum Development. (1989). *Toward the thinking curriculum: Current cognitive research.* Alexandria, VA: Author.

Bennett, W.J. (1988). *First lessons.* Washington, DC: U.S. Department of Education.

Biber, B. (1984). *Early education and psychological development.* New Haven, CT: Yale University Press.

Bredekamp, S. (Ed.). (1987). *Developmentally appropriate practice in early childhood programs serving children from birth through age 8* (exp. ed.). Washington, DC: NAEYC.

British Columbia Ministry of Education. (1990). *Primary program resource document.* Victoria, British Columbia: Author.

Chittenden, E., & Courtney, R. (1989). Assessment of young children's reading: Documentation as an alternative to testing. In D. Strickland & L. Morrow (Eds.), *Emerging literacy: Young children learn to read and write* (pp. 107–120). Newark, DE: International Reading Association.

Connecticut Department of Education. (1988). *Guide to program development for kindergarten.* Hartford, CT: Author.

DeVries, R., & Kohlberg, L. (1990). *Constructivist early education: Overview and comparison with other programs.* Washington, DC: NAEYC.

Dewey, J. (1916). *Democracy and education: An introduction to the philosophy of education.* New York: Macmillan.

Eisner, E. (1990). Who decides what schools teach? *Phi Delta Kappan, 71*(7), 523–526.

Eisner, W.E., & Vallance, E. (Eds.). (1974). *Conflicting conceptions of curriculum.* Berkeley, CA: McCutchan.

Elkind, D. (1976). *Child development and education.* New York: Oxford University Press.

Elkind, D. (1987). *Miseducation: Preschoolers at risk.* New York: Knopf.

Engel, B. (1990). An approach to evaluation in reading and writing. In C. Kamii (Ed.), *Achievement testing in early childhood education: Games grown-ups play* (pp. 119–134). Washington, DC: NAEYC.

Erikson, E. (1963). *Childhood and society*. New York: Norton.

FairTest (National Center for Fair and Open Testing). (1990). *Fallout from the testing explosion: How 100 million standardized exams undermine equity and excellence in America's public schools* (3rd ed.). Cambridge, MA: Author.

Ferreiro, E., & Teberosky, A. (1982). *Literacy before schooling*. Portsmouth, NH: Heinemann.

Garbarino, J. (1989). Early intervention in cognitive development as a strategy for reducing poverty. In G. Miller (Ed.), *Giving children a chance: The case for more effective national policies* (pp. 23–26). Washington, DC: National Policy Press.

Goodman, K., Goodman, Y., & Hood, W. (1989). *The whole language evaluation book*. Portsmouth, NH: Heinemann.

Hirsch, E. (1987). *Cultural literacy: What every American needs to know*. Boston: Houghton Mifflin.

Illinois Association for Supervision and Curriculum Development. (1989). *Early childhood screening*. Normal, IL: Author.

International Reading Association. (1989). *Literacy development and prefirst grade*. Newark, DE: Author.

Jones, E. (1989). *Emergent curriculum: Planning and letting go*. Unpublished paper. Pasadena, CA: Pacific Oaks College.

Kamii, C. (1982). *Number in preschool and kindergarten: Educational implications of Piaget's theory*. Washington, DC: NAEYC.

Kamii, C. (Ed.). (1990). *Achievement testing in early childhood education: The games grown-ups play*. Washington, DC: NAEYC.

Kamii, C., & DeVries, R. (1980). *Group games in early childhood education*. Washington, DC: NAEYC.

Katz, L. (1991). Pedagogical issues in early childhood education. In S.L. Kagan (Ed.), *The care and education of America's children: Obstacles and opportunities. Ninetieth yearbook of the National Society for the Study of Education* (pp. 50–68). Chicago: University of Chicago Press.

Katz, L.G., & Chard, S. (1989). *Engaging children's minds: The project approach*. Norwood, NJ: Ablex.

Kessler, S. (1991). Alternative perspectives on early childhood education. *Early Childhood Research Quarterly, 6*(2), 183–197.

Kliebard, H. (1986). *The struggle for the American curriculum*. Boston: Routledge & Kegan Paul.

Kramer, J.J., & Conoley, J.C. (Eds.). (1992). The eleventh mental measurements yearbook. Lincoln, NE: The Buros Institute of Mental Measurements, University of Nebraska.

Lloyd-Jones, R., & Lunsford, A.A. (Eds.). (1988). *The English Coalition Conference: Democracy through language*. Urbana, IL: National Council of Teachers of English.

Maryland State Department of Education. (1989). *Standards for implementing quality prekindergarten education*. Baltimore, MD: Maryland State Department of Education, Division of Instruction, Language, and Supplementary Programs. (ERIC Document Reproduction Service No. ED 238 525)

Meisels, S.J. (1985). *Developmental screening in early childhood: A guide* (rev. ed.). Washington, DC: NAEYC.

Missouri Department of Elementary and Secondary Education. (1989, May). *Project Construct: Curriculum and assessment specifications*. St. Louis, MO: Author.

National Association for the Education of Young Children. (1988). Position statement on standardized testing of young children 3 through 8 years of age. *Young Children, 43*(3), 42–47.

National Association of Early Childhood Specialists in State Departments of Education. (1987). Unacceptable trends in kindergarten entry and placement. Unpublished paper

National Association of Elementary School Principals. (1990). *Early childhood education and the elementary school principal*. Alexandria, VA: Author.

National Association of State Boards of Education. (1988). *Right from the start: The report of the NASBE task force on early childhood education*. Alexandria, VA: Author.

National Commission on Social Studies in the Schools. (1989). *Charting a course: Social studies for the 21st century*. Washington, DC: Author.

National Commission on Testing and Public Policy. (1990). *From gatekeeper to gateway: Transforming testing in America*. Chestnut Hill, MA: Author.

National Council of Teachers of Mathematics. (1989). *Curriculum and evaluation standards for school mathematics*. Reston, VA: Author.

Piaget, J. (1952). *The origins of intelligence in children*. New York: International Universities Press.

Rosegrant, T. (1989). The developmental characteristics of three-and-a-half- to five-and-a-half-year-olds and implications for learning. Unpublished paper.

Rothman, R. (1989). What to teach: Reform turns finally to the essential question. *Education Week, 1*(8), 10–11.

Shepard, L.A., & Smith, M.L. (1988). Escalating academic demand in kindergarten: Some nonsolutions. *Elementary School Journal, 89*(2), 135–146.

Smith-Burke, M.T. (1985). Reading and talking: Learning through interaction. In A. Jaggar & M.T. Smith-Burke (Eds.), *Observing the language learner* (pp. 199–211). Newark, DE: International Reading Association.

Spodek, B. (1977). What constitutes worthwhile educational experiences for young children. In B. Spodek (Ed.), *Teaching practices: Reexamining assumptions* (pp. 1–20). Washington, DC: NAEYC.

Spodek, B. (1985). Goals and purposes of educational programs for 4- and 5-year-old children. Final report of the Commission on Appropriate Education. Unpublished document.

Spodek, B. (1988). Conceptualizing today's kindergarten curriculum. *The Elementary School Journal, 89*(2), 203–211.

Spodek, B., & Saracho, O. (1990). Preparing early childhood teachers. In B. Spodek & O. Saracho (Eds.), *Early childhood teacher preparation. Yearbook in early childhood education* (vol. 1). New York: Teachers College Press.

Strauss, S. (1987). Educational-developmental psychology and school learning. In L. Liben (Ed.), *Development and learning: Conflict or congruence?* (pp. 133–157). Hillsdale, NJ: Erlbaum.

Teale, W.H. (1988). Developmentally appropriate assessment of reading and writing in the early childhood classroom. *The Elementary School Journal, 89*(2), 173–184.

Teale, W., & Sulzby, E. (Eds.). (1986). *Emergent literacy: Writing and reading*. Norwood, NJ: Ablex.

Vygotsky, L.S. (1978). *Mind in society: The development of psychological processes*. Cambridge, MA: Harvard University Press.

# Reaching Potentials Through Appropriate Curriculum: Conceptual Frameworks for Applying the Guidelines

*Sue Bredekamp and Teresa Rosegrant*

One of the most important tasks of good teachers is to provide conceptual frameworks for the learner to help make sense of what is being learned. The purpose of this chapter is to offer conceptual frameworks with which to make sense of and successfully apply the NAEYC and NAECS/SDE guidelines. It is important to note that the content of this chapter reflects the opinions of the authors, based on our work using the guidelines with teachers, and does not necessarily reflect the opinions of NAEYC or NAECS/SDE.

First, we will revisit the guidelines, offering some illustrative examples. Second, we will describe the big ideas or key concepts that undergird the guidelines. Then we will address some of those big ideas in more detail. A framework for describing the learning process—the cycle of learning—is offered; this framework provides a tool for determining age-appropriate and individually appropriate curriculum expectations, what content is realistic and attainable, and when to introduce the content. Among the other big ideas we discuss are whole child philosophy and child-centered curriculum; integrated curriculum; children's needs and interests, and the knowledge base of the disciplines. The chapter concludes with a description of a continuum of teaching behaviors that is congruent with the learning cycle. Before turning to the specifics of the

guidelines and their application, we begin by articulating our concept of curriculum, the hidden agenda behind this entire exercise.

## Curriculum and assessment: What do we have in mind?

A perspective about curriculum and assessment underlies everything that is said in this book. All curriculum decisions are value laden, and ours are no exception. We know that children spend many hours in child care centers, preschools, and primary grade schools. We believe that during those hours children are constructing their reality about many things, but especially about themselves as learners and human beings. Our job as teachers is to help children interpret their experiences and to involve them in decision making, not just make them perform or jump through the hoops that we have set up for them. We think that the primary purpose of curriculum should be to help children develop personal integrity and fulfillment while also enabling them to think, reason, and make decisions necessary to participate fully as citizens of a democracy.

To produce these kinds of people, we need meaningful curriculum, "mindful" rather than mindless experiences such as those to which so many children are exposed every day. The concept of a meaningful curriculum is described more eloquently by others. Katz and Chard (1989) and LeeKeenan and Edwards (1992) talk about engaging children's minds through the project approach. Duckworth (1987) describes learning and teaching as "the having of wonderful ideas." Gardner (1991) recommends that we help children develop the expert-like, deep understandings of a discipline by making schools more like hands-on museums and schooling more like serving apprenticeships. The excitement that surrounds the early childhood programs in Reggio Emilia, Italy (Katz, 1990; New, 1990), is primarily the discovery of meaningful curriculum in practice. In addition, the programs in Reggio Emilia appear to be models of cultural continuity and community involvement, key determinants of the meaningfulness of children's experiences. All of these perspectives are congruent with our goal of achieving mindful curriculum. Such a curriculum involves children mentally and physically in the life of the school. If the curriculum is mindful as opposed to mindless, children at work or play in school should be able to provide meaningful answers to the question, "What are you doing?" If they shrug their shoulders or answer "work," that may be a clue that curriculum is not mindful. Instead they might say something like, "We are making up our own holiday just for the people in our class" or "We are figuring out where the rain goes" (Reggio Emilia, Italy, Department of Education, 1987).

Mindful curriculum enables children to make sense of what they are learning and to connect their experiences in ways that lead to rich conceptual development. Mindless curriculum is similar to what Derman-Sparks calls "tourist curriculum" (1989; Chapter 8, this volume), the common approach to multiculturalism in which a culture is visited briefly, allowing only a surface exposure to artifacts rather than an understanding of the deep structural rules that define a culture. The problem of "tourist" curriculum is not limited to the area of multicultural studies. Too much of curriculum today fragments content and then moves on to the next subject, assuming that because a topic has been covered, it has been learned. "We can't do the farm in the spring; we did it in the fall," says a kindergarten teacher, or "You can't talk about the sun in kindergarten; "That's in the first grade curriculum—but you'd better cover the moon." Such an approach leads to schools full of uninterested tourists who view the school experience as though looking from a tour bus window. Occasionally the tour guide, their teacher, sparks their interest through a particularly entertaining story, but for the most part, the content is so thin that it slips right by. By contrast, mindful curriculum engages children in the challenge of learning; layers of

*MINDFUL CURRICULUM ENABLES CHILDREN TO MAKE SENSE OF WHAT THEY ARE LEARNING AND TO CONNECT THEIR EXPERIENCES IN WAYS THAT LEAD TO RICH CONCEPTUAL DEVELOPMENT.*

involvement are possible. The kindergarten class revisits the farm in the spring to observe the planting that resulted in the harvest they enjoyed in the fall. Kindergartners become so interested in their observations of the stages of the moon that they demand to know more about where the light comes from. Their understandings of these phenomena are deepened as a result.

What about assessment? The cause of much of the sad/bad curriculum in schools is sad/bad assessment, better known as overuse and abuse of standardized achievement testing. Assessment is the tail that wags the curriculum dog. If we want to see real curriculum reform, we must simultaneously achieve reform of assessment practices. We will never see meaningful, mindful curriculum as long as the country continues to settle for and be overly influenced by the results of mindless testing. For these reasons NAEYC and NAECS/SDE take strong positions about appropriate assessment, which are discussed in detail and illustrated with examples in Chapter 4.

NAEYC and NAECS/SDE define assessment as the gathering of useful information for the purpose of constructing understandings about children that guide educational decisions. The most appropriate use of assessment is in the service of instruction; assessment information should be used to make school experiences and life better for children. This is a high standard for assessment to meet, especially when its record is so poor, but it is essential. The concept of assessment that permeates the guidelines and this book is that teachers engage in an interaction with children and parents that enables each party to get feedback from which to adapt their behavior and adjust their thinking. Standardized, paper-and-pencil achievement tests do not serve this purpose, and, for this and other reasons, the use of such tests is inappropriate throughout early childhood. Screening and diagnostic measures do serve a useful purpose; when used correctly, they help identify and diagnose children's special needs, a process that ideally results in children's needs being served. (A more complete discussion of assessment for screening and diagnosis of special needs appears in Chapter 7.)

The assessment guidelines distinguish these purposes and are designed to guide assessment to be used in ways that help children rather than harm them. The greatest protection for children from the abuses of testing lies in this statement from the assessment guidelines (p. 25, this volume): "In constructing assessment procedures related to evaluating programs or determining program accountability, no other stated principles of curriculum or assessment are violated." That means that assessment procedures should not threaten children's psychological safety nor violate their physical needs—no more frightening kindergartners with warnings like, "During the test, I can't help you" or "You can't go to the bathroom during the test." If this guideline were actually implemented, reform of assessment in early childhood would be complete. Having articulated our primary objectives in this enterprise, we turn now to a more detailed discussion of the curriculum guidelines.

## The curriculum guidelines: A roadmap

One activity the NAEYC and NAECS/SDE Steering Committee used to develop the guidelines was to give actual curriculum—such as a state kindergarten curriculum guide, a school district's primary grade social studies curriculum, or a commercially available preschool curriculum—to groups of teachers to evaluate. First the steering committee asked the teachers to make a global judgment about the value of the curriculum for the intended age group of children. Did teach-

ers like it? Would they use it? Then the committee asked the same teachers to report what criteria they used to make their decisions. After the steering committee conducted this exercise several times, patterns began to emerge in the criteria that the teachers applied. These groups of early childhood professionals already had standards for evaluating and selecting curriculum; those criteria that emerged repeatedly became the curriculum guidelines. When the committee finished writing these criteria as principles, they discovered that there were 20. To make them more user friendly, the committee phrased each in the form of a question—20 questions to evaluate curriculum for young children.

The curriculum guidelines (pp. 19–22, this volume) can be divided roughly into three parts: Guidelines 1 to 3 lay the foundation, limiting the parameters by prescribing a theoretical framework and thus defining the type of curriculum desired; Guidelines 4 to 12 address the "what" of curriculum, the nature of the content; and Guidelines 13 to 20 describe the "how" of implementing appropriate curriculum. The guidelines do not separate content from process. This is because, as is stated in the position statement, content and process cannot be separated. Content and process are equally important, and each requires attention at every level of early childhood education.

The stability of any structure usually depends on its underlying foundation; the same is true of curriculum. Curriculum Guidelines 1, 2, and 3 describe the founda-

tion of good curriculum for young children, the theory of learning on which it is based, and the philosophy of education that permeates it. First and foremost, appropriate curriculum reflects an interactive, developmental, constructivist view of learning. But equally important, curriculum for young children must reflect a "whole child philosophy" (Guideline 2) and must be comprehensive, not limited to the achievement of narrowly defined skills (Guideline 3) or to development of one dimension of the person. These concepts are discussed in more detail later in this chapter.

Guidelines 4 through 12 address the "what" of curriculum; they are designed to guide selection of content for individuals and groups. Guidelines 4, 5, 6, and 7 activate knowledge of child development, guiding us to choose curriculum that is relevant, meaningful, and realistic, based on the needs, interests, and differences of individual children. Guidelines 8, 9, and 10 address the organization of curriculum planning, emphasizing that good early childhood curriculum builds on prior knowledge while not being limited to one sequence or one structure. Instead, good curriculum is conceptually oriented and integrated. Again, these concepts are addressed in greater detail in the next section of this chapter. The "what" of curriculum content is further determined by Guidelines 11 and 12, requiring that curriculum be worthwhile, have intellectual integrity, and be scientifically accurate. These guidelines are the primary focus of Volume 2 of this work, in which we turn to the disciplines to assist with curriculum decisions.

Guidelines 13 through 20 address the "how" of curriculum. Many of these points are further described in NAEYC's position statements on developmentally appropriate practice (Bredekamp, 1987). The curriculum developer in isolation may be able to meet Guidelines 1 through 12, but Guidelines 13 through 20 require action on the part of the implementor as well as the developer. These guidelines further articulate what we know about how children learn: children need to be active constructors of their own knowledge who learn from social interaction.

Guidelines 17 and 18 constitute the basics of curriculum for young children, reflecting Maslow's hierarchy of needs (1968). The simple fact is that children's biological needs must be met first if we expect them to learn; moreover, their needs for psychological safety and security must be respected if they are to succeed. With their physical needs met and their safety assured, children then may develop a sense of belonging—the feeling of being an integral part of the group—that is essential for them to experience a sense of competence and an enjoyment of learning. These principles should go without saying, but unfortunately, they are often violated. For example, Guideline 17 is unaffectionately referred to as "the bathroom rule." Some teachers tell us that on the day they are to be observed by the principal, they caution the children about going to the bathroom because if they do, the teacher will be marked down for classroom control! Some administrators brag that they have eliminated outdoor play to allow for more instructional time. Such shortsighted practices place curriculum goals above children's physical needs. Guideline 18 is the "stomachache rule" because when this guideline is violated, children become anxious or stressed, and symptoms such as stomachaches manifest. The practical application of this guideline is that if the curriculum gives children (or teachers) a stomachache, then it is probably not appropriate. Curriculum should contribute to, not threaten, children's feelings of psychological safety.

If children's physical and psychological needs are respected, then it is much more likely that Guideline 19 can be met—children can gain a sense of competence and an enjoyment of learning. This goal should not be confused with the notion that projects or activities should be selected solely because they will be fun. Too often we have seen curriculum described as developmentally appropriate because "the children just love it." Learning does not have to be painful, but it should not be vacuous entertainment either. The enjoyment referred to in Guideline 19 is the feeling of accomplishment and confidence that occurs when hard work is completed or a difficult problem is solved.

Guideline 20 reflects what we know about child development and about individual diversity; curriculum must be flexible both in design and implementation because no one curriculum could ever fit every child or every group.

The 20 curriculum guidelines considered individually may not seem daunting or particularly innovative. Nevertheless, a high standard is set for evaluating curriculum against the guidelines: a group of early childhood professionals should agree by consensus that the curriculum complies with every principle of the guidelines. Ignoring or violating even one principle, such as not suggesting alternatives to encourage flexibility, makes the curriculum unacceptable.

# Organizing elements of guidelines (key concepts, big ideas)

The 20 principles embodied in the guidelines are not unrelated to each other; they derive from several key concepts or overarching ideas. If meaningful curriculum is the goal, what are the elements that comprise it? Obviously there are at least 20, but we think that 6 of these are paramount; these 6 ideas are key concepts of the guidelines. Many of them have been discussed for more than a century and have almost become bromidic; nevertheless, it is time to reclaim these key concepts and to state clearly our intentions in promoting them.

*Figure 1.* THE LEARNING CYCLE

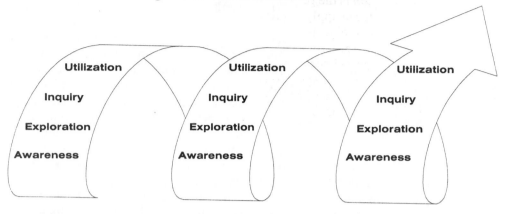

Meaningful curriculum

• is based on how children learn and addresses the entire learning cycle;

• reclaims the whole child and redefines *child centered;*

• provides depth of understanding and promotes conceptual development through integrating experiences;

• is individually appropriate, based on children's needs and interests;

• derives from the knowledge base of the disciplines and has intellectual integrity; and

• results from interactive teaching.

Each of these points is described more fully below and referenced to the related guidelines.

## The cycle of learning: A description of how children learn

The Curriculum and Assessment Guidelines are based on an interactive-constructivist view of learning. From this perspective, learning is a process, a movement from the more concrete, personalized understandings of very young children to the conventional understandings of society. We envision the learning process as a cycle that reflects the process of constructing knowledge but also applies to the acquisition of other forms of knowledge, including physical and social-conventional (DeVries, 1987). This cycle is not developmental in the pure sense of the word because the process itself does not change as the person grows; children experience the cycle of learning—and so do adults—whenever they acquire a new skill or gain new knowledge. First we describe the learning cycle more fully, and then we offer examples to illustrate its utility. Table 1 summarizes the learning cycle but does

not adequately convey its nonlinear, cyclical character, which is visually presented in Figure 1.

To learn something new, children must become aware, be able to explore and inquire, and then use and apply what they have learned (Rosegrant & Cooper, 1986). This process occurs over time and reflects movement from learning that is informal and incidental, spontaneous, concrete referenced, and governed by the child's own rules, to learning that is more formal, refined, extended, enriched, more removed in time and space from concrete references, and more reflective of conventional rule systems. The cycle depicts movement from learning that is primarily exploratory to learning that is more goal directed, movement from invention to convention. The process is similar for learning in all domains, not just cognitive but social and physical as well.

The cycle of learning begins in awareness. *Awareness* is broad recognition of the parameters of the learning—events, objects, people, or concepts; awareness comes from exposure, from experience. The next step in the cycle is exploration. *Exploration* is the process of figuring out the components or attributes of events, objects, people, or concepts by whatever means available; young children activate all of their senses during exploration. While exploring, children construct their own personal meaning of their experiences. **Awareness and exploration are essential but are not sufficient for complete understanding; personal meanings must be adapted to the shared meanings of a culture or society.** *Inquiry* is the term we apply to the adaptation process during which children examine their conceptual understandings and compare them to those of other people or to objective reality. At this point in the cycle, the learner develops understanding of commonalities across events, objects, people, or concepts. Children begin to generalize personal concepts and adapt them to more adult ways of thinking and behaving. *Utilization* is the functional level of learning, at which children can apply or make use of their understanding of events, objects, people, or concepts. The learning becomes useful for a variety of purposes. The learning cycle repeats because when the learner utilizes knowledge, skills, or dispositions, new awareness is created about what is not known or understood. Similarly, when the learner observes models operating at the utilization level, heightened awareness is created. As Gardner (1991) states, "It is highly desirable for children to observe competent adults or older peers at work—or at play . . . youngsters readily come to appreciate the reasons for the materials as well as the nature of the skills that equip the master (utilizer) to interact with them in a meaningful way" (p. 206).

To illustrate this cycle, think of the process of learning to write. Three- and 4-year-olds usually demonstrate an awareness of print from their prior experiences of being read to by adults or observing that signs convey messages. Some 4s and most 5-year-olds begin

---

### *Table 1.* CYCLE OF LEARNING AND TEACHING

|  | WHAT CHILDREN DO | WHAT TEACHERS DO |
|---|---|---|
| **Awareness** | Experience<br>Acquire an interest<br>Recognize broad parameters<br>Attend<br>Perceive | Create the environment<br>Provide opportunities by introducing new objects, events, people<br>Invite interest by posing problem or question<br>Respond to child's interest or shared experience<br>Show interest, enthusiasm |
| **Exploration** | Observe<br>Explore materials<br>Collect information<br>Discover<br>Create<br>Figure out components<br>Construct own understanding<br>Apply own rules<br>Create personal meaning<br>Represent own meaning | Facilitate<br>Support and enhance exploration<br>Provide opportunities for active exploration<br>Extend play<br>Describe child's activity<br>Ask open-ended questions—"What else could you do?"<br>Respect child's thinking and rule systems<br>Allow for constructive error |
| **Inquiry** | Examine<br>Investigate<br>Propose explanations<br>Focus<br>Compare own thinking with that of others<br>Generalize<br>Relate to prior learning<br>Adjust to conventional rule systems | Help children refine understanding<br>Guide children, focus attention<br>Ask more focused questions—"What else works like this?" "What happens if . . . ?"<br>Provide information when requested—"How do you spell . . . ?"<br>Help children make connections |
| **Utilization** | Use the learning in many ways; learning becomes functional<br>Represent learning in various ways<br>Apply learning to new situations<br>Formulate new hypotheses and repeat cycle | Create vehicles for application in real world<br>Help children apply learning to new situations<br>Provide meaningful situations in which to use learning |

---

to explore print by scribbling, drawing, using their own inventive spelling to write words, and rereading what they have written. Six-year-olds begin to more carefully examine print, looking for patterns and detecting similarities and differences in letters and words. Most 7- and 8-year-old children are beginning to utilize the conventional rule systems that govern written language to function as effective readers and writers.

The cycle of learning repeats itself as children's concepts and skills become more elaborated. Experiences at each level of the cycle actually create awareness of other things. This cycle—awareness to utilization—describes what children are doing at any given time. What teachers do looks different depending on where individual children are in this cycle of learning, as illustrated in Table 1. Not only must the teacher adjust her or his behavior depending on where the group of children are in the learning cycle, but the teacher must also identify where each child is on this continuum, and plan and interact accordingly. For instance, if a 6-year-old comes to school not having had opportunities to become aware of and explore print, the school needs to provide these experiences. This child cannot be expected to successfully begin with the conventions of print, as most of the other 6-year-olds will. Instead, time must be provided to create awareness and foster exploration, albeit not as much time as would have been given to this process more naturally. Similarly, another 6-year-old in the group may have had numerous prior opportunities to become aware of, explore, and examine print, and this child may proceed to utilize the knowledge of print in writing.

The cycle of learning can also be illustrated in the process of learning to read. The ability to recognize letters is one important predictor of successful reading, but adults often erroneously assume that by itself, direct instruction in letter recognition will achieve this end. Like the development of other knowledge, the ability to recognize letters begins in awareness and exploration. Awareness is created beginning in infancy, when children look at cloth and cardboard books. Toddlers, 3-year-olds, and 4-year-olds should have many opportunities to become aware of letters in meaningful contexts by being read to and by seeing environmental print. Some 4-year-olds and most 5s will explore letters in many contexts and learn to recognize those that are most meaningful first. Some 5s and most 6-year-olds examine letters more closely, adjust their personal perceptions to the conventional uses of letters, and are able to utilize the ability to recognize letters in a variety of contexts. Again, the normative expectation that 6-year-olds are at an inquiry level in letter recognition ability is predicated on their having had opportunities to become aware of and explore letters in a variety of contexts. If they have not had those

opportunities, then an expectation of understanding the conventional letter system at age 6 is unrealistic.

## Using the learning cycle as a framework for determining age-appropriate and individually appropriate curriculum

Determining age-appropriate and individually appropriate expectations is the key to making good curriculum decisions. Such decisions are best made at the classroom level, where teachers know the individual children and the community. Many important curriculum decisions are made at a level far removed from the individual child, however, such as when the school district adopts a textbook series for each grade level or when the curriculum specialist for a child care system adopts a commercially available curriculum or develops one for all centers.

As indicated earlier, curriculum has many sources, among which are child development knowledge, knowledge of individuals, community expectations, and the content of the disciplines. In developing and/or selecting appropriate curriculum content, all of these sources are activated; but for the curriculum to be developmentally appropriate, knowledge of child development and learning must be considered. If curriculum expectations are not realistic and attainable for the age group in general, then it is less likely that the curriculum can be made individually appropriate or that the goals can be achieved, regardless of community expectations or other variables.

The utility of the learning cycle is best seen in its application as a framework for determining what content, goals, and objectives are age appropriate and individually appropriate. Ensuring that curriculum content is not only age appropriate but also adjusts for individual differences is a difficult task. Because learning and development are so individualized, it is neither possible nor desirable to establish uniform age-appropriate expectations; however, it is possible to identify parameters to guide decisions about the appropriateness of curriculum expectations. It is also possible to identify goals for the full age range served in an early childhood program (such as the sample goals on p. 18, this volume). Specific content and learning objectives appropriate for each age group will vary, however. For example, curriculum to promote literacy development will look quite different for 3-year-olds than for 8-year-olds. Similarly, expectations of what children are capable of understanding and doing will vary according to the age and experience of the children.

Normative expectations of children of different ages vary greatly depending on the specific curriculum objective or content. For example, the ability to express thoughts and feelings verbally so as to be clearly

© Vivienne della Grotta

understood by others should be well developed in most 4-year-olds. Awareness and exploration of verbal language naturally occurs in infancy and toddlerhood. This means that utilization of verbal language would be a focused goal in preschool and kindergarten. Verbal language ability then becomes further refined and elaborated as it is utilized for many different purposes throughout the primary grades.

The utility of this framework can also be illustrated by applying it to a mathematics example. One of the K–4 curriculum standards of the National Council of Teachers of Mathematics (1989) deals with measurement. Of course, the expectation of children's understanding of measurement should vary enormously depending on age and individual experience. An appropriate expectation of 3- and 4-year-olds is awareness and exploration of relative size differences. Fours, 5s, and 6s should explore the concept of measurement using their own nonstandard units of measure, such as how many blocks long the building is or how many of their own hands tall they are. Having grasped the concept of measuring by inventing their own units of measure, 7- and 8-year-olds can then begin to apply the standard units of measurement.

We have been cautious to describe the learning process as a cycle because it is not hierarchical; utilization is not necessarily a more highly valued goal than are awareness and exploration. In fact, depending

on the context, awareness may be the appropriate goal for all learners during the period of early childhood, or it may be the desired goal for most learners throughout life. For example, it is important for every educated individual to be aware of the need to recycle valuable resources, while far fewer people need to understand and utilize the technical mechanisms of conservation. Similarly, it is just as important to be aware of and appreciate poetry as it is to write it; no doubt the poets would prefer this balance. Especially for young children, utilization (mastery) is not necessarily the goal. The younger the child, the more the process of learning is continuous, and therefore, measuring outcomes becomes a hazardous task. If the expectation is mastery, the task will of necessity be highly delimited. What a very young child can master may not be a useful or desirable outcome.

Utilizing the learning cycle as a framework to conceptualize both age-appropriate and individually appropriate curriculum expectations has several advantages. It emphasizes the need for teachers at all levels to understand the entire continuum of learning. It helps to emphasize the value of awareness and exploration in the learning process, but it also acknowledges that creating interest and allowing for exploration are only part of the continuum of learning. Depending on the specific curriculum goal and the individual children in the group, teachers assist the inquiry process whereby children's learnings are extended, refined, and adjusted to the conventional adult constructs and are thereby applicable in many contexts. Children in any group are at various stages along the continuum of learning relative to the curriculum content and depending on their individual experiences. Attention to the full learning continuum corrects the error of premature expectation of mastery, just as it corrects the error of assuming that exploration is the goal in every learning situation. Finally, the framework forces us to recognize that if children lack experiences, the school has the responsibility to provide those experiences or assist families to provide the experiences rather than to punish the child by forcing him or her to repeat a grade.

Most of the examples cited thus far illustrate the applicability of the learning cycle to the construction of logical-mathematical knowledge. The learning cycle is equally applicable to the acquisition of physical knowledge and skills. For example, children develop concepts about floating and sinking by first becoming aware of the phenomenon during baths. After many opportunities to explore and experiment with objects that float and sink through waterplay or from real-life experiences, children develop their own hypotheses about why objects float or sink (big ones sink and little ones float, perhaps). But through repeated experiences and adult support, at some point the children are forced to reexamine these personal theories and adapt their views to the widely accepted and conventionally known perspective of science. The same cycle applies when we acquire a physical skill at any age. Children learn to ride a bike by observing others and exploring on their own (using the process of trial and error to achieve balance and smoothly operate the pedals). Then after trying many of their own strategies more or less successfully, they are usually open to coaching by adults and older peers, which helps them to become expert bike riders. Later, when they learn to ski or drive a car, they revisit the cycle of learning again.

Even social-conventional knowledge, the agreed-upon accumulation of facts that constitutes much of school learning, is best acquired if the learning cycle is respected in the instructional process. Letters, numbers, colors, shapes, holidays, and the calendar are all examples of social-conventional knowledge. Opportunities for awareness and exploration contribute to greater understanding and more successful utilization of such knowledge.

The preceding examples apply the learning cycle primarily to the cognitive and physical domains, but it is also useful to think of the cycle of learning in relation to other areas of development, such as social skills. A common curriculum goal in early childhood programs is the acquisition of high-level social problem-solving strategies. This ability begins in awareness when children participate in parallel play next to other children. Then as children have more opportunities to play with others, they explore the possibilities of social interaction over time during the preschool years. By age 5 or 6, children are assisted by adults to move into the inquiry level, where they begin to engage in truly cooperative play that requires reciprocity. By ages 7 and 8, most children are able to use high-level social strategies such as negotiation, working cooperatively in groups, and establishing lasting friendships. This movement through the learning cycle is highly individual, depending on experience. For example, when children experience full-day child care at a very early age, their awareness and exploration of peers occurs earlier and they often demonstrate empathy and social play skills that appear advanced for their age.

## Whole child philosophy/child-centered curriculum

Basing curriculum decisions on how children learn (Guideline 1) is predicated on the assumption that the child is at the center of the curriculum. Unfortunately the phrase *child-centered curriculum* is often misunderstood both by general educators and by parents as equating to child determined or child dictated. As Katz (1992) points out, child-centered curriculum is too often interpreted as "child indulgent," and a more descriptive term would be "child sensitive." The goal of child-centered curriculum is to base curriculum decisions first and foremost on the needs of children and the ways in which children learn. It is our belief that the essence of child-centered curriculum is an approach that emphasizes the whole child. Guideline 2 dictates that curriculum attend to the whole child by calling for content goals to address all domains—social, emotional, cognitive, and physical, but these goals are not simply developmental in nature. Instead, the goal is to help children achieve optimum developmental potential so as to be fully prepared to participate as citizens of a democracy.

*THE HUMAN BRAIN IS A PATTERN DETECTOR; IT FUNCTIONS MOST EFFECTIVELY WHEN PROCESSING MEANINGFUL INFORMATION. INTEGRATED CURRICULUM, THEREFORE, WORKS BECAUSE IT MAKES MAXIMUM USE OF THE BRAIN'S CAPACITY FOR LEARNING.*

"Whole child philosophy" is early childhood jargon as old as "developmentally appropriate," yet it is much in need of reclamation. Despite the fact that early childhood educators use the term freely, there are differences in emphasis even among those who outwardly support the concept. For example, many early childhood educators who function at the preschool level err on the side of neglecting the cognitive dimension or not establishing clear objectives and strategies that contribute to achieving their goals for the whole child; we have termed this situation "the early childhood error," but it has a counterpart in "the elementary error." The elementary error is that in elementary school, although goals are clear, they are too often limited to the cognitive dimension. Social and emotional competencies are not seen as the purview of the school but are assumed to be formed prior to school entrance. For too many teachers in the primary grades, discipline is something to be handled in order to get on with the curriculum. The development of social competence is left to the free-for-all of recess or the competition of games during physical education. Fortunately, this situation is changing as elementary schools discover the benefits of cooperative learning strategies and as curriculum models develop that foster positive social interaction and caring (Solomon, Watson, Delucchi, Schaps, & Battistich, 1988). Similarly, physical education is moving toward fuller integration in the curriculum and deemphasis on competition in the early years (AAHPERD, 1992).

The concept of attending to the whole child is further supported by the recent work defining progress toward achieving Goal 1 of the National Education Goals. In an attempt to describe an outcome for the early years of life, the National Education Goals Panel formulated the goal, by the year 2000 all children will start school ready to learn. Although much work still needs to be done on operationalizing and determining appropriate ways of assessing progress toward achieving this goal, the Goals Panel endorsed a multidimensional definition of readiness: physical well-being and motor development, social competence, approaches toward learning, language and literacy, cognitive development, and general knowledge (NEGP, 1992). This is important acknowledgment of the significance of the whole child in relation to the preschool and early elementary years.

### Integrated curriculum: A meaning-centered approach

One of the major themes of the Curriculum and Assessment Guidelines is the importance of making learning meaningful for children, building conceptual development and deep understanding. The goal is meaningfulness, but the strategy is integrated curriculum. Integrated curriculum is another well-worn early childhood construct that has recently been discovered by other levels of education, including middle and secondary schooling (see, for example, Brandt, 1991). During early childhood the concept of integration derives from the integrated nature of development—what happens in one developmental dimension, such as physical growth, inevitably influences other dimensions of development, such as cognitive and social development. For example, as the child acquires mobility, he is exposed to a broader range of objects and interpersonal interactions, which in turn enhance his cognition and support language and social development. The interrelatedness of developmental domains, especially in very young children, virtually dictates an integrated approach to programming. As children get older the benefit of integrated approaches to instruction expands because it not only reflects the nature of development but is also consistent with learning theory and research on brain development (Caine & Caine, 1990; Shoemaker, 1991). The human brain is a pattern detector; it functions most effectively when processing meaningful information. Integrated curriculum, therefore, works because it makes maximum use of the brain's capacity for learning.

Integrated curriculum is a phrase that refers to several different strategies designed to enhance meaningfulness and support conceptual development encompassing thematic and holistic approaches—as well as interdisciplinary or infusion approaches, such as writing across the curriculum (Shoemaker, 1991). Efforts to integrate curriculum should not be artificial nor should they be forced and limiting ("We can't read your book on butterflies today because we are studying animals, not insects"). Everything does not have to relate to a single theme or a single topic, especially if the relationship is not natural. A variety of strategies for integrating the curriculum are utilized during early childhood, such as the project approach (Katz & Chard, 1989) and webbing across themes or disciplines (Krogh, 1990).

Most importantly, integrated curriculum approaches do not neglect skills development. Children are expected to learn to spell from whole language approaches; the difference is that spelling is integrated with writing and reading, and the expectation of mastery is given later priority. More traditional approaches stress acquisition of basic skills prior to moving to more meaningful integrated strategies, such as problem solving and composition. As Shoemaker (1991) points out, "... the brain processes parts and whole simultaneously. Good teaching neglects neither ... and leads to learning that is cumulative and developmental" (p. 794).

## Individualizing curriculum: Planning for needs and interests

One of the most frequently discussed but rarely implemented educational phenomena is individualization of instruction. In fact, individualization is the primary reason to implement developmentally appropriate teaching practices because providing options for children, rather than expecting all of the children to do the same thing at the same time, increases the likelihood of adjusting for individual differences. In addition, individual variation is the most dominant theme of all developmental literature. No matter how accurately one specifies expectations for an age group, the outcome is always an average around which real children's performance will range.

In practical terms the concept of individualizing is translated into *planning for children's needs and interests.* Recently it has come to our attention that this, too, is an often misinterpreted aspect of early childhood philosophy. Jeannette McCollum (personal communication, April 15, 1992) points out that early childhood educators tend to interpret individualization as responding to children's *interests,* while early childhood special educators individualize according to children's *needs* in relation to individually determined goals and objectives. Once again, we encounter an artificial and unnecessary dichotomy. It is hoped that by promulgating the Curriculum and Assessment Guidelines, which clearly emphasize both needs and interests, this false dichotomy can be put to rest. It is also hoped that the relationship between needs and interests will be clearly identified.

Every program has goals for the group and also for individuals. The distance between an individual's current status and the desired objective is a need. Good curriculum provides several strategies for achieving objectives in recognition of the fact that no one strategy is likely to succeed for every child. An alternative, more commonly used approach is to teach all of the children the same thing the same way the first time and provide remediation for the individuals who fail to succeed. It is clear that the second approach leads to greater stigmatization and communicates that some children are failures, even though the approach may have failed rather than the child. More holistic approaches to learning, such as those described in developmentally appropriate practice, will lead to acquisition of program objectives for most children through a relatively informal, spontaneous, experiential approach. Nevertheless, any approach will not work equally well for all children; therefore, teachers must be skilled observers of children and must adapt their approaches when children fail to learn or when a more directive strategy is needed.

One of the more successful ways to meet children's needs is to consider their interests. Again, consideration of interests does not mean indulging children or abdicating responsibility; it means that children are more likely to find curriculum meaningful and engaging when it relates to and respects their interests. Interests are both predictable and individual. There are predictable interests that individuals share because they are human beings of a certain age cohort living in a given culture (for instance, 16-year-olds in the United States are almost universally interested in automobiles, driving, and independence, not necessarily in that order). In the case of young children, it is easy to predict that most preschoolers are interested in themselves or that most 7-year-olds are interested in their peers of the same gender, but within those predictable interests are individual, almost idiosyncratic interests. All of the 4-year-olds in preschool seemed to enjoy animals, but Jonathan's interest in raccoons became almost an obsession. He had to have every book in the library on raccoons; he required a raccoon birthday party invitation and Christmas ornaments; and for Halloween, nothing would do but a raccoon costume. Jonathan's teacher encouraged his interest in raccoons because it became a natural vehicle through which to promote his learning.

The relationship of interests and culture has already been established, but this relationship cannot be overemphasized. When children find school a culturally safe and comfortable place to be, they are naturally more interested. Interests are perhaps most determined

# Figure 2. Teaching Continuum

| NONDIRECTIVE | MEDIATING | DIRECTIVE |
|---|---|---|
| Acknowledge / Model / Facilitate / Support / Scaffold / Co-construct / Demonstrate / Direct | | |

by culture. For this reason, culturally salient books, materials, ways of communicating, values, and topics must be infused in the curriculum if children are to be successful. Achieving a culturally comfortable and, therefore, interesting curriculum is easier when fewer cultural groups are represented; parents must be involved to ensure successful communication. Curriculum developers and teachers must address the issue of cultural diversity and view it as essential for meeting children's needs and interests. (See Section 3 for a more complete discussion of culturally appropriate curriculum.)

## Intellectual integrity derived from the knowledge base of the disciplines

One impetus for developing the Curriculum and Assessment Guidelines was the observation of too many examples of "mindless" curriculum in programs for young children. To address this issue, the guidelines call for curriculum that not only has "intellectual integrity" relevant to the knowledge base of the disciplines but also is worth knowing. Numerous examples could be cited to demonstrate the problem. On one hand are examples of curriculum that is trivial, meaningless, and wastes children's time, such as a month-long kindergarten unit on teddy bears. Equally disturbing are examples of curriculum that has been oversimplifed to the point of inaccuracy or activities that misrepresent reality or create confusion rather than clarity.

An example of an activity that lacks intellectual integrity was done by S. Bredekamp as an inexperienced teacher with her preschool class. The children were engaged in a study of "myself" that included several activities about faces. The teacher planned what she thought was the "cutest" activity—to make potato-head faces. She had seen in a book how the top of the potato could be cut off and replaced with cotton balls on which grass seed could be grown, with proper watering, to simulate hair! The teacher spent several days engaged in this activity, rushing in each morning to see if the grass (hair) had grown overnight, hoping that the seeds would sprout before the potatoes rotted. Unlike the teacher, the children failed to engage with this activity at all, and she had to literally beg them to look at the potato heads each day before she finally threw them away. The potato-head activity has many

problems, but its primary fault seems to lie in its lack of intellectual integrity. Grass doesn't grow on cotton balls, grass doesn't grow on potatoes, and potatoes don't grow hair! It seems fortunate that the children did *not* engage with this project because if they had, it is hard to imagine what learning would have resulted and what relationship that learning would have had to reality.

The potato head and the teddy bears are examples of curriculum that appear to be active and hands-on and, therefore, are assumed—inaccurately—to be developmentally appropriate. Unless the content of the curriculum activity or project has a sound foundation in the knowledge base and has intellectual integrity, its inclusion is not justified. (Volume 2 of this publication addresses the content of the disciplines and the question of what is worth knowing in more detail.)

## Interactive teaching

Teaching young children is a highly complex activity. Ironically, it is often portrayed simplistically in dichotomies such as child-initiated versus teacher-directed or in jargon-like phrases such as "facilitate learning." The truth is that teachers of young children make hundreds of decisions each day about which specific teaching behavior or form of adult assistance is appropriate for this child in this situation at this point in her or his process of learning. To help visualize the complexity of the options teachers face, we offer a continuum of teaching behaviors (see Figure 2). These behaviors are also options for parents as they interact with their children. We envision the teaching continuum as an array of behaviors ranging from nondirective to directive. Between those two extremes are many options varying in degree of intrusiveness. Each of these teaching behaviors is described in more detail below.

Every one of these behaviors occurs in adult-child interactions. The percentage of time each behavior is used will vary depending on the activity and the child. All of these behaviors are appropriate at certain times and under certain conditions. Disproportionate use of any one behavior renders it ineffective.

The least directive teaching behavior is to withhold attention. All adults withhold their interaction from children at times. Withholding may be appropriate when the adult knows that a child can do something

© Jean-Claude LeJeune

information to begin a project or process and by providing cues or prompts or other forms of coaching.

Facilitate is a word that is used with great frequency in describing teaching young children but with little specificity as to what is really involved. Facilitating is usually temporary assistance to help children get to the next step as the child is ready. It is similar to the kind of help adults offer by holding the back of the bike for a brief moment until the child gains a sense of balance. Facilitation is also apparent when a teacher encourages children to write on a chalkboard so that they can experiment without concern for errors.

Supporting learning is similar to facilitating but differs in the degree of adult involvement. In a facilitating situation the child has greater control, for example, sending a message to let go of the back of the bike, while in offering support the teacher and child together determine when the support is no longer necessary. Supported learning is similar to providing a fixed scaffold like training wheels on the bicycle, which allow the child to participate but with clearly available assistance.

Scaffolding is a popular term for teaching since Vygotsky's work (1978) has become widely popularized in educational circles. The concept of scaffolding is not new to early childhood educators, but it is an especially descriptive word for setting up challenges and assisting children to work "on the edge" of their current competence or for pushing the limits of their current developmental level. If curriculum and assessment are truly to achieve the goal of "reaching potentials" for all children, then scaffolding is an essential teaching behavior. Too often, "developmentally appropriate" has been misinterpreted as not being too hard or as forcing an exact match to children's capability (as though that were possible or desirable). Appropriate curriculum and assessment always take children where they are but challenge them to move ahead. Successful scaffolding is predicated on teachers' knowledge of the entire continuum of not only child development but of learning in various domains. Teachers must first know the general continuum; then they must observe and know their children and where they are in the learning cycle.

Beyond scaffolding are other more directive teaching strategies. At times teachers co-construct or actually do a project or an activity with the child. In this situation the teacher and the child are both learners and both teachers simultaneously. In preschool classrooms co-construction is seen when teachers build a block structure with a child or play tea party in the house area as equal actors. In primary schools teachers co-construct when they work with children to draw maps or to construct models for science or social studies lessons.

without assistance. Certainly withholding attention is frequently used to extinguish inappropriate behavior such as temper tantrums or bathroom language. Teachers also withhold response when they give children time to respond, often called *wait time.*

Acknowledging is giving attention and positive encouragement. This level of interaction often keeps children involved in the activity, but overuse of praise has been found to lessen children's motivation for a task. Again, it is important to find the right balance.

Modeling is both implicit and explicit in teachers' repertoire. The implicit form of modeling is less directive, while the explicit version is probably more so. In modeling, teachers display for children the desirable ways of behaving in the classroom. For instance, if shouting is not permitted in school, then teachers should not shout themselves. If polite conversation is valued, then teachers should speak courteously and kindly to children. This is the implicit form of modeling. Modeling can be more explicit in its intent, however. The teacher models by providing just enough

Yet more directive is when teachers demonstrate for children. The teacher is the active participant, while the children observe the outcome of the demonstration. At times demonstration is appropriate, especially when an activity can be done in a way that is clearly wrong or unsafe. Demonstration comes naturally to adults who interact with young children, so it is important to determine whether the situation warrants demonstration or just modeling. Too many classrooms find teachers demonstrating a lesson such as floating and sinking to an entire group of disinterested observers; principles of floating and sinking are better explored firsthand, with teachers serving as facilitators. Unless the tub of water is so deep as to risk drowning, demonstration could be an intrusion on children's learning.

Direct instruction can be defined many ways, but our continuum defines it in the narrow sense for situations in which the parameters are very tight and children must be given specific directions to do something one way. For example, when a child with a disability does not learn to feed herself through observation of adult models and practice over time, teachers directly instruct the child to ensure success and decrease dependence. Direct instruction falls on the more intrusive end of the continuum, not because it is undesirable, but because it places the teacher between the child and the learning. The teacher directs the learning within narrowly defined dimensions of error. "This is the way to tie your shoe; follow these directions" or "Here are the steps in the recipe; they have to be completed in this order." Early childhood education is not a decision between teacher-directed and child-initiated learning; both are essential components of a good classroom for young children. The true dilemma is which of the many teacher interactions is best for this child in this situation working toward this goal?

Beyond the end of the continuum, the most directive adult behavior is intrusion. Although the word is strong and certainly has negative connotations, it is nonetheless the most appropriate response in some circumstances, especially with very young children. If a child is brandishing a knife in another child's face during a cooking experiment, the teacher must intrude (presumably the teacher has already carefully guided children in safe rules regarding use of knives). Such circumstances should not occur too frequently, however, if the environment and the learning opportunities are developmentally appropriate. Thus, another reason to provide appropriate curriculum is to remove from the teacher the role of police officer. If intrusion is seldom exercised, it will be more effective when it is really needed.

By describing a continuum of teaching interactions, we hope that we have dispelled the myth that early

*TOO OFTEN, "DEVELOPMENTALLY APPROPRIATE" HAS BEEN MISINTERPRETED AS NOT BEING TOO HARD OR AS FORCING AN EXACT MATCH TO CHILDREN'S CAPABILITY (AS THOUGH THAT WERE POSSIBLE OR DESIRABLE). APPROPRIATE CURRICULUM AND ASSESSMENT ALWAYS TAKE CHILDREN WHERE THEY ARE BUT CHALLENGE THEM TO MOVE AHEAD.*

childhood teachers do not teach and that children control the classroom; nothing could be further from the truth. In fact, the verb that best describes what good early childhood teachers do is "orchestrate"—the teacher orchestrates the learning environment by coordinating and facilitating numerous activities, moving around, monitoring children's social and cognitive needs, assisting when needed, encouraging and acknowledging children's efforts, and challenging them to new levels of learning. Such interactive teaching is directly related to the cycle of learning, as is illustrated in the following example related to us by Diane Trister Dodge (personal communication, October 21, 1990).

### Interactive teaching and the cycle of learning: An example

When Diane was teaching kindergarten, she created awareness in her classroom by providing an aquarium for the children to observe. One little boy in particular became engaged in his study of the aquarium and observed it carefully over several days. After much exploration this boy came to Diane one day and announced with great conviction, "We have to put more water in the fish tank because the fish are drinking the water." Obviously, from his exploration, he had observed the water level going down over time, and he formed a hypothesis to explain the phenomenon, based on his past experience and personal understanding of what would make sense. At this point Diane was faced with the entire continuum of teaching interactions. She could have committed the "early childhood error" of assuming that exposure to this experience was sufficient for learning and withheld further interaction. In this case she probably would have stifled a laugh, made a mental note to tell all of her friends this cute story, and left the child to continue his exploration with no further enlightenment. Another option she could have pursued would have led to the "elementary error"—attempting to help the child leap to the utilization level; she might have seen this teachable moment as the opportunity to instruct the young boy about evaporation and molecular theory. It would have been necessary to simplify the concepts, of course, and so the lecture would have gone something like, "No, in the water are tiny things called *molecules* that you can't see because they are so small, and they go up into the air, which also has tiny molecules." Meanwhile, it is easy to imagine what would have happened to the child's interest in the aquarium as a result of this informative lecture. Instead, Diane chose to support his learning, to provide an opportunity for him to test his hypothesis further. She said, "Oh, do you think that if we put another tank of water with no fish in it, the water would stay the same? Let's try it and find out." Which they did, and it didn't. We are not so naive as to believe that this child constructed an understanding of molecular theory on the basis of this experience, but we do know that his participation was engaged, his thinking challenged, his hypothesis tested, his interest encouraged, and his ownership enhanced, and he was forced to be accountable for his own learning. Now that's good teaching.

\*　　\*　　\*　　\*　　\*

In this chapter we have presented many ideas—some new, but most are part of the well-established canon—in an attempt to provide conceptual frameworks for making sense of and applying the Curriculum and Assessment Guidelines. We think that the guidelines are potentially valuable tools for improving curriculum and assessment, and we hope that these frameworks help the guidelines reach their potential.

## References

American Association of Health, Physical Education, Recreation, and Dance. (1992). NASPE/COPEC feature: Developmentally appropriate physical education for children. *Journal of Physical Education, Recreation, & Dance, 63*(6), 29–60.

Brandt, R. (Ed.). (1991). *Educational Leadership, 49*(2), 4–75.

Bredekamp, S. (Ed.). (1987). *Developmentally appropriate practice in early childhood programs serving children from birth through age 8* (exp. ed.). Washington, DC: NAEYC.

Caine, R., & Caine, G. (1990, October). Understanding a brain-based approach to learning and teaching. *Educational Leadership, 48*(2), 66–70.

Derman-Sparks, L., & the A.B.C. Task Force. (1989). *Anti-bias curriculum: Tools for empowering young children.* Washington, DC: NAEYC.

DeVries, R., with Kohlberg, L. (1987). *Constructivist early education: Overview and comparison with other programs.* Washington, DC: NAEYC.

Duckworth, E. (1987). *"The having of wonderful ideas" and other essays on teaching and learning.* New York: Teachers College Press.

Gardner, H. (1991). *The unschooled mind.* New York: Basic Books.

Katz, L. (1990). Impressions of Reggio Emilia preschools. *Young Children, 45*(6), 11–12.

Katz, L. (1992, April). *Future visions for early childhood education.* Speech presented at the NAEYC Leaders Conference, Washington, DC.

Katz, L., & Chard, S. (1989). *Engaging children's minds: The project approach.* Norwood, NJ: Ablex.

Krogh, S. (1990). *The integrated early childhood curriculum.* New York: McGraw-Hill.

LeeKeenan, D., & Edwards, C.P. (1992). Using the project approach with toddlers. *Young Children, 47*(4), 31–35.

Maslow, A. (1968). *Toward a psychology of being.* New York: Van Nostrand Reinhold.

National Council of Teachers of Mathematics. (1989). *Curriculum and evaluation standards for school mathematics.* Reston, VA: Author.

National Education Goals Panel. (1992). Report of the Technical Planning Subgroup on Goal 1. Unpublished paper.

New, R. (1990). Excellent early education: A city in Italy has it. *Young Children, 45*(6), 4–10.

Reggio Emilia, Italy, Department of Education. (1987). *The hundred languages of children.* Reggio Emilia, Italy: Author.

Rosegrant, T., & Cooper, R. (1986). *The talking text writer: Professional guide.* New York: Scholastic.

Shoemaker, B. (1991, June). Education 2000: Integrated curriculum. *Educational Leadership, 48*(9), 793–797.

Solomon, D., Watson, M., Delucchi, K., Schaps, E., & Battistich, V. (1988). Enhancing children's prosocial behavior in the classroom. *American Educational Research Journal, 25*(4), 527–554.

Vygotsky, L. (1978). *Mind in society: The development of psychological processes.* Cambridge, MA: Harvard University Press.

# Reaching Potentials
# Through Appropriate Assessment

*Tynette W. Hills*

The NAEYC and NAECS/SDE Curriculum and Assessment Guidelines describe assessment as a process with potential for benefiting individual children and improving early childhood programs. The purpose of this chapter is to help ensure that assessment achieves this potential by elaborating on the Assessment Guidelines, showing the connection between assessment and curriculum, and providing examples of appropriate assessment strategies that conform to the guidelines. This chapter addresses several issues relevant to the role of assessment in early childhood education: how appropriate assessment helps to ensure that the needs of children are met; improves choices for curriculum content and instructional practice; helps teachers collaborate with parents for the benefit of children; and demonstrates that early childhood programs are fulfilling their mission to children, sponsoring agencies and institutions, communities, and the larger society.

The Curriculum and Assessment Guidelines clearly call for the integration of assessment with curriculum content and instructional strategies. This chapter addresses assessment separately because assessment has been underemphasized in early childhood education, not integrated in most teacher preparation programs, and relatively neglected in many curricula. Where assessment has been addressed, it has often been narrowly defined (limited to testing), and the information obtained has not been sufficiently helpful to teachers. The topic of assessment is given separate attention in this book to provide an opportunity to thoroughly address the issues. Presenting this information as a separate chapter, however, does not mean

that assessment should be considered independently from the other aspects of curriculum; in practice, they are inseparable.

This chapter, like the assessment guidelines, is limited to addressing services for children 3 through 8 years of age. (For guidelines relevant to screening and assessment of infants and toddlers, see Meisels & Provence, 1989.) This chapter addresses the following questions:

**1.** What is assessment? What purposes should it serve in developmentally appropriate programs?

**2.** Who should be involved in assessment? What does each party need to know?

**3.** What should be assessed?

**4.** How should assessment be accomplished?

## What is assessment? What purposes should it serve in developmentally appropriate programs?

The guidelines define assessment as "the process of observing, recording, and otherwise documenting the work children do and how they do it, as a basis for a variety of educational decisions that affect the child" (p. 10, this volume). Assessment involves the multiple steps of collecting data on a child's development and learning, determining its significance in light of the program goals and objectives, incorporating the information into planning for individuals and programs, and communicating the findings to parents and other involved parties.

## Some current assessment practices

When groups of early childhood educators are asked what they associate with the word *assessment,* they list such terms as testing, screening, observation, records, and report cards. Distressingly often, they speak of assessment methods that are incongruent with the goals and objectives of their programs. Sometimes kindergarten and primary teachers sound as if they are reading from an atlas—Iowa, California, Metropolitan!—as they cite or indict group standardized achievement testing, which Bredekamp (Gold, 1988) has termed "one of the dismaying rites of spring in schools throughout the country."

Johnson (1991) relates a touching story about the way the mandated standardized test intrudes, curtailing the great variety of whole language and other rich learning experiences that children typically have in first grade. Johnson describes the children's bewilderment and her own dismay at the marked changes that are wrought in the program. During this period in March, the children cannot talk to each other, they must all do the same things at exactly the same time, and they must respond to directions and materials that make little sense to them. It is a long time, Johnson says sadly, before she finds another picture with "I love you Msr. Jonhsn" in the message box on her desk.

The national obsession with standardized testing that these concerns signify is a major reason for the development of the Curriculum and Assessment Guidelines. NAEYC and NAECS/SDE, like numerous other organizations, object to overuse, misuse, and abuse of formal, standardized testing, epitomized by standardized achievement tests that are unrelated to the ongoing activities of classrooms. These organizations call for assessment practices that are more appropriate for young children and more consistent with teachers' purposes and needs (see pp. 22–26, this volume). In fact, an unprecedented concern has been demonstrated about the extent of testing, its prevalence, the uses to which test information is put, and its impact on curriculum and teaching practice (National Commission on Testing and Public Policy, 1990; Mitchell, 1992; U.S. Congress, Office of Technology Assessment, 1992).

Overreliance on standardized testing has left teachers, administrators, and parents with significant problems in assessment of individual students. One school district (Polakowski, Spicer, & Zimmerman, 1992) found the following discrepancies between their program goals and the district-adopted standardized tests:

**1.** The tests failed to give a valid and reliable basis for describing children and ascertaining their progress.

**2.** The standardized tests for 5- to 8-year-olds failed to measure children's progress toward what the programs actually taught.

**3.** Scores on the achievement tests, which are based on assumptions of linear and unidimensional changes, did not correspond to young children's growth and development.

Perrone (1990) provides the following historical context in discussing how the nation has arrived at a point where formal tests mandated by local and state administrators and funding sources can be at such odds with the intent and values of educational programs. Over a 30-year period the nation and the states have increasingly linked resources for education with large-scale program evaluation. Standardized tests, readily available from a growing test industry, are the same everywhere, inexpensive, and relatively quick—in short, the fast food of assessment. Perrone's work explains the uneasiness about testing that is widespread among early childhood educators.

Currently, educators are studying a variety of assessment strategies that go far beyond the limits of standardized testing:

• "kidwatching"—"learning about children by watching how they learn" (Goodman, 1985, p. 9), a concept associated with the child study movement of the 1930s and rejuvenated by the whole language movement;

• "keeping track"—collecting raw descriptive data on individual children, to be summarized, interpreted, and quantified (Engel, 1990);

• "documenting"—observing and collecting evidence of children's learning (Chittenden & Courtney, 1989);

• "naturalistic" (Wood, 1988) and "authentic" assessment—assessing children's performance in a real-life context (Meyer, 1992); and

• "performance assessment"—assessing how children carry out specific tasks that simulate, represent, or replicate real-life challenges (Brandt, 1992).

All of these terms describe alternatives to formal standardized testing as the mainstay of assessment

---

*THE NATIONAL OBSESSION WITH STANDARDIZED TESTING IS A MAJOR REASON FOR THE DEVELOPMENT OF THE CURRICULUM AND ASSESSMENT GUIDELINES. NAEYC AND NAECS/SDE, LIKE NUMEROUS OTHER ORGANIZATIONS, OBJECT TO OVERUSE, MISUSE, AND ABUSE OF FORMAL, STANDARDIZED TESTING, EPITOMIZED BY STANDARDIZED ACHIEVEMENT TESTS THAT ARE UNRELATED TO THE ONGOING ACTIVITIES OF CLASSROOMS.*

programs. All of these practices are potentially consistent with the guidelines for appropriate assessment (NAEYC & NAECS/SDE 1991, p. 22–26, this volume).

## Purposes of assessment

Assessment in early childhood programs provides information necessary for these important educational decisions that affect the child:

1. Instructional planning and communicating with parents

   a. What are this child's strengths, needs, and learning processes?

   b. How is this child doing?

   c. How will this child's instruction and guidance be planned?

   d. What and how can the teacher best communicate with the parents about the status and progress of their child?

2. Identification of children with special needs (for a more complete discussion of this topic, see Chapter 7)

   a. Can this child's needs be met in this program?

   b. If not, how does this program need to be supplemented, or what program is required?

3. Program evaluation and accountability

   a. Is this program, as now implemented, meeting its goals and objectives?

Assessment, curriculum, and instruction (teaching practices) must be united in the service of development and learning. Vygotsky's (1978) "zone of proximal development" depicted in Figure 1 (Hegland & Hills, 1988) offers a helpful way of looking at the interaction of teaching and assessment. The zone of proximal development lies between what the child can presently accomplish independently and what the child can potentially do in a supportive environment. Possible supports include the mediation of the teacher, another child, or equipment and materials. Vygotsky believed that assessment of potential as well as actual, independent problem solving is essential to knowing the capabilities of the child. All children can do more with assistance than they can manage alone, but the direction of growth, development, and learning is toward independence.

Emerging abilities are demonstrated first in an interpersonal context and later independently, according to Vygotsky. Within the boundaries of the zone of proximal development, which constitutes a "bandwidth of competence" (Brown & Reeve, 1987), the child can demonstrate abilities with varying kinds and amounts of aid. Observing and supporting the child, the teacher integrates instruction and assessment, all the while coming to understand the child's thinking processes more fully. Assessing what children can do when assisted provides a richer picture and a better estimate

## Figure 1. VYGOTSKY'S ZONE OF PROXIMAL DEVELOPMENT

Instruction and assessment involve continuous interactions of the teacher and the child, based upon . . .

**Observations of:**   Child's spontaneous behaviors

Child's assisted behaviors

**In relation to:**   Teacher's goals and objectives

■ ■ ■ ■ ■ ■ ■ ■ ■ ■ ■ ■ ■ ■ ■ ■ ■ ■ ■ ■ ■ ■ ■ ■ ■ ■ ■

**Zone of Proximal Development**

○                              ○                              ○

Child cannot           Child does with          Child does
do                          assistance                 alone

of status and progress than assessing independent attainments alone and simultaneously helps the teacher evaluate and plan teaching strategies.

# Who is involved in assessment? What do they need to know?

The key players in assessment in early childhood programs are children who are assessed, teachers who assess, and audiences for assessment information. The position of NAEYC and NAECS/SDE is that the child is at the center of assessment; all assessment activities should result in benefits to children. Further, the teacher is the primary assessor in the early childhood program, as the individual who is closest to the child, most responsible for the quality of the program, best positioned to coordinate the needs of individual children with the program goals and objectives, and most likely to have the information that parents and other interested persons need.

The nature and intensity of parents' needs for assessment information set them apart as stakeholders. Parents need the most specific information about individual children. Administrators, policy boards, government officials, and others have legitimate needs for assessment information related to programs and large groups of children; their needs are extensive, not intensive, and unrelated to data on individual children.

All of the adults involved closely with assessment issues have responsibilities—they are accountable. Teachers, administrators, and parents must wrestle with the issues of what is worth knowing and how to communicate those values to children.

## The role of the child

Children can have four roles in assessment: as the subjects of assessment; as sources of assessment information; as observers and critics of their own thinking processes and progress; and as beneficiaries of the ways the information is used.

Several characteristics of very young children affect assessment. First, young children are acutely sensitive to their surroundings. This sensitivity means that they may be easily distracted and may have emotional reactions to assessment procedures that may skew their behavior. The way an assessment task is presented or the way a child is required to respond may alter or impede his demonstration of competence. The comfort level the child has with the assessor also influences how the child responds to questions or manipulates objects for certain kinds of tasks. To produce a reliable picture, assessment must take place in a variety of situations that reflect the objectives of the program, make the child comfortable, and represent the child's typical range of activities.

Second, young children are characterized by rapid developmental change, meaning that they must be assessed frequently. They are especially prone to dynamic changes in social and emotional development, for example, in inhibiting impulses and delaying gratification. Third, they have limited interest in being assessed—an adult's agenda—especially when the assessment procedures interfere with their normal range of movement, talk, and expression of feelings. They are naturally interested in engaging in activities that fit their needs and desires, in feeling good about themselves and their accomplishments, and in pleasing significant adults. As they develop they grow in interest and awareness of their own thinking processes and their progress. These developing metacognitive capacities are an important part of assessment plans.

The way adults assess gives young children a message about what is important. Early childhood educators must continually reflect on both how the assessment is likely to affect the children and what is communicated about what the teacher values.

## The role of the teacher

Teachers are not only the primary assessors, they are the primary users of assessment information. Teachers need information about every one of the children—how they are progressing, how they think and solve problems, and how they think about their own learning. Teachers cannot decide what, how, and when to teach without knowing what is happening with the children.

In practice, teachers continually assess as they observe the children's learning processes and examine their products—paintings, block constructions, social interactions, developing oral and written language, and all the rest. They continually draw conclusions and make decisions based on their observations, even though the process itself may be intuitive and unreflective. Effective early childhood programs require assessment decisions based on continual collection of evidence of what children are doing and how they are faring, followed by teachers' reflections on their observations and the data at hand.

The teacher's responsibilities for assessment are to

1. integrate instruction and assessment fully in planning and carrying out the program;

2. use knowledge of young children to choose or design assessment processes;

3. analyze the results to find their meaning for the program and the children;

4. apply what has been learned to planning next steps and improving the program; and

5. communicate with parents and involve them in an exchange of information about their child's learning and development.

## The role of parents

Parents are a primary audience for what is learned from assessment of their own children. They need to know that their children are well cared for and that they are making progress. Parents want to understand the program and feel confident about it. They want concrete evidence about what is happening and what their children are experiencing.

Graves (1983) points out the kinds of information about language learning that are important to parents in terms of both how their children are progressing and what teachers are doing about it. These concerns generalize to all areas of learning:

• How is my child doing? Is my child improving?

• Do you teach the necessary skills?

• Do you help my child correct mistakes?

• How can I help at home? How will I know how to help?

The assessment information most important to parents allows them to see their own children's growth.

As the world's greatest living experts on their own children, parents have knowledge about their children that is invaluable to teachers. They know what their children can do in a comfortable, familiar social setting (this is partly what is involved in the frequent report from parents that children demonstrate at home some achievements that teachers fail to credit to them in school). Parents' responses to questionnaires about their children's developmental histories as they enter the program and parents' periodic reports of what they

© Hildegard Adler

observe at home are rich resources for a teacher's plans for individual children and for evaluation of the program's effectiveness.

## *The role of administrators*

Unlike teachers and parents, administrators do not need detailed information on individual children. Instead, they need to know how groups of children are doing in relation to a standard of expectation. Administrators are accountability agents; they must monitor how programs fulfill their goals and objectives and assess needs for broad program changes.

Currently school administrators are required to give significant time and energy to large-scale program evaluation, often implemented through formal, standardized testing programs beginning by Grade 2 or 3. Pressure for high scores on standardized tests—reinforced by media reports, politicians, government officials, and educational reformers (Stiggins, 1985)—weighs heavily on school superintendents and principals, who are accountable to the public for the outcome of publicly funded programs. Similarly, administrators of child care programs must respond to the requirements of funding sources, mandates of policy boards, and expectations of parents, many of whom pay tuition or choose where they use vouchers for child care.

Administrators have an equally important responsibility to be instructional leaders, supporting the kind of assessment that teachers need to improve the quality of children's experiences. Too often administrators lack experience and training in early childhood education. When these dual roles conflict, administrators should seek in-service training on young children's development and learning, curriculum and assessment, and teachers' roles in early childhood education. Administrators so informed may be empowered to help teachers observe and evaluate children's performance and reduce un-

examined reliance on mass standardized testing for program evaluation and teacher assessment (Stiggins, 1985).

## What should be assessed?

The goal of assessment is to acquire sufficient knowledge about each child, and about a group of children, in relation to program goals and objectives to fulfill the purposes of assessment described earlier. Because developmentally appropriate programs for young children address the "whole child"—physical, social, emotional, and intellectual—the assessment plan should include strategies that will gather information on a broad range of children's activities and functioning. This means that assessment processes must focus on children in relation to what is known about developmental directions (the continuum of development) in acquiring knowledge, skills, attitudes, and dispositions (see Chapters 5 and 6) in addition to children's individual learning strategies and attainment of specific goals and objectives.

In recent times there has been a quiet avalanche of theory, research, and demonstration in curriculum and learning (e.g., Glazer, 1988; Resnick & Klopfer, 1989). This curriculum research emphasizes the learner's own role in constructing knowledge and acquiring skills, leading to a reconceptualization of how young children integrate their acquisition of concepts, skills, and dispositions. Common themes include the following:

**1.** For children to construct more mature and complex concepts and solve novel problems, they must examine new information in relation to what they already know.

**2.** Children's interest in their own learning is a positive, motivating influence in what they can do.

**3.** Children's intellectual and affective capabilities develop in a social context and are influenced by the quality of social interactions.

**4.** Children develop increasing ability to regulate their own performance and behavior, thinking about their own thinking and assessing what is required to solve the learning tasks they face.

*P*ARENTS NEED THE MOST SPECIFIC INFORMATION ABOUT INDIVIDUAL CHILDREN. *A*DMINISTRATORS, POLICY BOARDS, GOVERNMENT OFFICIALS, AND OTHERS HAVE LEGITIMATE NEEDS FOR ASSESSMENT INFORMATION RELATED TO PROGRAMS AND LARGE GROUPS OF CHILDREN; THEIR NEEDS ARE EXTENSIVE, NOT INTENSIVE, AND UNRELATED TO DATA ON INDIVIDUAL CHILDREN.

*Figure 2.* MATCHING PURPOSE AND TYPE IN ASSESSMENT

| *Purpose* | *Types of Assessment* | |
|---|---|---|
| | **Formal** | **Informal** |
| To ascertain a child's preparedness to benefit from a particular planned program | Readiness tests (criterion referenced) | Observation; parents' reports |
| To identify children who *may* need specialized placement (e.g., special education) or a modified, individualized classroom program | Developmental screening tests (to be followed by developmental evaluation for those identified) | Error analysis; structured observation |
| To evaluate the appropriateness of teaching programs and teaching strategies | Appropriate criterion-referenced achievement tests | Teacher-made tests and procedures; observation; analysis of work samples |
| To evaluate a child's progress | Appropriate criterion-referenced achievement tests | Teacher-made tests and procedures; observation; analysis of work samples |
| For determining classification and placement | Developmental assessment tests (normative standardization) with high reliability and predictive validity | |

These themes are as relevant to assessment as to curriculum and instruction. The sample early childhood program goals (p. 18, this volume) are consistent with the view of children and their learning represented in these themes—emphasis on the *whole* child, with intellectual, affective, and interpersonal capabilities intertwined and interactive. Assessment programs that do not encompass all of the domains of child development risk underassessing children's capabilities, missing some children's needs or strengths, and delimiting the information that teachers and parents need for optimal understanding and support. Similarly, assessment strategies that are not sensitive to cultural differences in learning style and rate and those that are not designed for children from linguistically diverse backgrounds cannot provide an accurate picture of children's strengths and needs. (For a more detailed discussion of these issues, see Chapters 9 and 10.)

## How should assessment be accomplished?

Selection of assessment procedures should be determined first by the purpose of the assessment. Figure 2 displays purposes matched to types of assessment, both formal and informal (Taylor, 1984; Meisels, 1985).

Informal types of assessment, done systematically and well, can serve all purposes except the purpose of identifying and diagnosing children with special needs (for a complete discussion of assessment of children with special needs, see Chapter 7; for guidelines on screening and assessment of infants and toddlers, see Meisels & Provence, 1989). In fact, informal methods should be the primary form of assessment in early childhood programs to assure that teaching and assessing are complementary and that developmentally ap-

*Figure 3.* ASSESSMENT—A CONTINUUM

| | |
|---|---|
| ←-------------------------→ | |
| Informal | Formal |
| ←-------------------------→ | |
| Low constraints on behavior | High constraints on behavior |

**Types of Assessment**

| | | | |
|---|---|---|---|
| ←-------------------------→ | | | |
| Observation | Analysis of work samples | Structured work samples | Tests |

propriate approaches are employed. The primary strengths of standardized tests, *if they are properly designed and properly used,* are that they can eliminate biases in assessment of individual children and that they provide data that can be aggregated, permitting comparisons of groups to a standard. Early childhood educators who rely on less formal, less constraining assessment strategies will also want to plan carefully so that their assessment programs assure objectivity and accountability.

The key difference between formal and informal assessment is the level of intrusiveness into children's lives—the degree of constraint placed on their behavior. The assessment plan should include a range of procedures to meet the needs of all children. Figure 3 shows a continuum of assessment, from informal to formal, moving from observation-based assessments through documentation of children's accomplishments and on to formal, standardized testing (Teale, Hiebert, & Chittenden, 1987; Hegland & Hills, 1988).

The nature of young children from birth through 5 years of age and the programs that typically serve them rightfully emphasize informal, observation-based assessments, as represented on the left pole of the continuum. In contrast with many kindergarten and primary programs, especially in public schools, preschool and child care programs are more likely to be evaluated by the expectations of parents or the program standards of funding sources (such as accreditation or Head Start performance standards). Appropriately, preschool and child care programs are less likely to be measured against predetermined outcomes for individual children and groups of children, which is the form accountability sometimes takes in school-based programs. As children grow older and proceed through successive levels of school, most of them are subjected

*ASSESSMENT STRATEGIES THAT ARE NOT SENSITIVE TO CULTURAL DIFFERENCES IN LEARNING STYLE AND RATE AND THOSE THAT ARE NOT DESIGNED FOR CHILDREN FROM LINGUISTICALLY DIVERSE BACKGROUNDS CANNOT PROVIDE AN ACCURATE PICTURE OF CHILDREN'S STRENGTHS AND NEEDS.*

to assessment procedures that are more formal, more constraining, and more dependent on tests.

A complete discussion of the properties of formal standardized testing is beyond the scope of this chapter. Nevertheless, it is important for early childhood educators, both teachers and administrators, to be informed about that type of assessment for them to advocate what is best for children (Stiggins, 1985; NAECS/SDE, 1987; NAEYC, 1988; Brandt, 1992). Helpful sources of information about kinds of standardized tests, valid uses for them, and necessary psychometric properties include Goodwin and Driscoll (1980), Langhorst (1989), Meisels (1985, 1987), and Meisels and Provence (1989).

### Observation-based assessment

In this chapter the focus is on assessment, broad and authentic, that can take early childhood educators where testing cannot go in ascertaining what and how children are learning. Observation is the most effective strategy for getting to know young children; therefore, approaches based on observation are the primary forms of assessment and the most congruent with the guide-

*Figure 4.* LINKING THEORY AND PRACTICE THROUGH OBSERVATION

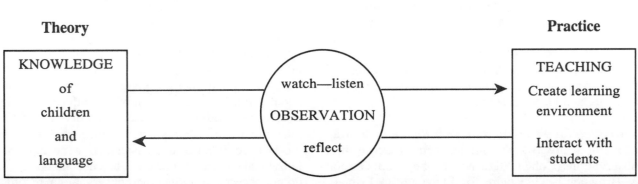

Reprinted from p. 5 of "Introduction and Overview" by Angela Jaggar in Observing the Language Learner, *ed. by Angela Jaggar & M. Trika Smith-Burke (© 1985). Reprinted with permission of Angela Jaggar, the International Reading Association.*

*A WIDE ARRAY OF METHODS ARE AVAILABLE FOR TEACHERS TO RECORD THEIR OBSERVATIONS. ASSESSMENT OF YOUNG CHILDREN CANNOT BE THE EDUCATIONAL EQUIVALENT OF FAST FOOD.*

lines for assessment (NAEYC & NAECS/SDE, p. 22–26, this volume). Observation can lead to collection of valid, reliable information without intruding on or transforming the daily classroom life and without constraining the children's behavior so as to limit their demonstration of competence.

*The importance of reflection.* Jaggar (1985, p. 5) points out that observation and reflection link theory and practice, helping teachers to make sound judgments about children and to continue in their professional growth (see Figure 4). Understanding children's development and learning provides a basis for decisions about practice. The process Jaggar describes places the teacher in the role of observer, somewhat apart from the action and therefore more objective and reflective about the children.

Teachers know a great deal about children and are constantly observing them. E.A. Chittenden, senior research psychologist at the Educational Testing Service (personal communication, July 22, 1992), seeks to "demystify assessment." He interviews teachers, asking questions like *How do you think Erin is doing with reading . . . or math? What makes you think so?* or *On what do you base your comments?* Asked such questions, teachers either offer the evidence or decide that they are not sure and need to observe the child more closely.

The connotation of *observe* is that one stands apart from the action, noticing important things that others may miss and being more detached and objective (Genishi, 1985). Systematic planning for observation helps teachers to become observant and use what they learn. Systematic planning for observation-based assessment involves a series of steps: (1) establish purpose and focus; (2) observe and record; (3) compile what was recorded, both for individual children and for the group; and (4) reflect on the records and refocus teaching and learning activities.

*Methods for observing and recording.* A wide array of methods are available for teachers to record their observations (Cohen, Stern, & Balaban, 1983; Gordon & Browne, 1985; Centre for Language in Primary Education, 1988; Beaty, 1990). Some are time consuming but rich in information, like anecdotal records. Others can be done more quickly, like checklists.

Some can be done after the observed event, like logs and journals. Some are designed to be used over time, like rating scales. Some can be employed with the assistance of others, such as parents and volunteers, or with technology, such as cameras, tape recorders, and video cameras. None are simple; none are likely to reduce teacher effort. But, as H.L Mencken pointed out, for every complex problem there is a simple solution, and it's wrong! Assessment of young children cannot be the educational equivalent of fast food.

A teacher's decision about how to observe and record depends on the purposes and the focus of assessment, whether on individual children or groups, and the instructional setting. Gordon and Browne (1985) classify methods of recording observations as narratives, time sampling, event sampling, and modified child-study techniques. This classification, with additional points from Beaty (1990), is shown in Figure 5.

*Uses of observation.* Observing how young children use language, oral or written, is an important focus in observation-based assessment. Viewing the functions of language means finding out how the children use language in the ongoing life of the classroom—to communicate about themselves, to find out something they want to know, to respond to others, and to negotiate social transactions. Pinnell (1985) developed a checklist for observing language functions, based on the categories developed by Halliday (1975), that is presented in Figure 6. Teachers of young children can readily recall observing these language functions during typical activities, such as in the dramatic-play center or the block area, on the playground, and in the arts and crafts area.

Young children's interpersonal relationships are an important target for assessment and are most readily assessed through observation. Because the quality of sociodramatic play of young children is associated with their literacy development—and the quality of their peer interaction, with long-term competence—it is essential that assessment include social-personal behaviors. Pellegrini and Glickman (1990) recommend observing and recording in situations in which the children feel comfortable and free to interact with others, such as during outdoor play.

Observing and recording yield descriptive information about children. Interpretation of that information is the final step in relating what teachers observe to their own planning; frequently this step is neglected. Some teachers lack confidence and hesitate to write reports on individual children, while other teachers do observe but do not necessarily reflect their observational records in their planning. Teachers need supervisory help, professional development, and on-site training to integrate assessment results with daily classroom practice.

## *Figure 5.* METHODS FOR OBSERVING AND RECORDING

**I. Narratives**—attempts to record as much as possible of what happens within the focus of the observation.

**A.** Diary description—a chronological record of individual children's behavior, made after the behavior occurs; used to provide information about children whose behaviors the teacher needs to understand more fully. Examples: aggressive, avoiding, compliant, disruptive, passive, withdrawn behavior in certain kinds of interpersonal situations; ways of engaging materials and/or interacting with others in specified learning activities.

**B.** Anecdotal record—a descriptive narrative, recorded after the behavior occurs; used to detail specific behavior for children's records and for teachers' planning, conferencing, etc.

**C.** Running record—a sequential record over a given time, recorded while the behavior is occurring; used to document what children are doing in the particular situation (with a focus on social or preacademic/academic activity); used for teachers' planning for individuals or groups.

**D.** Specimen description—detailed notes on an identified situation, recorded while the behavior is occurring, often with the aid of video or audio recordings; used to discover cause-and-effect relationships in individual children's behaviors, to analyze classroom management, etc.

**E.** Log or journal—a recording of brief details about each child in the group, usually made after the behavior occurs; used to describe the status and progress of every child in the group over time.

**Narrative records based on observations have the advantages of being open ended and flexible, and they can provide a wealth of information about children and the program. They are time consuming to both record and interpret.**

**II. Time Sampling**—an observation of what happens within a given period of time, coded with tallies or symbols while the behavior is occurring; used to document the frequency of specific behaviors.

**Time sampling can be more objective than narrative records. It is less time consuming, and it offers a way to observe and record two or more children simultaneously. Unlike narratives, however, it is closed ended, limited to what happens in the specified time interval, and lacking in behavioral and contextual detail.**

**III. Event Sampling**—an observation of an event that has been defined in advance and what happens before and after, recorded briefly while it is taking place; used to observe and record children's social-personal interactions with the teacher and other children as a basis to plan desirable interventions.

**Like time sampling, it is objective and potentially helpful to teachers trying to gain insight into individual behavior and classroom management issues. Like time sampling, event sampling is closed ended and limited, thus lacking the richness of the narrative methods.**

**IV. Modified Child Study Techniques**—a variety of techniques originally used in child study research, adapted for use by teachers, including the following:

**A.** checklist—a list on which the teacher (or parent or other adult) checks the behaviors or traits observed before, during, or after the behavior occurs

**B.** rating scale—a list of behaviors made into a scale, using frequency of behavior, level of mastery, etc., which the observer checks before, during, or after the behavior

**Checklists and rating scales have the advantage of being relatively easy to design, undemanding of time, and applicable to more than one child at a time, but they are limited to the specified traits or behaviors, lacking information on the context or quality of the behavior, and they are subject to the observer's interpretation.**

**C.** Shadow study—a detailed, in-depth observation of one child at a time, done by multiple staff members, using mostly narrative methods; used to gain a more comprehensive understanding of individual children and, so doing, enhance understanding of all children. A shadow study is time consuming, but the views of multiple observers can provide a rich, relatively objective picture of the child's behavior. Those who engage in shadow studies value their enhanced understanding of children and the professional growth that results.

## *Figure 6.* A FUNCTIONAL VIEW OF LANGUAGE

Viewing the functions of language means finding out how the children use language in the ongoing life of the classroom—to communicate about themselves, to find out something they want to know, to respond to others, and to negotiate social transaction (Pinnell, 1985).

Halliday (1975) identified seven categories of language that are important for all children to experience in their homes, communities, and schools:

1. **Instrumental language**—to get what we want

2. **Regulatory language**—to manipulate/control others

3. **Interactional language**—to establish and define social relationships

4. **Personal language**—to express individuality and personality, including feelings

5. **Imaginative language**—to express fantasy, including dramatic play roles

6. **Heuristic language**—to inquire, investigate, wonder about, and figure out

7. **Informative language**—to communicate information, report facts, and report conclusions

Pinnell (1985, pp. 57–58) offers more expanded definitions of these categories.

---

### OBSERVING LANGUAGE FUNCTIONS

#### *Functions of Language Observation Form*

Name:_____
      (individual, small group, or large group)

Time:_____
      (time of day)

Setting:_____
      (physical setting and what happened prior to observation)

Activity:_____
      (activity, including topic/subject area)

| *Language Function* | *Examples* |
| --- | --- |
| Instrumental_____ | _____ |
| Regulatory_____ | _____ |
| Interactional_____ | _____ |
| Personal_____ | _____ |
| Imaginative_____ | _____ |
| Heuristic_____ | _____ |
| Informative_____ | _____ |

**Note:** Check each time a language function is heard and/or record examples.

---

*Reprinted from pp. 59 & 67 of "Ways to Look at the Functions of Children's Language" by Gae Su Pinnell in* Observing the Language Learner, *ed. by Angela Jaggar & M. Trika Smith-Burke (© 1985). Reprinted with permission of the International Reading Association.*

Sometimes teachers report that they do not have time to observe or that observation takes them away from teaching. Teachers' instructional and management practices are related to the degree of difficulty they have in observing and keeping records. When they foster autonomy and initiative in children, teachers are more likely to be able to take the role of observer and are more likely to find the time to make brief records or use checklists.

*The power of observing and recording.* Smith (1991) recounts the experience of a kindergarten teacher, Carol, whose class included a little girl who was the most challenging child in Carol's 20-year career. Juanita could not curb her impulsivity, was in constant motion, and seemed oblivious that other children were present. Carol found ways to reach Juanita—a gentle touch, a reassuring hug, and something special to hold in the story circle. Within two months, the situation was under control. Asked how she did it, Carol recounted the desperation that set her to writing a journal; Carol had written about Juanita every night. Soon she began to see patterns of cause and effect, relationships between Juanita's behavior and the classroom context, and effective steps that she could take, using her journal to carry on a conversation with herself about what was occurring. Journal writing enabled her to stand apart from the daily interaction, reflect on what was happening, and gain insight.

Regarding observation of the functions of language (see Figure 6, p. 52), Pinnell (1985) points out that teachers can learn

1. about an individual child's competence by documenting the ways he or she uses the various functions of language; and

2. about the language environment in the classroom by determining which functions occur and where, and which do not.

These comments can be generalized to other well-designed assessments based on observation. Systematic observing and recording can provide valid, reliable information from which teachers can alter and enrich their curriculum, instruction, and the learning environment.

## Samples of children's performance in daily classroom life

Examining what children do, what they produce, and how they do it in the natural course of classroom events is essential for teachers' and parents' understandings of how the children are doing and how the program is serving them. This approach to assessment is consistent with the concepts of "keeping track of children," "documenting," and naturalistic or "authentic" assess-

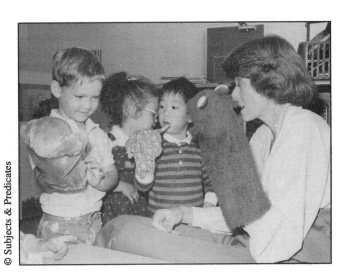

© Subjects & Predicates

ment since it appraises what children typically do, without altering the curriculum for assessment's sake. Using the kinds of assessment activities described below, teachers of young children obtain evidence of progress toward program objectives and information to guide instructional planning.

*Progress in written language.* Combined with observation-based methods, performance samples ideally should collect information on young children's progress by sampling their (1) concepts of the function and conventional forms of written language; (2) understanding and recall of stories read to them; (3) abilities to read familiar environmental print, such as signs or food labels; (4) approaches to reading texts prior to conventional reading; (5) awareness of sound–symbol relationships and word structures; (6) approaches to writing prior to conventional writing; and (7) ideas about letters and their sounds (Teale, 1988, pp. 176–177).

Figure 7 is a sample of "writing" produced by a kindergarten child in the fall (her dictation) and then other samples produced in the winter and spring after many experiences with writing materials in several interest centers in the room. Her samples show progress and understandings associated with literacy.

Several assessment schemes are available to help teachers determine where children are in invented or creative spelling. Teachers' knowledge of a child's own construction of spelling rules can help teachers decide what spelling skills to teach and when. Sowers (1988) offers a simple hierarchy of spelling skills and some recommendations for engaging children in conversations about their writing. An "instructional conversation" (p. 66) or interview is essential because only the child can tell why she did it that way. An instructional conversation might include acknowledging the child's spelling, pointing out the beginnings and endings of words, asking what certain letters in the child's words

## Figure 7. Emergent Writing Sample

We had a ride in the farm wagon.

Seda

mean, and asking her to apply her knowledge of sound–symbol correspondence to other instances of her writing. Figure 8 illustrates these assessment strategies for literacy.

Bingham (1988), a teacher in a multilevel primary classroom, uses legal-size folders to collect children's writing samples to document their progress over the year. In addition to her own tracking of the growth in children's skills, she finds the folders invaluable for parent conferences, selecting samples several months apart. She examines children's work for improvement in clarity of expression, increased information and detail, willingness to revise and edit, improved letter formation, and movement toward conventional spelling and mechanics.

***Mathematics.*** Similarly, teachers should document children's progress in all areas of the curriculum through collecting samples of their work—their drawings representing their mathematical and scientific ideas, photographs of block constructions with notations of their problem solving, or audio tapes or transcripts of their reading, for just a few examples. Suggestions for methods of collecting and documenting children's written language (Centre for Language in Primary Education, 1988) are useful for other areas of learning as well: a checklist for ensuring that samples are collected for all of the children, folders in which children store drafts of their works in progress, and a designated spot where children can place things needing the teacher's help. Figure 9 illustrates a recorded conversation on children's concepts of age and size.

The groundbreaking curriculum and evaluation standards of the National Council of Teachers of Mathematics (1989) set forth curriculum standards in 13 areas of mathematics for kindergarten through Grade 4. An example of children's understanding of patterns, one area of the K–4 standards, appears in Figure 10 (Laurence Wiley, personal communication, August 4, 1992). To assess young children's growth in mathematics, it is important to focus on

• children's problem-solving strategies—observing the way they go about solving a problem and listening to them explain how they did it;

• the thinking process they use—observing the way they use concrete objects, drawings, and their own bodies to represent mathematical ideas and observing how they progress in using conventional symbol systems; and

• the understandings they develop and apply—observing and documenting how they use mathematical concepts and skills in real-life contexts and their explanations of what they did and how they knew what to do.

***Teachers' shared reflections.*** When working with teachers to develop alternative assessment strategies, Chittenden (personal communication, July 22, 1992)

## Figure 8. Emergent Literacy—Inventive or Developmental Spelling

i Knwe you woe be Angry !
C Icame Home frmississippi

**A Hierarchy of Inventive Spelling**

1. String of letters
2. Beginning sounds only
3. Beginning and ending sounds
4. Beginning, middle, and ending sounds

Marissa, age 5, in the spring of her kindergarten year, wrote a note to her dad.

---

encourages teachers to meet in small groups, bringing with them samples of children's work. These samples become the focus of discussion as the child's teacher shares perceptions about a child's progress and has her own understandings clarified and modified by sharing with the others. This kind of interaction about the issues of children's learning brings a social dimension to a teacher's reflection and has the potential to enhance insight.

### Samples of children's performance in structured tasks

The continuum of assessment (Figure 3, p. 48) places structured work samples between analysis of typical performance samples and standardized tests, in degree of formality and constraints on children's usual behavior. On numerous occasions teachers or other professionals will ask children to do certain things in order to assess their progress and identify their thinking and problem-solving strategies. At such times it is essential that the children feel safe, confident, and comfortable and that they understand what is being requested. In these situations, as in all assessment, the Guidelines for Curriculum and Assessment should not be violated.

Teachers who incorporate structured tasks in their assessment programs do so because they want to be sure that they can rely on the data they are collecting on the children—that the data are fair, not biased by subjectivity or chance; and that subsequent use of the same approach will reveal any changes that have occurred (Clay, 1985). Used appropriately, these more

### Figure 9. Children's Discussions of Concepts of Age and Size

Yvonne Smith, a teacher at Central Park East Elementary School in New York City was interested in her children's thinking about age, size, and other mathematical concepts. She took this running record of a discussion in her classroom of 4- and 5-year-olds.

S: I'm 6 years old. I'm the oldest kid in this class. When I came, I was 3 and the youngest kid in the class.

J: You're not older than Gina; she's bigger than you.

G: Yes, she is. I'm only 5. I'll be 6 in May.

J: When you're 6, then you'll be older than Sara. (G looks skeptical, but slightly pleased.)

F: Oh, no! When Gina turns 6, Sara will be an older 6.

S: Yeah, I'll always be older than Gina.

*Teacher*: Why do you think Gina will be older than Sara when Gina turns 6?

J: Because Gina is older than Sara when they were 5.

M and F: Oh no!

M: Sara is always older than Gina. Her birthday comes first.

J: But Gina's bigger.

S: So what? Just because I'm smaller doesn't mean Gina's older than me.

F: Bigger doesn't mean older.

*(E.A. Chittenden, July 22, 1992. Used with permission.)*

*Figure 10.* PATTERNS AND RELATIONSHIPS

In an art lesson on patterns, 8-year-old Christopher produced the paper pattern below.

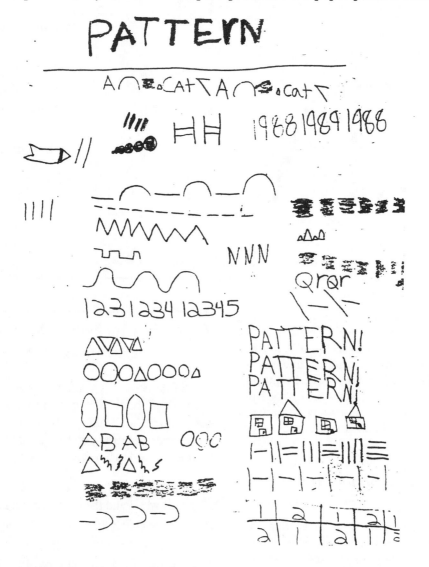

## What the Teacher Can Observe and Document

The teacher interested in integrating curriculum and assessment can observe Christopher's mathematical concepts in his production in an art activity.

**1.** He has drawn repeating patterns—in which the core repeats—such as ABABAB (which he has actually shown that way!) in several examples and ABCDEFABCDEF (top example).

**2.** He has drawn growing patterns—in which the core grows—in several examples.

**3.** He has even drawn one example (third from bottom, right-hand column) showing interlinked vertical and horizontal planes with a growing core.

## What the Teacher Must Ask the Child

One example has alternative interpretations—the repeated three circles and a triangle. Was he thinking of the three circles as a unit and therefore as an ABAB pattern, or was he creating an AAAB pattern? Only Chris knows what he meant. The teacher can find out by asking, *How would you describe this pattern? Can you think of another way to describe this pattern?*

formal, test-like assessments meet standards of validity and reliability because they involve learning tasks and situations that are consistent with goals and objectives for children and are like typical classroom activities.

Many kinds of structured performance assessments are available, including games, interviews, demonstrations of reading or other performance, and special assignments to an individual child or groups of children. The following is a sampler of some of these more structured strategies, in all of which the teacher sets the task and records the child's responses—sometimes asking probing questions, always listening and watching.

*Games.* Kamii and Rosenblum (1990) recommend playing games—such as the one that follows—with children as a simple and practical way to assess the way they think about numerical concepts. A card game that a teacher can use with all first graders, one or two at a time, allows them to demonstrate what they understand about making 10 with two smaller numbers. The teacher may record on an observation form what arithmetic strategies the child uses to arrive at each of the combinations (p. 151), as a way to keep track of individual progress and provide information for the teacher's planning.

*Interviews (or instructional conversations).* Clay's (1985) design for assessing young children's knowledge of reading has been widely used in this country. Her "Concepts of Print" assessments are based on assumptions that beginning to read involves what a young child knows about books and print—ways to address books, the ability to distinguish between letters and between words, ideas about word structure, and other conventions of print, such as the functions of space and punctuation. Carried out in a one-on-one interview format, using booklets that are similar to typical children's books, this procedure taps the child's familiarity with reading materials, helping teachers discover what children have learned about books and reading prior to entering kindergarten or first grade.

Conferences with children about language and literacy are also frequently used to understand the child's language in and out of the program, his favorite stories, and his self-perceptions as a language user (Centre for Language in Primary Education, 1988). This strategy is especially important for speakers of languages other than English (for a discussion of assessment of linguistically diverse children, see Chapter 10). In assessment of mathematics, interviews can inform teachers about children's algorithms, reasoning, and metacognitions. The interviews may be recorded on the spot or audiotaped for later coding (see examples in Centre for Language in Primary Education, 1988; Engel, 1990).

*EXAMINING WHAT CHILDREN DO, WHAT THEY PRODUCE, AND HOW THEY DO IT IN THE NATURAL COURSE OF CLASSROOM EVENTS IS ESSENTIAL FOR TEACHERS' AND PARENTS' UNDERSTANDINGS OF HOW THE CHILDREN ARE DOING AND HOW THE PROGRAM IS SERVING THEM.*

*Contracts.* Contracts are a plan for what a child will do in the course of a day or for a longer period of time, consistent with the age of the child, to which both child and teacher agree. The plans are written or illustrated with drawings or are combinations of print and representations (Day, 1988). Contracts provide a record of each child's activities and progress. When it is individually appropriate, a young child may check off the tasks or activities completed. Contracts give children frequent feedback on their progress, and, especially when accompanied by work samples, they can provide parents with tangible evidence of what their children are doing. Often, younger preschool children are engaged in programs that involve systematic planning (Hohmann, Banet, & Weikart, 1979). Their name tags can be hung on a chart in progression of learning centers they use, the information can be tallied, and the children's oral reports of what they did and their work samples can provide significant assessment information.

*Directed assignments.* When children are beginning to read independently, they may be asked to read a certain passage aloud and then retell the story. The passage may be selected by the teacher or chosen by the child from a collection of books the teacher shows and describes briefly. Recording at the time or later, if audiotaping is available, the teacher analyzes the reading sample for accuracy, self-corrections, and kinds of mistakes, that is, mistakes that preserve the meaning contrasted with those that change it. Often called "miscue analysis" (Goodman, 1973), this assessment strategy is described more fully elsewhere (Centre for Language in Primary Education, 1988; Chittenden & Courtney, 1989, pp. 107–120) and is illustrated in Figure 11. Young children who are pre-readers may listen to a teacher or an older child read a story and then be asked to retell it. The retelling yields information about the child's attentiveness, comprehension, and awareness of story structure.

Baratta-Lorton (1976) recommends that teachers assess young children's understandings of mathematical concepts by asking them to use concrete, manipu-

# Figure 11. Two Reading Records From a Child's Folder

**Second record (right page):**

Child's name M
Teacher M.J.   Grade 1
Date 5/12/87

2nd Reading
Next Day

FLY WITH ME

Fly with me.

Fly with me up and up.

Fly with me down and down.
                through
Fly with me into the clouds
fly with me
and around and around.
TA
Look out for the hill.   isolated "L", then said "look"

Look out for the bridge.
                          TA
Look out for the ground!   isolated "g"
                           used picture

(40 words)

| text | substitution |
|------|--------------|
| into | through |
| and | fly with me |

Later I isolated words in text. she was able to read all of them.

look
flying
me
and
up

**First record (left page):**

TA = Teacher Assistance
|| = Pause

Teacher Read Title

1st Reading

FLY WITH ME

      W  TA
Fly with me.   isolated w

                  TA
Fly with me||and up.           looked back to page 2
                               Re-read sentence on page 2 several times
Fly with me down||and down.    then read "and"

Fly with me into the||clouds   Looked at picture

 TA        TA
and around and around.   Looked back to page 2 but this time
                         couldn't remember "and"
Let's go fly over
||Look out for the hill.   added "over"

Let's go fly over a river   added "over"
Look out for the bridge.
                 again
Let's not fly out for again
Look out for the ground!

Long
Pause

(40 words)

| text | substitution |
|------|--------------|
| with | "w" |
| and | — |
| around | let's |
| look | go |
| out | fly |
| for | |

| text | substitution |
|------|--------------|
| the | a |
| bridge | river |
| ground | again |

Reprinted from "Assessment of Young Children's Reading: Documentation as an Alternative to Testing" (Figure 4) by Edward Chittenden and Rosalea Courtney in Emerging Literacy: Young Children Learn to Read and Write, ed. by Dorothy S. Strickland and Lesley Mandel Morrow (© 1989). Reprinted with permission of Edward Chittenden and the International Reading Association.

## *Figure 12.* ASSESSMENT OF A DIRECTED ASSIGNMENT IN MATHEMATICS

The teacher's assignment to pairs of children working together (spring of first grade):

There are 49 children in the classes that are going on a field trip. How many cars are needed if each car can take 5 children?

Yuka and Thomas together produced the solution shown below.

### What the Teacher Can Observe and Document*

**1.** Together the children demonstrate the concept of grouping, supplying concrete representation of the remainder (9).

**2.** They are close to understanding the base 10 number system, with a rudimentary understanding of base 5 (note the tallies for 5 passengers and the curved lines linking the cars and the trailers). They know that fewer than 10 children need a last, *whole* car: they cannot be transported on a part of a car.

**3.** They are composing and decomposing numbers.

**4.** They demonstrate understanding of halving and doubling (e.g., that 10 is composed of 5 & 5, 20 of 10 & 10, etc.), the basis of powerful strategies in mathematical thinking, for example, the basis of understanding fractions.

Early childhood educators trained in mathematics will also recognize that the children have represented the structure of a binary tree.

### What the Teacher Must Find Out From the Children

If the teacher has not observed Yuka and Thomas during their problem solving, he must ask them for additional information that is important for assessment.

**1.** Did you start your drawing up here (top) or down here (bottom)?

**2.** What did you do next? and then? and then?

**3.** Why did you decide to draw cars and then trailers?

Because the teacher is always concerned about individual status and progress, he will want to find out what parts of the representation were done by each partner. Ideally, the teacher will want to know how the thinking and actions of each partner influenced the other and final solution (see Figure 1, p. 45, this volume).

*Thanks to Laurence Wiley, mathematics consultant, New Jersey Department of Education.

lative objects in responding to questions. She presents sample assessment strategies for one-to-one correspondence and conservation of number, for example, having children use buttons, blocks, and other commercial or found materials. A directed assignment in mathematical problem solving for older children is shown in Figure 12.

## Constructing a profile of progress

Given the variety of assessment strategies and tools now available, the need to have a broad range of knowledge about childhood development and learning, and chronic shortages of time and energy, how can early childhood educators plan assessment programs that fulfill all of the purposes and satisfy legitimate audiences? How can a teacher build an adequate base of assessment for curriculum planning and for communicating with parents?

One answer that is gaining increasing attention and support is portfolios. An assessment portfolio consists of a collection of a child's work that represents what the child has done over a period of time. Sometimes portfolios are seen as belonging to the child, and the child shares with the teacher in decisions about what to include (Grace & Shores, 1991). Portfolios typically include samples of the child's writings, such as journal entries, stories, and reports, including some first drafts as well as finished products (Tierney, Carter, & Desai, 1991); samples of the child's representations in mathematics; work samples in reading, such as audio tapes of oral reading and story retelling; teachers' comments and assessments; and creative expressions, like original artwork or photographs of the child's block constructions. Portfolios are not just educational scrapbooks; they are systematic collections of similar products constructed at regular intervals that can be compared to assess children's progress over time.

The South Brunswick early childhood portfolio began as a means to allow a teacher to build a record that would follow a child's progress from the start of kindergarten through second grade (Polakowski, Spicer, & Zimmerman, 1992). This assessment portfolio has been a work in progress for several years, evolving in response to the teachers' experience of what is useful, revision of curriculum, and the needs and desires of parents and members of the board of education. Currently emphasizing language arts, the portfolio includes the child's self-portrait at the beginning of each year; an interview with the child on favorite pastimes and reading at home; a parent questionnaire; an assessment of conventions of books and print at the beginning and end of kindergarten; the Word Awareness of Writing Activity (humorously known as the WAWA) to tap emerging understanding of

*AUTHENTIC ASSESSMENT, INTEGRATED WITH DEVELOPMENTALLY APPROPRIATE CURRICULUM CONTENT AND INSTRUCTIONAL PRACTICES, CASTS TEACHERS AS CHILD DEVELOPMENT RESEARCHERS AND ORCHESTRATORS OF DYNAMIC TEACHING AND LEARNING ENVIRONMENTS.*

word structure and symbol–sound relationships in kindergarten and first grade; unedited writing samples; and an assessment of the child's retelling of a story as read by the teacher or, when appropriate, read independently.

Because the teachers, by now thoroughly sensitized to assessment needs and strategies, have found anecdotal records and checklists both too time consuming and often unnecessary, the basic portfolio contents have been simplified. The commitment to equal attention to all children, however, is absolute. To assure that all children are carefully assessed, the teachers review what they know about the children twice a year and record on a class record sheet whether the child is attentive and participates in both small and large groups, has a disposition to read and write willingly, and is able to retell a story. If the answers are positive, no additional information is added to the portfolio; if not, various checklists that require closer monitoring are added. (Another example of the use of portfolios is provided in Chapter 11.)

In Redwood City, California, the early childhood portfolio consists of checklists for math and language arts, an inventory of reading and literature, a Grade 1 reading profile, observational items for determining social growth, and writing samples (Casey & Espinosa, 1992). The school is currently pilot-testing assessment of audio tapes of children's reading. (For a more complete description of the Redwood City primary education program, see Chapter 12.)

For portfolios involving social studies, teachers can ask children to select examples from their work that fit prescribed categories, such as learning something new, something that was difficult, something that shows a solution to a problem, or work that brought a sense of pride (Adams & Hamm, 1992). Work samples in art should document children's progress in the division and use of space, awareness of shapes, fine-motor control and eye–hand coordination, and sensitivity to materials (Cherry, 1990).

Those who have used portfolios bear witness to the richness of the record they store. Children have high interest in their own work, and they love to see the evidence of their own growth. Selecting and discussing work to be kept in a portfolio enhances children's awareness of their own learning. Portfolios are also of great interest to parents, who gain insight into their children's efforts and a better understanding of the program. In celebration of the educational road they have traveled from the beginning of kindergarten, second graders in South Brunswick write an essay entitled "On Being Eight" in the spring. The essay becomes one of the final entries in their portfolios, which are then presented with joyful ceremony to their parents!

# Assessment in the service of teachers and children

Assessment not only has the potential to improve instruction, as illustrated above, but it also has the potential to serve teachers and children.

## How developmentally appropriate assessment serves teachers

The assessment processes described in the guidelines and outlined in this chapter help early childhood educators with their critical responsibilities in teaching and learning. Developmentally appropriate assessment practices empower teachers because

• they are consistent with the values that teachers of young children typically hold;

• they confirm and validate what those teachers know about children; and

• they give teachers the information to do their jobs better and communicate to parents and others with confidence.

Appropriate assessment enhances the professional role of teachers, lifting them far above the "meter reader" metaphor that captures the misgivings many have felt as they scored daily worksheets, end-of-unit tests in basal texts, and standardized tests (Calfee & Hiebert, 1988). This kind of assessment, integrated with developmentally appropriate curriculum content and instructional practices, casts teachers as child development researchers and orchestrators of dynamic teaching and learning environments. Authentic assessment also forms a basis for teachers to evaluate their own efforts as dedicated professionals, fitting comfortably with their implicit theories about what is significant for children to learn and do.

The adults who care for children and understand them are responsible for fostering their welfare. Teachers must work to enhance their own skills in appropri-

ate assessment while simultaneously advocating for others' support. Advocacy can include circulating the Curriculum and Assessment Guidelines, informing parents and administrators, and demonstrating how appropriate assessment strengthens early childhood programs.

Because teachers of young children practice their craft in diverse settings, it is important to join forces and lend each other inspiration and strength. Two of the most important objectives for collaborative effort are

1. eliminating the overuse, misuse, and abuse of standardized tests, which do disservice to young children—by restricting their educational opportunities—and to teachers—by masking the wealth of information available through a balanced assessment program; and

2. developing and using authentic, developmentally appropriate assessments that can achieve all of the major purposes of assessment.

## How developmentally appropriate assessment benefits young children

Young children in the 1990s need teachers to meet their needs and to do what is appropriate for them, offering programs that allow them to feel competent even while they are growing in their abilities and understandings; that value their uniqueness and respect their out-of-school lives, including their parents and families; and that get them engaged in authentic learning experiences that best serve their long-run interests.

The contribution that developmentally appropriate assessment can make to those ends will depend upon the extent to which assessment processes are

• continuous;

• directed to all developmental areas;

• sensitive to individual and cultural diversity;

• completely integrated with curriculum and instruction;

• based on a defensible theory of child development and learning;

• collaborative between teachers and parents;

• helpful to teachers in their planning to meet the needs of children and the goals of the program; and

• unequivocally in the best interests of the children.

The children deserve nothing less.

## References

Adams, D.M., & Hamm, M.E. (1992). Portfolio assessment and social studies: Collecting, selecting, and reflecting on what is significant. *Social Education, 56*(2), 103–105.

Baratta-Lorton, M. (1976). *Mathematics their way.* Menlo Park, CA: Addison-Wesley.

Beaty, J. (1990). *Observing development of the young child.* Columbus, OH: Charles Merrill.

Bingham, A. (1988). Using writing folders to document student progress. In T. Newkirk & N. Atwell (Eds.), *Understanding writing* (2nd ed.) (pp. 216–225). Portsmouth, NH: Heinemann.

Brandt, R. (1992). On performance assessment: A conversation with Grant Wiggins. *Educational Leadership, 49*(8), 35–37.

Brown, A.L., & Reeve, R.A. (1987). Bandwidths of competence: The role of supportive contexts in learning and development. In L.S. Liben (Ed.), *Development and learning: Conflict or congruence?* (pp. 172–223). Hillsdale, NJ: Lawrence Erlbaum.

Calfee, R., & Hiebert, E. (1988). The teacher's role in using assessment to improve learning. In *Assessment in the service of learning: Proceedings of the 1987 ETS Invitational Conference* (pp. 45–61). Princeton, NJ: Educational Testing Service.

Casey, B., & Espinosa, L. (1992). Integrating developmentally appropriate curriculum and assessment practices: Redwood City School District. In B. Day, L. Malarz, & M. Terry (Eds.), *The education and care of young children* (pp. 38–42). Alexandria, VA: Association for Supervision and Curriculum Development.

Centre for Language in Primary Education. (1988). *The primary language record.* Portsmouth, NH: Heinemann.

Cherry, C. (1990). *Creative art for the developing child* (2nd ed.). Carthage, IL: Fearon.

Chittenden, E., & Courtney, R. (1989). Assessment of young children's reading: Documentation as an alternative to testing. In D.S. Strickland & L.M. Morrow (Eds.), *Emerging literacy: Young children learn to read and write* (pp. 107–120). Newark, DE: International Reading Association.

Clay, M.M. (1985). *The early detection of reading difficulties* (3rd ed.). Auckland, New Zealand: Octopus, Heinemann.

Cohen, D.H., Stern, V., & Balaban N. (1983). *Observing and recording the behavior of young children* (3rd ed.). New York: Teachers College Press.

Day, B. (1988). *Early childhood education* (3rd ed.). New York: Macmillan.

Engel, B. (1990). An approach to evaluation in reading and writing. In C. Kamii (Ed.), *Achievement testing in early childhood education: Games grown-ups play* (pp. 119–134). Washington, DC: NAEYC.

Genishi, C. (1985). Observing communication performance in young children. In N.A. Jaggar & M.T. Smith-Burke (Eds.), *Observing the language learner* (pp. 131–142). Newark, DE: International Reading Association.

Glazer, R. (1988). Cognitive and environmental perspectives on assessing achievement. In *Assessment in the service of learning: Proceedings of the 1987 ETS Invitational Conference* (pp. 37–43). Princeton, NJ: Educational Testing Service.

Gold, D. (1988, Mar. 30). Early testing said to have "long-term negative effects." *Education Week,* p. 6.

Goodman, K.S. (1973). *Miscue analysis: Applications to reading instruction.* Urbana, IL: ERIC/National Council of Teachers of English.

Goodman, Y.M. (1985). Kidwatching: Observing children in the classroom. In A. Jaggar & M.T. Smith-Burke (Eds.), *Observing the language learner* (pp. 9–18). Newark, DE: International Reading Association and National Council of Teachers of English.

Goodwin, W.L., & Driscoll, L.A. (1980). *Handbook for measurement and evaluation in early childhood education.* San Francisco: Jossey-Bass.

Gordon, A.M., & Browne, K.W. (1985). *Beginnings and beyond: Foundations in early childhood education.* New York: Delmar.

Grace, C., & Shores, E.F. (1991). *The portfolio and its use: Developmentally appropriate assessment of young children.* Little Rock, AR: Southern Association on Children Under Six.

Graves, D. (1983). *Teachers and children at work.* Portsmouth, NH: Heinemann.

Halliday, M.A.K. (1975). *Learning how to mean: Explorations in the development of language.* London: Edward Arnold.

Hegland, S., & Hills, T.W. (1988, July). *Using assessment for classroom planning.* Paper presented at the First National Institute for Head Start Coordinators, Washington, DC.

Hohmann, M., Banet, B., & Weikart, D.P. (1979). *Young children in action: A manual for preschool educators.* Ypsilanti, MI: High/Scope.

Jaggar, A.M. (1985). Introduction and overview. In A.M. Jaggar & M.T. Smith-Burke (Eds.), *Observing the language learner* (pp. 1–7). Newark, DE: International Reading Association.

Johnson, K. (1991). The test that wounds. *Educational Leadership, 48*(5), 100–101.

Kamii, C., & Rosenblum, V. (1990). An approach to assessment in mathematics. In C. Kamii (Ed.), *Achievement testing in the early grades* (pp. 147–162). Washington, DC: NAEYC.

Langhorst, B. (1989). *Assessment in early childhood education: A consumer's guide.* Portland, OR: Northwest Regional Education Laboratory.

Meisels, S.J. (1985). *Developmental screening in early childhood.* Washington, DC: NAEYC.

Meisels, S.J. (1987). Uses and abuses of developmental screening and school readiness testing. *Young Children, 42*(2), 4–6, 68–73.

Meisels, S., & Provence, S. (1989). *Screening and assessment: Guidelines for identifying young disabled and developmentally vulnerable children and their families.* Washington, DC: National Center for Clinical Infant Programs.

Meyer, C.A. (1992). What's the difference between *authentic* and *performance* assessment? *Educational Leadership, 49*(8), 39–40.

Mitchell, R. (1992). *Testing for learning: How new approaches to evaluation can improve American schools.* New York: The Free Press.

National Association for the Education of Young Children. (1988). Position statement on standardized testing of young children 3 through 8 years of age. *Young Children, 43*(3), 42–47.

National Association of Early Childhood Specialists in State Departments of Education. (1987). *Unacceptable trends in kindergarten entry and placement.* Unpublished document. (Available from early childhood specialists, state education agencies, state capitals.)

National Association for the Education of Young Children & the National Association of Early Childhood Specialists in State Departments of Education. (1991). Guidelines for appropriate curriculum content and assessment in programs serving children ages 3 through 8. *Young Children, 46*(3), 21–38.

National Association of Elementary School Principals. (1990). *Early childhood education and the elementary school principal.* Alexandria, VA: Author.

National Commission on Testing and Public Policy. (1990). *From gatekeeper to gateway: Transforming testing in America.* Chestnut Hill, MA: Author.

National Council of Teachers of Mathematics. (1989). *Curriculum and evaluation standards for school mathematics.* Reston, VA: Author.

Pellegrini, A.D., & Glickman, C.D. (1990). Measuring kindergartners' social competence. *Young Children, 45*(4), 40–44.

Perrone, V. (1990). How did we get here? In C. Kamii (Ed.), *Achievement testing in the early grades: The games grown-ups play* (pp. 1–13). Washington, DC: NAEYC.

Pinnell, G.S. (1985). Ways to look at the functions of children's language. In A. Jaggar & M.T. Smith-Burke (Eds.), *Observing the language learner* (pp. 57–72). Newark, DE: International Reading Association.

Polakowski, C., Spicer, W., & Zimmerman, J. (1992). Linking assessment to accountability/linking curriculum to appropriate assessment: South Brunswick school district. In B. Day, L. Malarz, & M. Terry (Eds.), *The education and care of young children* (pp. 47–53). Alexandria, VA: Association for Supervision and Curriculum Development.

Resnick, L.B., & Klopfer, L.E. (1989). Toward the thinking curriculum: An overview. In L.B. Resnick & L.E. Klopfer (Eds.), *Toward the thinking curriculum: Current cognitive research* (pp. 1–18). Alexandria, VA: Association for Supervision and Curriculum Development.

Smith, D. (1991, March). *The teacher as significant other in the preschool, kindergarten, and primary classroom: The challenge of change.* Paper presented to the Annual Conference of the California Association for the Education of Young Children, Los Angeles, CA.

Sowers, S. (1988). Six questions teachers ask about invented spelling. In T. Newkirk & N. Atwell (Eds.), *Understanding writing* (2nd ed.) (pp. 62–68). Portsmouth, NH: Heinemann.

Stiggins, R.J. (1985). Improving assessment where it means the most: In the classroom. *Educational Leadership, 43*(2), 69–74.

Stiggins, R.J. (1991). Assessment literacy. *Phi Delta Kappan, 72*(7), 534–539.

Taylor, R.L. (1984). *Assessment of exceptional students.* Englewood, NJ: Prentice Hall.

Teale, W.H. (1988). Developmentally appropriate assessment of reading and writing in the early childhood classroom. *Elementary School Journal, 89*(2), 173–183.

Tierney, R.J., Carter, M.A., & Desai, L.E. (1991). *Portfolio assessment in the reading-writing classroom.* Norwood, MA: Christopher-Gordon.

U.S. Congress, Office of Technology Assessment. (1992). *Testing in America's schools: Asking the right questions.* Washington, DC: U.S. Government Printing Office.

Vygotsky, L.S. (1978). *Mind in society: The development of higher psychological functions.* Cambridge, MA: Harvard University Press.

Wood, K.D. (1988). Techniques for assessing students' potential for learning. *The Reading Teacher, 41*(4), 440–447.

SECTION

# Reaching Individual Potentials

*In Section I of this book, principles of appropriate curriculum and assessment are presented, described, and illustrated with examples. The guidelines, or principles, provide the basis for the many curriculum and assessment decisions that occur at all levels. Curriculum is not just the goals and objectives (or outcomes, if you will), nor is it limited to the strategies or methods of teaching and evaluating. Although vital decisions occur at the levels of goal setting and program organization, many (perhaps most) curriculum and assessment decisions occur at the classroom level; these are the decisions such as what activities will occur, which materials will be used, how the day will be structured, what will happen first and next, and what the daily plans look like. Perhaps the title of a book (Dittmann, 1977) that NAEYC published many years ago said it best: "Curriculum is What Happens." That book had a subtitle that was often neglected when the ideas were*

*quoted: "Planning is the Key." Curriculum does encompass everything that happens, but what happens does not occur randomly or by chance. Instead, effective curriculum requires thoughtful planning and implementation. It is to this level of curriculum and assessment that we turn in Section II.*

*In Chapter 5, drawing on the principles of appropriate curriculum and assessment, we present a model of curriculum planning designed to help all children reach their potentials—leading to programs that are individually appropriate. Then in Chapter 6 we demonstrate the application of this model of curriculum planning and implementation with 3- through 5-year-olds and with 6- through 9-year-olds. Chapter 7 presents the principles of best practice for achieving the individual potentials of children with special needs.*

# Reaching Individual
# Potentials Through
# Transformational Curriculum

*Teresa Rosegrant and Sue Bredekamp*

**T**he process of curriculum development occurs in at least four phases: (1) theoretical; (2) planning; (3) implementation; and (4) assessment. The theoretical phase of curriculum development provides teachers with an understanding of *why* they make certain decisions. The planning phase provides teachers with a framework for guiding what those decisions become. The implementation phase is what happens in the classroom—how, when, and where teaching and learning occur. The assessment phase provides information on why, how, when, and where children learn, enabling teachers to review and revise the curriculum. A theoretical perspective is operational and articulated prior to initiating specific planning. The curriculum guidelines and the discussion of the guidelines in Chapter 3 provide the theoretical basis for the curriculum design we describe here. (Other theoretical perspectives exist and could also be used to guide program development.)

In this chapter we take the application of the Curriculum and Assessment Guidelines to the more specific level of planning and implementation in the classroom. First we review the various perspectives that inform curriculum and examine what each perspective brings to the picture. Then we offer a new framework, a model of curriculum planning that we call *transformational curriculum,* that draws on the strengths of all of these perspectives while focusing attention on the

individual child. In Chapter 6 we follow with specific strategies for using the model of transformational curriculum in planning and implementation. The assessment phase of curriculum planning is ongoing, as described in Chapter 4.

## Perspectives that inform curriculum

In Chapter 3 we identified meaningful curriculum as our overarching goal, and we presented several key concepts from the curriculum guidelines that are essential to achieve meaningfulness: integrated curriculum, whole child philosophy, intellectual integrity, and children's individual needs and interests. Each of these key concepts provides an important perspective that informs curriculum. The many sources of curriculum include, but are not limited to, these perspectives (see guidelines, pp. 9–22, this volume). Meaningful curriculum results from thoughtful planning and organization that draws on at least these four perspectives. Rephrased, the four perspectives that inform curriculum planning are

**1.** conceptual organizers or other integrated, meaning-centered approaches (such as themes, units, or projects);

**2.** child development knowledge (normative information relevant to the cognitive, socioemotional, language, and physical domains);

**3.** the knowledge base of the subject-matter disciplines (such as science, social studies, mathematics, language arts, health, physical education, and the arts); and

**4.** the continuum of development and learning, both hypothetical and actual, of the children in the group (whether broadly defined—such as birth to 3, 3- through 5-year-olds, or 6- through 8-year-olds—or more narrowly prescribed).

By identifying and listing these perspectives separately, we do not intend to imply that they are mutually exclusive; elements of each encroach on the others. Likewise, each of these perspectives informs both the content of curriculum and the processes of learning and teaching because, as indicated earlier, content and process are inseparable elements. Each of these perspectives on curriculum planning brings important information to the curriculum that should not be neglected, which is described in more detail below.

### How conceptual organizers—"meaning-centered" approaches—inform the curriculum

Conceptual organizers are the "meaning-centered" approaches that are designed to enhance comprehension and depth of understanding of curriculum content. We begin with this perspective in our discussion of curriculum because our goal is "mindful" or meaningful curriculum for young children. The term *meaning-centered* is used here to encompass the various approaches to conceptually organizing or integrating curriculum, such as themes, webs, units, or projects. Conceptually organized curriculum

• provides enriched meaning and understandings, layers of understanding with depth and texture;

• starts where children are—children can engage immediately;

• is informed by children's interests, both cultural and individual;

• engages the child first-hand with concrete referents available;

• provides ways of organizing information—classifying and categorizing—that make sense and help children connect the learning to what they already know; and

• places learning in context—experiences occur in natural or actual settings.

Conceptually organized curriculum has the advantage of making discipline-based knowledge accessible to young children. The curriculum starts from children's meaningful experiences, building on and activating prior knowledge. If meaning-centered approaches are used appropriately (taking into consideration age-, culturally, and individually appropriate information),

© Nancy P. Alexander

then children inevitably want to learn more. Without conceptual organizers, purely discipline-based instruction is much less motivating and engaging for children, who then resort to rote learning. Meaning-centered curriculum helps move children to the inquiry level of the learning cycle, enhancing their interest and desire to make sense of the learning. The emphasis on meaning and connectedness defines early childhood curriculum through the primary grades. Curriculum for older children and adults can be more abstract, although trends in education at the middle- and secondary-school levels also emphasize meaning-centered, conceptually organized curriculum (Shoemaker, 1991).

## How knowledge of child development informs curriculum

Child development knowledge is another important information source for planning curriculum. Normative child development data (Katz & Chard, 1989, p.17) provides teachers with information about what is age appropriate. This information is used by curriculum planners and teachers in at least four ways:

**1.** *Child development information provides teachers with theoretical perspectives for understanding how and why children behave.*

This information helps teachers create appropriate expectations for children's behavior. These expectations form the basis for classroom rules and routines. Knowledge of child development is also used as a framework for understanding and selecting appropriate strategies for guiding children's behavior—using appropriate discipline techniques and supporting children's social and moral development.

**2.** *Child development provides information about what children can do and understand within normative guidelines.*

This information helps teachers set broad parameters, age-appropriate expectations, for when children may be ready and able to accomplish new tasks and move to new levels of ability. Knowledge of what is age appropriate helps teachers to plan challenging and interesting classroom projects and activities that foster various forms of learning and also to select materials and media that are a good fit developmentally.

**3.** *Child development provides teachers chronologically based data on when children generally reach certain developmental milestones.*

Age-related data gives teachers information that can be used to organize and sequence what types of activities occur throughout the year. An understanding of developmental milestones enables teachers to plan the learning environment and introduce materials when

*FAILURE TO ATTEND TO CHILD DEVELOPMENT INCREASES THE LIKELIHOOD OF ERROR, THE POTENTIAL OF MISSING THE MARK ENTIRELY, BY EITHER OVERESTIMATING OR UNDERESTIMATING CHILDREN'S ABILITY AND INTEREST. IN SHORT, ATTENDING TO AGE-APPROPRIATE EXPECTATIONS INCREASES THE LIKELIHOOD THAT A PROGRAM WILL BE ABLE TO ADJUST TO INDIVIDUAL DIFFERENCES.*

children are more likely to benefit from and enjoy their use. Developmental data help teachers understand the role of experience in learning so that children who have had less experience in an area can be provided enriched experiences to enable them to succeed at new tasks. When children appear to have sustained difficulties, knowledge of typical child development enables teachers to refer children for help from specialists and/ or to modify the types of activities within the classroom for specific children.

**4.** *Child development information supports the concept of individual and cultural variation.*

The knowledge base of child development is not static; our understanding of individual and cultural variation is constantly being expanded with new research. The study of child development theory and research provides teachers with various perspectives for interpreting and supporting the development of individual children.

Child development information relevant to all developmental domains (physical, social, emotional, and cognitive) provides a baseline from which curriculum developers and teachers can plan. Predictions can be made about what children within given age ranges are able to do and what they are interested in doing. Attention to the "commonness" among children, what abilities and interests they share, enables programs to get in the general range of acceptability. Failure to attend to child development increases the likelihood of error, the potential of missing the mark entirely, by either overestimating or underestimating children's ability and interest. In short, attending to age-appropriate expectations increases the likelihood that a program will be able to adjust to individual differences.

## How the disciplines inform curriculum

To a large extent the content of the curriculum derives from the disciplines, such as mathematics or science. Much of what children need to know and be able to do in school is derived from the subject-matter disciplines. Attention to the knowledge base of the disciplines ensures that curriculum has intellectual integrity, as discussed in Chapter 3. The disciplines shape curriculum for young children in numerous ways; we mention just a few of the most important contributions. Discipline-based knowledge provides children ways of

• learning about the world;
• describing what is learned;
• structuring knowledge;
• testing assumptions and challenging understandings; and
• defining and solving problems.

From the discipline of science, for example, children learn about the physical and biological aspects of the world in which they live. The discipline provides several key concepts or ways of describing this knowledge, such as change, cause-and-effect, and systems. In addition the discipline of science offers structures or paradigms for understanding these key concepts. The scientific method is the way science tests its assumptions and challenges those understandings. Science emphasizes problem solving; problems (or questions) generate hypotheses that can then be tested by systematic experimentation.

Discipline-based curriculum has the potential of providing enormous depth and breadth of content, a highly rich educational experience, but there are disadvantages to a purely discipline-based approach to organizing curriculum, especially for young children. A discipline-based approach is an expert-based system. Only the experts—the scientists, the mathematicians, and the artists—can claim a thorough understanding of the discipline; such knowledge is not accessible to very young children. To improve accessibility, subject-matter-based curriculum often oversimplifies important constructs for presentation to young audiences, resulting in inaccuracies or confusion. Science is particularly challenging for young children because their magical thinking may take precedence over the logical, though not clearly observable, explanation. If the change resulting from the experiment does not occur in plain view, children are more likely to attribute it to magic or to some other personally meaningful hypothesis than to the true cause. As a result, discipline-based knowledge needs to be incorporated in a meaning-centered, conceptually organized approach that also reflects what is known about how children develop cognitively.

## How a developmental/learning continuum informs curriculum

A developmental/learning continuum is the organizing of desired goals or outcomes to guide planning and keep track of children's progress. Such a continuum is not a rigid sequence, nor is it necessarily linear, because the order in which children acquire knowledge or achieve a desired outcome will vary. A developmental/learning continuum provides a general framework from which to plan, but specific curriculum planning requires attention to the individual children in relation to the relevant continuum of development and learning. First the planner must outline a hypothetical continuum of specific developmental and learning objectives that guides curriculum planning. This trajectory tells the teacher where to begin; provides a reasonable order to the curriculum (at least a pattern, not a rigid sequence); and sets goals or outcomes, endpoints toward which the effort is directed. For such a continuum to be useful, however, it cannot be viewed as separate from the continuum of development and learning that occurs within each child. The hypothetical learning continuum must be modified and adjusted in relation to each individual child in the group. For instance, a child may not have had sufficient prior experience to benefit from an activity that is of value to most of the other children; likewise, a child may already be beyond the endpoint of the teacher's hypothetical continuum. In short, the curriculum plan must be individually as well as developmentally appropriate.

Teachers use the concept of a continuum of development and learning in many ways, but primarily to determine when, where, and how to provide individual assistance to children, such as in the following:

• *identifying "teachable moments"—figuring out the timing when assistance will be most effective*

Teachers constantly determine what a child has achieved and understands and what the child is not perceiving. The concept of teachable moments relates to identifying an individual's readiness for a particular task.

• *matching the learner's style and pace*

Awareness of individual differences keeps teachers from giving too much or too little support and prevents them from going too fast or too slow.

• *providing the right kind of support*

Teachers need to know individual children to decide which of the myriad of possible teaching behaviors, from acknowledging to directing, is appropriate in a given situation. For instance, teachers need to recognize whether a child actually needs help or just encouragement. If assistance is required, teachers need to figure out why and how children are confused. The same group of children who don't understand a given concept, such as one-to-one correspondence, may be confused about the concept in very different ways. Using the same explanation or strategy for all of these children will most likely be unsuccessful.

• *providing adequate scaffolding—the appropriate amount of support*

Teachers need to understand individual children to be able to help each of them do what they want to do but are incapable of without help. Teachers provide assistance, or scaffolding, that supports the learner to move to a new level of ability or understanding, focusing on meaningfulness, without taking away the child's ownership and motivation.

• *fostering a strong sense of self-concept*

Teachers need to know individual children to help foster a positive sense of self, to ensure a culturally safe classroom, and to ensure that children gain a sense of competence. Teachers need to be acutely aware of where children are on their own continuum of development and learning and to make sure that children have enough successful experiences so that their self-esteem is not undermined.

The concept of a developmental/learning continuum reflects the dynamic dimension of child development (Katz & Chard, 1989, p. 18), which deals with the way human beings change over time. While normative information provides a framework for comparison (information about what most children are capable of at different chronological ages), there is a wide range of individual variation that is well within the normal range. In addition, each individual demonstrates a unique continuum of development and learning that results from the interaction between maturation and experience. The concept of a developmental continuum occurring within each child is represented in the "individually appropriate" aspect of the definition of what is "developmentally appropriate" (Bredekamp, 1987, p. 2). This information is obtainable only from observing and interacting with the child and from parents, who observe their child in other contexts.

Having explored the various perspectives that inform curriculum and having identified the usefulness of each, we turn now to a discussion of how these perspectives have influenced curriculum in the past and offer a new paradigm for curriculum planning in the future.

## A new paradigm for curriculum planning: Transformational curriculum

The NAEYC and NAECS/SDE guidelines call for meaning-centered, integrated, "mindful" curriculum, but such curriculum is only achieved if the other perspectives that inform curriculum are activated—child development knowledge, discipline-based knowledge, and knowledge of the individual developmental/learning continuum of each child. The curriculum guidelines therefore require that curriculum not only be meaning centered but that it be age appropriate (reflect knowledge of child development domains), be individually appropriate (based on children's needs, interests, and individual differences), and have intellectual integrity (reflect the knowledge base of the disciplines). In short, the NAEYC and NAECS/SDE guidelines call for attention to all four perspectives that inform curriculum planning. Traditional approaches to curriculum draw on one or two of these perspectives but are not often adequately informed by all perspectives at the same time.

To plan and implement curriculum that draws on all four of these perspectives requires more than integration; it requires transformation. In effect, the curriculum guidelines call for a new model of curriculum planning that is a step beyond the integrated curriculum approaches—what we call "transformational curriculum." Transformational curriculum combines not just two of the perspectives on curriculum planning mentioned above but synthesizes all four perspectives. A transformational approach to curriculum planning results in mindful curriculum because it

• is conceptually organized, using a meaning-centered approach;

• draws on the knowledge base of the disciplines; and

• considers information about child development in all domains (the whole child); and

• considers the individual developmental continuum of each child in the group (whether multiage or one chronological year).

Transformations are changes. We use the adjective *transformational* to describe this approach to curriculums because it is based on the assumption that not only does such a curriculum change the learner but the learner also affects and changes the curriculum. The model of transformational curriculum planning is depicted in Figure 1. The child remains at the center of the curriculum, transformed by the interaction with the curriculum but influencing and transforming the curriculum in return. By this, we do not mean that the child controls the curriculum; but if learning is to be an interactive process, then curriculum must change in response to the learner. During the planning process teachers involve children by assessing what the children already know about a topic as well as what they want and need to know. Then, during implementation, teachers continually assess the needs and interests of children in relation to curriculum goals and adapt the curriculum and instructional strategies to be more responsive.

Although Figure 1 centers on the individual child, except in rare instances, such as tutorials, learning occurs in the sociocultural context of groups; therefore Figure 1 places the child in a sociocultural context that is influenced by many factors, especially the cultures of the families served and the larger community. Curriculum decisions always occur in cultural contexts; cultural values are one of the many sources of curriculum. In the model of transformational curriculum, culture is not viewed as a separate source of curriculum but rather as the context within which children learn and as the context within which all curriculum decisions are made. Culture is therefore seen as influencing all four perspectives that inform curriculum decisions; for example, the culture of the children and the community affects the selection of conceptual organizers for curriculum because what is

meaningful to children and of value to the community is influenced by diverse cultural experiences. Culture certainly influences decisions about which discipline-based knowledge is included and how it is interpreted; for example, in American schools decision-making skills are fostered because they are essential for citizens of a democratic society. The inclusion or exclusion of specific curriculum content often reflects the cultural values of a region, state, or community. Likewise, child development knowledge is not culture free. Child development research is always embedded in cultural context and may be limited to one cultural group; therefore, child development knowledge must be carefully evaluated for its generalizability to the population being served if such data is to accurately inform curriculum decisions. Programs serving children whose primary language is not English, for example, should be informed by research that is conducted on similar populations with similar opportunities for second-language acquisition. Finally, the continuum of development and learning exhibited by individual children is influenced by the sociocultural context of the classroom, in which much learning is socially constructed, and by the culture of the community. The sociocultural context of curriculum is com-

*Figure 1.* TRANSFORMATIONAL CURRICULUM

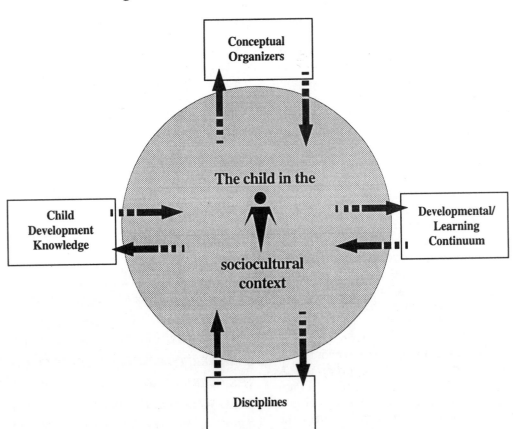

© Florence Sharp

plex and cannot be adequately represented in a two-dimensional model. (For a more detailed discussion of the sociocultural context of curriculum, see Section III of this volume.)

## Reaching potentials through transformational curriculum

To help all children reach their potentials as developing human beings and learners, a transformational curriculum is needed. Such a curriculum is meaningful; intellectual; and developmentally, culturally, and individually appropriate. Perhaps this sounds like an attempt to be all things to all people—to satisfy critics by putting in a little bit of each perspective; actually nothing could be further from the truth. Each perspective on curriculum is important, but it is only in the interaction among the different perspectives that their true value is realized; attention to any one or even two without attention to the others opens the margin for error. A few examples will illustrate the importance of this interaction.

Achieving "mindful" curriculum requires meaning-centered, conceptually organized curriculum. Such curriculum has several advantages over purely discipline-driven curriculum. The primary advantage seems to be that in meaning-centered approaches, children are the agents of their own learning rather than the audience for learning. Nevertheless, meaning-centered approaches can also fail miserably if they do not attend to the disciplines, as well as to information about what is age, culturally, and individually appropriate. A series of unrelated or "undisciplined" projects is not curriculum; if the conceptual dimension of curriculum planning is considered in isolation from the others, the curriculum may be too idiosyncratic, lacking in direc-

tion or focus, or limited to "fun" activities that lack integrity. Similarly, projects, themes, and other integrating approaches can be inappropriate if they do not respect children's development and prior experience, such as when children in the inner-city school stare blankly during the farm unit or when preschoolers in Arizona "study" the winter season by gluing cotton balls on paper snowmen. This same content can be transformed into meaningful learning experiences, however: the city children could begin with what they know about food and move into learning about the farm and other food sources; the children in Arizona could observe their own weather, record what winter is like in the desert, and compare this data to weather reports from other parts of the country.

Attention to the knowledge base of the disciplines ensures that the curriculum has integrity and accuracy and is worthwhile, but attention to this dimension alone can lead to the error in which curriculum objectives are not provided in meaningful context and are unrelated to the child's needs and interests. The results of such curriculum are apparent in Kamii's research (1989) on children who successfully learn the "tricks" to solving place-value problems (cross out this number and write in the next-smallest number) but are unable to solve a meaningful problem that requires understanding of place value. On the other hand, discipline-based approaches that are meaning centered, age appropriate, and individually appropriate result in children's reconstructing the expert understandings of the discipline (see Kamii, 1985, 1989; DeVries & Kohlberg, 1990; Gardner, 1991).

Knowledge of child development domains provides the basis for formulating age-appropriate expectations, but again this information is useless in isolation. The norms do not tell us much that is helpful about any one child; that child's own continuum of development and learning must be studied. For example, the typical sequence of motor development in infancy is well known—basically, babies crawl, stand, cruise, and walk; but most people know at least one baby who never crawled and now walks fine. Child development knowledge is not the content of the curriculum; child development information is useful in guiding decisions about what content is possible, desirable, and appropriate, and when.

*A SERIES OF UNRELATED OR "UNDISCIPLINED" PROJECTS IS NOT CURRICULUM; IF THE CONCEPTUAL DIMENSION OF CURRICULUM PLANNING IS CONSIDERED IN ISOLATION FROM THE OTHERS, THE CURRICULUM MAY BE TOO IDIOSYNCRATIC, LACKING IN DIRECTION OR FOCUS, OR LIMITED TO "FUN" ACTIVITIES THAT LACK INTEGRITY.*

Finally, the dynamic perspective on curriculum—the continuum of development and learning—must be addressed. This interaction can only occur at the classroom level because the teacher must engage with the learners as individuals and determine where they are in relation to the continuum of objectives. She must know the general continuum to be expected (the hypothetical idealized continuum) so that she can identify when children need help and when they need more challenge. For instance, research on literacy learning provides support for a generalized continuum of emergent writing in which children scribble, draw, and form initial consonants, non-phonetic letter strings, phonetic letter strings, and invented spellings; but such neat sequences are always violated by individual children. Four-year-old Drew rarely picked up a marker and seldom chose to draw, but after many months of careful observation of others, he formed all four letters in his name quite legibly. Most teachers can cite examples of children who began reading before they knew all of the letters and sounds, so a continuum of learning and developmental outcomes must be used flexibly. Unfortunately this approach can be misused if the idealized continuum is set up as a rigid standard and children who do not match it are judged as failures, or if children are not really looked at as individuals and are placed in "homogenous" groups for instruction. The real potential of this approach to curriculum is individually appropriate instruction, which is possible if knowledge of the child's actual continuum of development and learning is used to modify and adjust the curriculum.

## Transformational curriculum in practice

We visualize four perspectives that inform curriculum within a sociocultural context—conceptual organizers to ensure meaningfulness, child development knowledge to enhance age appropriateness, discipline-based knowledge to ensure that curriculum has intellectual integrity and is worth knowing, and the developmental/learning continuum to ensure that the curriculum is individually appropriate—as intertwined strands of one strong rope. For the rope to hold, all strands need to be strong. In preschool classrooms in which the child development strand is sometimes disproportionately emphasized, the content of the curriculum may become too shallow (sometimes called the "greeting card" approach to curriculum). Likewise, too often in primary classrooms in the past, the discipline strand has been disproportionately thick, neglecting variance in individual children or failing to acknowledge cultural differences. As we attempt to achieve balance, however, we must also be cautious that we do not unduly weaken any strand. Math educators are justifiably concerned when they hear teachers who use meaning-centered approaches say, "but we do math everywhere!" In reality they may have integrated math

to the point that its knowledge base disappears. If any one strand gets too strong, others are probably weakened. The child development strand in curriculum is sometimes so weak that it breaks down regularly through setting curriculum goals that are unrealistic or assuming that learning results because children have all been exposed to the same experience.

One of our favorite examples of the importance of all four strands was a first-hand experience in Teresa Rosegrant's kindergarten classroom (personal communication, September 15, 1992). As part of a unit on growing things, the class studied the growth of the frog. Presumably the project reflected all of the important dimensions of curriculum planning, beginning with a visit to the pond to collect tadpoles. The class carefully set up the environment to raise the tadpoles and watch their transformation into frogs. Science books and pictures supplemented the first-hand experiences, ensuring that information was scientifically accurate. Children charted and graphed the growth of the tadpoles. The teacher had carefully prepared the children for the tadpoles' transition to frogs, which the children had been observing first-hand over several days. Nevertheless, the first morning that true frogs appeared in the aquarium, the children were absolutely stunned. The typical question was, "Where did those frogs come from?" Despite all of the teacher's reminders and explanations, the children kept asking, "When did you put those frogs in there?" Recently, when Teresa met some of the children from that class who are now second graders, they said, "Remember when we got those frogs!" Even with her considerable knowledge of child development, Teresa was reminded that her excellent curriculum plan could not overcome the children's preoperational thinking. Such experiences demonstrate the importance of attending to all four perspectives in planning and implementing appropriate curriculum, a more detailed discussion of which follows in Chapter 6.

## References

Bredekamp, S. (Ed.). (1987). *Developmentally appropriate practice in early childhood programs serving children from birth through age 8* (exp. ed.). Washington, DC: NAEYC.

DeVries, R., & Kohlberg, L. (1990). *Constructivist early education: Overview and comparison with other programs.* Washington, DC: NAEYC.

Dittmann, L. (Ed.). (1977). *Curriculum is what happens: Planning is the key.* Washington, DC: NAEYC. (Out of print)

Gardner, H. (1991). *The unschooled mind.* New York: Basic Books.

Jones, E., & Reynolds, G. (1992). *The play's the thing . . . Teachers' roles in children's play.* New York: Teachers College Press.

Kamii, C. (1985). *Young children re-invent arithmetic: Implications of Piaget's theory.* New York: Teachers College Press.

Kamii, C. (1989). *Young children continue to re-invent arithmetic: 2nd grade.* New York: Teachers College Press.

Katz, L., & Chard, S. (1989). *Engaging children's minds: The project approach.* Norwood, NJ: Ablex.

Shoemaker, B. (1991). Education 2000: Integrated curriculum. *Educational Leadership, 48*(8), 793–797.

# Planning and Implementing Transformational Curriculum

*Teresa Rosegrant and Sue Bredekamp*

In the previous chapter a model of transformational curriculum is presented that is based on the curriculum guidelines and informed by all of the important perspectives for ensuring that children reach their potentials. Transformational curriculum is conceptually organized and meaningful, drawing on knowledge of child development, discipline-based knowledge, and the dynamic continuum of development and learning that each individual presents. The purpose of Chapter 6 is to describe the processes of curriculum planning and implementation based on this model and to provide examples in practice for three age groups: young preschoolers (2- and 3-year-olds), kindergartners, and second graders (7- and 8-year-old children in primary school).

In this chapter we begin with a discussion of goals because all curriculum emanates from goal setting; then we describe the process of planning transformational curriculum; next we discuss implementation issues; and finally we demonstrate planning and implementation, with vignettes from three classrooms. Volume 2 of this book presents curriculum planning—organized by the subject-matter disciplines—that is meaningful, conceptual, and reflects knowledge of age-appropriate, culturally appropriate, and individually appropriate expectations. Volume 2 also includes a discussion of curriculum planning for infants and toddlers.

## Goals for young children

Before specific planning can begin, the "common" goals of the curriculum must be established. Curriculum planners must begin by answering the fundamental question, What kind of children do we want? (See p. 18 for a sample goal statement.) The answers to this question affect decisions about the program's goals. The goals for children, in turn, determine curriculum and assessment decisions. Certainly, each of the four perspectives that inform transformational curriculum also informs goal setting. Goals must be meaningful, relevant, and conceptual to ensure that children gain depth of understanding. Goals must have intellectual integrity and be derived from the knowledge base of the disciplines to ensure breadth in the curriculum. Goals must be realistic and attainable, reflecting child development knowledge, and also address the "whole" child. Goals must be derived for groups and individuals based on needs and interests. The overarching goal of curriculum is for children to reach their potentials as contributing members of a democratic society. Obviously potential is not fully achieved during early childhood, but the foundation is laid. It is especially important that experiences in early childhood do not narrow children's options nor restrict their potential achievements in the future.

Goals for children are not limited to the acquisition of knowledge and understanding, processes and skills; goals also address the development of positive attitudes and dispositions. Dispositions are inclinations to behave in a certain way or habits of mind (Katz, 1991). There are many dispositions that relate to success in school and in life; certainly, among the most important for teachers to cultivate is the disposition to go on learning, as Katz points out. In their research on developing literacy using the microcomputer as a tool with various ages of children, including children with disabilities, Rosegrant and Cooper (1986) found that certain dispositions or learning behaviors are essential for acquiring literacy. These important learner dispositions are persistence, focused participation, hypothesis testing, risk taking, and self-regulation. Each of these dispositions was found to be significantly related to children's progress. Moreover, a low level of one or more of these behaviors was consistently observed in children who continued to have difficulty learning to read and write. Curriculum for young children must be planned and implemented so as to foster these desirable dispositions, each of which is described in more detail below.

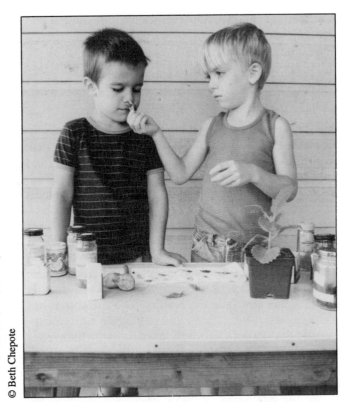
© Beth Chepote

## Persistence

Most teachers and parents would not be surprised by the fact that *persistence* is an important determinant of success in learning. Learning important skills such as reading and writing is not always easy. To develop skills and extend thinking, children must stay with a task—even when it is difficult. Persistence is harder for children who feel that their efforts more often result in failure than in progress. The role of the teacher and the environment is to support children until they reach a new level of achievement. This support—whether provided by a teacher, a parent, another child, or a computer that gives appropriate feedback—is necessary to strengthen and maintain the disposition to persist at learning tasks.

## Focused participation

*Focused participation* is another term to describe engagement. Children need to attend to the learning task not just by passively listening (although listening is important in certain contexts) but with a high level of participation and attention. Children who experience too much failure or frustration are less likely to attend to learning tasks or to actively participate. Focused participation is such an important predictor of children's success and is so highly correlated with experiencing success that teachers' goal should be that children experience success most of the time. This means that the curriculum must start where the child is; if the expectations are not developmentally appropri-

ate, then failure is more likely. By using a learning continuum, the adult can chart each child's progress and modify activities and experiences when needed. The challenge is to support the development of a sense of competence in all children so that their focused participation is maintained.

## Hypothesis testing

So much of children's learning occurs as they develop and test hypotheses. The process of *hypothesis testing* is especially apparent as children acquire verbal language and then again as they acquire literacy and numeracy. Children's invented spellings are a clear example of their testing hypotheses about written language. Throughout early childhood, hypothesis testing is seen repeatedly as children construct assumptions about how things work in the world and then try out their assumptions to see if they are adequate, adjusting them over time. Hypothesis testing is the major activity during the exploration to inquiry phases of the learning cycle; it is much like the scientific method at its most applied level. This approach to learning is pragmatic, a far more efficient strategy than the random trial-and-error of the young toddler. The disposition to formulate and test hypotheses tells us that a child is developing understanding and establishing rules about how the world works and what makes sense. Learning activities and projects must be sufficiently open ended to allow children some intellectual freedom to construct their own hypotheses, interpretations, and understandings.

### Risk taking

Learning anything new is a step into the unknown that requires some risk taking, especially at the beginning stages. The risk lies in trying to execute a task before it has been mastered, similar to the crawling and toddling that precedes walking. In fact, toddlers are perhaps the greatest risk takers in the world, and their risk taking—including its requisite bumps and spills— is critical to their development and learning. Some risks that children take result in negative feedback. If children continually experience negative feedback on their performance, they become more tentative in their efforts. They are less willing to take risks to display their efforts and face the results. They find that not trying is easier than trying and risking failure. Consequently they experience even less success, which leads to less effort—a vicious cycle. Taking risks is an essential part of learning. If the disposition to take risks is to be cultivated successfully, teachers must provide a learning environment that starts where children are and that is appropriate for the range of abilities among the children. This way the children are relatively engaged and feel successful before being asked to try something new that is probably more difficult. In such an environment children can easily explore without fear of making mistakes. Such a learning environment provides the number of successful experiences that children need to feel competent. In addition, it supports constructive error as a natural part of learning.

### Self-regulation

A goal of all parenting *and* teaching in early childhood has to be to develop self-confident, self-regulated human beings. No society in the world can continue to function unless most of its citizens regulate their own behavior and make appropriate, ethical decisions. Self-regulation begins in toddlerhood, when children's natural inclination to exert their autonomy is used to help them learn to make choices ("You can wear the green one or the red one"; "You can eat a hamburger or soup"); but self-regulation becomes even more important as children begin to live and work in groups. The development of self-regulation, as well as the other desirable dispositions mentioned above, should be clear goals of the curriculum and outcomes of all good early childhood programs.

The Curriculum and Assessment Guidelines describe a learning environment in which all of the dispositions described above, as well as others, are nurtured and developed. Curriculum that encourages choice and active participation supports the dispositions to persist, engage, test hypotheses, safely take risks, and regulate one's own behavior. Likewise, assessment strategies that encourage self-evaluation and reflection also contribute to these important dispositions. Each learner can be expected to exhibit varying levels of the desirable dispositions described above. Learners who demonstrate high levels of all of these behaviors tend to also be high in interest, ownership, and accountability for their own learning. Likewise, low levels are related to a lack of interest, ownership, and accountability (Rosegrant & Cooper, 1986). Curriculum must promote the development of these desirable learner dispositions while also helping children acquire knowledge and skills.

# Planning transformational curriculum for young children

How and what teachers do to make classrooms into places where children can reach their potentials as learners is discussed in this section, in which we take a closer look at the planning process. In the following section we will examine the steps needed to implement curriculum plans in the classroom. Principles of planning and implementation are described in general and then illustrated with examples for different age groups in the final section of the chapter.

Planning and implementing appropriate curriculum can be described in many ways; this description addresses the essential elements of successful curriculum development at the classroom level. To achieve meaningful, developmental, and dynamic curriculum, purposeful and organized planning is required. Curriculum planning is a fundamental task of teachers. We have found that to be meaningful, purposeful, and organized, planning must occur in several stages. First a *conceptual organizer,* or unifying concept, is established, based on the program's goals. A *brainstorming* stage follows, during which ideas are generated but not evaluated. Then a *research-and-recording* stage occurs, during which ideas are developed and put down on paper. An *extending-and-refining* stage follows, during which ideas must turn into methods or teaching strategies. The *scheduling-and-arranging* stage, during which the ideas are related to the learning environment and the daily time schedule, completes the planning process.

### Identifying conceptual organizers—the unifying concept for planning

The first task in planning involves generating ideas for a conceptual organizer around which to plan a unit of study. The conceptual organizer is the unifying concept that ensures that curriculum is meaningful.

Examples of meaningful, conceptual organizers might be "friends" for a first grade class; "mammals" for 7- and 8-year-olds; or "growing things" for kindergarten. Whatever is selected, the conceptual organizer(s) must be sufficiently broad to encompass many program goals and must be sufficiently flexible to generate pedagogical constructs that can be arranged on a continuum. The concept must also be appropriate for the range of abilities and experiences of the children in the classroom and relevant to their interests and individual and cultural backgrounds. The purpose of organizing around unifying concepts is to achieve the goal of meaningful, conceptual curriculum; however, the finished plan also draws on information from child development, the disciplines, and the needs and interests of individual children. Once the unifying concept is determined, the planning process begins in earnest with brainstorming.

## Brainstorming

The brainstorming stage of planning is more easily accomplished using a team approach. Ideas flourish within a social context. This is not only true for children but also for adults. Two or more teachers working together are likely to have little difficulty generating a rich set of ideas. The free-flowing generation of ideas may be difficult for less experienced teachers to achieve without some research. To assist in generating ideas, many teachers use favorite books, such as *Story S-t-r-e-t-c-h-e-r-s* (Raines & Canady, 1989, 1991, 1992) or *And What Else?* (Massam & Kulik, 1986). Another useful strategy for brainstorming is "webbing" (Krogh, 1990), in which several related topics are generated from a central, overarching theme. Webbing is an especially effective strategy for conceptually organizing curriculum. Teachers frequently involve children in the brainstorming phase, especially during the primary grades, as will be illustrated later.

Brainstorming usually takes the form of a long list of ideas, most efficiently displayed on large pieces of poster or butcher paper. Content ideas, process ideas, and types of activities are all put on the list, as are poems, songs, and games. The goal at this stage is to generate a number of ideas that later can be refined and adapted to the children in the group. Collecting some books and information prior to brainstorming sessions can be helpful, especially if the topic is new to the planning team. Involving specialists from within the school or from the community can also provide a broader range of ideas because, for instance, an art or music teacher is more likely to have a well-developed set of ideas within his or her specialty area. In programs in which such specialists are not available, other teachers may have hobbies or areas of interest from which to draw; artists or musicians from the community may also be consulted.

*CURRICULUM THAT ENCOURAGES CHOICE AND ACTIVE PARTICIPATION SUPPORTS THE DISPOSITIONS TO PERSIST, ENGAGE, TEST HYPOTHESES, SAFELY TAKE RISKS, AND REGULATE ONE'S OWN BEHAVIOR. LIKEWISE, ASSESSMENT STRATEGIES THAT ENCOURAGE SELF-EVALUATION AND REFLECTION ALSO CONTRIBUTE TO THESE IMPORTANT DISPOSITIONS.*

## Research and recording

At the research-and-recording stage of planning, teachers turn their general list of brainstormed ideas into several specific lists so that their rough ideas can be organized and analyzed. This process should be informed by all of the perspectives on curriculum planning, using the curriculum guidelines in the form of questions (see p. 22). Most importantly, the initial brainstormed list must be connected to specific goals and objectives for children. If clear connections to curriculum goals are not obvious, then the topic is not appropriate and should be discarded.

Once the large brainstormed list is separated into several small lists, each section of the plan can be filled in. Other issues will arise, such as the need to search for book titles and authors, tapes and records, and games. Many ideas need to be worked out and described in more detail. Activities need to be carefully planned and written down. Arrangements need to be made, such as inviting guests, planning field trips, or requesting things from home. Basically this is the stage of the planning process during which ideas are more fully developed, refined, and sometimes rejected.

## Extending and refining

The next step is to organize the ideas into long- and short-term goals, general and specific goals, and group and individual goals. This process requires thinking about a continuum, a sequence or pattern of development and learning of skills and concepts that is used to organize the learning environment and the daily projects and activities. A continuum implies that some relationships exist; events tend to occur in some orderly fashion. The continuum model does not imply a rigid sequence, however; events can occur simultaneously or they can occur in a different order, but there is a general trend toward higher levels of understanding and greater complexity. There is also sufficient predictability about the pattern of development and learning in a given area to guide planning. Use of a continuum requires that the teacher be sufficiently familiar with child development and learning to make reasonable predictions while also being sufficiently flexible to adapt for individual variation. The hypothetical sequence is always altered in terms of order, related skills, the overall timing of introducing new abilities or understandings, and how long those issues remain central to classroom activities and projects. The underlying purpose is to refine and extend the goals of the unit of study.

## Scheduling and arranging

At least four elements of scheduling and arranging the classroom require some forethought in curriculum planning. These elements are time, space, group management, and activities. Much more could be said on these topics than space permits here. Rather than present specifics we offer some principles that must be considered in planning.

*Time.* The specific time schedules used by teachers vary considerably depending on many factors, such as the length of the program day (half day, school day, extended day) and the location of the program (for example, how much time children can play outside during the winter). Perhaps the most important determinant of the time schedule, though, is the age and developmental level of the children. The principle that

applies is that the younger the child, the more these routines are informal and dictated by the child's own time schedule. For any age group at least four principles of timing—which are interrelated—must be considered:

**1. Schedules include daily rituals and routines that establish expectations.**

Every program has daily rituals and routines within which certain activities occur. Children quickly develop expectations for themselves and other people because there is considerable redundancy in the behaviors required. Rituals and routines contribute to a feeling of security because children can predict what will happen and when. Examples of ritualized and routine periods are a time in the morning to plan the day, morning news, sharing times, singing time, story time, transitions, meals and snacks, and rest periods.

**2. Schedules need a balance of open-ended and structured time.**

Time should be provided in which children choose activities and the choices are open ended. Some time periods are more structured, during which the class functions as a whole group (group discussion, taking a walk, eating lunch). Because so many routines are of necessity structured in group programs ("We all have to go outside now"), teachers must consider those routines in establishing a balance of open-ended and structured time.

### 3. Schedules should allow sufficient time.

Too often children just begin an activity or a project and time is up. Research (Christie & Wardle, 1992) shows that children need large blocks of time (at least 30 to 45 minutes, often longer) in which to fully engage in dramatic play (like shoe store), block building, journal writing, or other complex activity. Some overly structured, teacher-directed activities require less time because children do not really engage. The teacher must establish a general time schedule and adapt when children become thoroughly engrossed or back off when something isn't working. The principle of sufficient time is well known to teachers in the primary grades, who often complain about being interrupted by institutional time clocks or by pull-out programs that fracture the continuity of children's experiences.

### 4. Schedules encourage children to develop awareness of time.

The predictability of scheduling helps children acquire an understanding of the complex concept of time. Toddlers and 3-year-olds gain awareness of time by teachers' repeatedly framing their day for them— "This morning, we will . . . ," "After lunch . . . ," and "Tomorrow . . . ." Preschoolers and kindergartners get more detailed time references, such as "Five more minutes until clean-up" and "Next week is my birthday." Primary grade children use the calendar to record their activities and plan for the future.

*Space.* An important part of planning is determining how space is used. Principles to consider in arranging space include safety, access, and efficiency. Classrooms for young children through the primary grades must be inviting spaces, arranged in learning centers that support a variety of different kinds of activities and experiences. Learning centers must be arranged to support a high degree of autonomy in children, as well as social interaction. Some typical areas for 3- through 8-year-olds are a block area, art area, manipulative materials area, science area, reading or library area, and imaginative play areas where children can role-play aspects of daily experience and explore objects. Imaginative areas change depending on the theme of study; examples include household play, shoe store, office, transportation, grocery store, beauty and barber shop, bakery, and fast food restaurant. Learning centers include a number of structured experiences that are selected and developed to challenge children and provide opportunities to extend children's knowledge of curriculum concepts. Many of the activities within a learning center are done in small groups so that children can develop cooperation and communication skills. Although a specific sequence is not prescribed within these activities, there is some orderliness in what occurs. Beginning in kindergarten and primary grades, children may keep weekly folders that document what they do in learning centers, especially when centers contain activities relevant to a theme of study, such as a rocks-and-minerals center or an occupations center.

The physical environment in an early childhood program has the potential to become an additional "teacher" if the materials are sufficiently rich and engaging and the space is well organized. Space arrangement varies on a number of dimensions (Prescott, Jones, Kritchevsky, Milich, & Haselhoe, 1975; Kritchevsky, Prescott, & Walling, 1977), and those involved in the planning process should pay attention to ensuring that these dimensions are provided for; for instance, space must be arranged so as to provide variety on the dimensions of quiet and active, soft and hard, and open-ended and structured, to name a few.

*Group management.* Arranging the space in interesting learning areas serves many purposes, among which is achieving self-regulation/management among the children. The potential of such a classroom is that children learn to make meaningful choices and live with the consequences of their decisions. In such classrooms children also acquire social problem-solving skills and deepen their understandings through social interaction. Many teachers institute external management systems, such as color-coding areas or assigning children to activities, to ensure efficient crowd control. In working with numerous groups of teachers, we have observed that implementing such systems may assist a teacher in making the transition from controlling all of the classroom behaviors to an environment with more shared decision making. The problem with such systems, however, is that they remain external to the child; they do not accomplish the goal of internal self-regulation. To achieve this goal children must be guided to make choices, and they must develop internal strategies for guiding their own behavior. Many successful strategies are used by teachers. One effective strategy is to engage children in planning and reflection about their choices (Hohmann, Banet, & Weikart, 1979). In general, teachers can guide children toward self-management, using questions such as, What do you want to do? What do you need to do that? Did you do it? How did you do? Are you satisfied? Would you do anything different next time? Did you clean up for the next person?

For child-initiated activity to achieve its potential, teachers must be astute observers and provide appropriate support as needed. For instance, teachers should observe which materials or activities are not chosen by children and why, which materials or activities children need help with, and which materials children continue to use in the same way. Then the teacher can provide systematic support to help children more effectively use materials, expand their options, and make their activity more complicated. Periodically, in her kindergarten class, Teresa Rosegrant plans a 30-minute period of relatively structured activity, during which she focuses on a material or activity that children have not selected or with which they are unfamiliar. For about 10 minutes, with the entire class, she or one of the children demonstrates some ways to use the material, and then for 20 minutes children play with the objects in small groups, sharing their ideas about how to use the materials. This form of scaffolding is also regularly provided to individual children throughout the day. Teresa also uses transitions to teach children to regulate their own behavior rather than to simply wait. During transition to lunch children can read books independently; they quickly become adept at getting a selection of books and pairing off. During another transition point children must select a puzzle, and as the year goes on, the children become very clever at identifying activities that may be considered "puzzles." The point is that there are many ways in which teachers can assist children to regulate their own behavior; in so doing children also develop important social skills and problem-solving abilities.

Scheduling must consider the ways in which children experience groups. The younger the child, the less time should be spent in whole-group activities and the more time should be individually determined. Teachers need to be sure that grouping patterns accomplish several goals: mix ability levels; mix developmental/age levels; mix genders; and vary by size, with a larger proportion of time in small groups than in whole-group or individual activity.

*Activities.* The types of activities planned drive scheduling to some extent. Again, some basic principles apply. Activities that require close supervision should be scheduled, along with other activities in which children can function more autonomously. Many activities need prior preparation and planning on the part of the teacher; children should not be asked to wait while teachers scramble around looking for flour or other necessary ingredients. Activities should be planned with the learning cycle in mind. What is the goal—awareness, exploration, inquiry, or utilization? Activities should vary across the learning cycle for the entire group, and when children are not operating at the expected level, experiences at another level of the cycle should be provided. Another principle is that there should be a variety of forms of activity; the "balance" of activities will vary with the age of the child. With young preschoolers (2s and 3s), for example, play will occupy a majority of the time and whole-group activity will be limited. Two- and 3-year-olds should hear stories; lap book reading and small, self-selected clusters, however, are more appropriate

than story time for the whole group. Whole-group story time may be introduced with older 4s and 5-year-olds.

Forms of activity for young children are numerous, including, but not limited to, dramatic play; playful exploration (with materials such as clay, sand, and water); gross-motor play; dramatizations (puppets, flannel boards, and plays); constructing (from open-ended projects to making models); using manipulatives; learning centers; miniature play (Legos); writing journals; writing stories; making books; reading books; listening to audiotapes; discussions; solving problems; experimenting; observing; field trips; electronic media, such as computers, slides, and videotapes; guest speakers; physical games and activities; music and instruments; movement; and art forms, such as fingerpainting, tempera, markers, crayons, and collage.

Selection of activities should be designed to promote the acquisition of knowledge and skills while also fostering positive learner dispositions, such as those described above—persistence, focused participation, risk taking, hypothesis testing, and self-regulation. Some activities lower children's risk taking and persistence; lacing cards for 2s and 3s is such an activity, as is demanding handwriting mastery in kindergarten. Young children do need many opportunities to develop fine-motor skills with a variety of implements, but if the task is too difficult—as forming letters properly on the line usually is for kindergartners—then children's dispositions to participate and to persist decrease. Some activities diminish these positive dispositions, while others promote them; for instance, play and projects contribute to the development of desirable learner dispositions, while other activities, such as filling in worksheets, diminish them.

Play and projects are especially useful because these activities support mindful, meaning-centered curriculum and can be easily adapted to children's interests and actually foster interests. (A complete discussion of the value of play and projects is beyond the scope of this chapter; for more information, see Katz & Chard, 1989; Scales, Almy, Nicolopoulou, & Ervin-Tripp, 1991; Wassermann, 1991; Jones & Reynolds, 1992; and Shores, 1992.) When children are interested and have high levels of the learner dispositions described here, their sense of ownership increases. Children who are interested in learning and feel ownership of the tasks are more personally accountable for their own learning. Accountability is a word that tends to be associated with teachers' performance, but another way of thinking about accountability during early childhood is to see it as a legitimate objective to develop in the learners themselves (as described in Chapter 4). If children are deeply engaged in the meaningful curriculum of the school, then they will exercise personal accountability over their work. As children move through the learning cycle in relation to a given task, their interest, ownership, and accountability should increase. Unlike play and projects—which increase interest, ownership, and accountability—filling in worksheets or reproducing adult-made models tends to have the opposite effect. Models do have appropriate uses and are not necessarily inappropriate *if not overused,* but the most difficult problem with providing too many models is that children do not gain ownership of their own work, and their accountability decreases. Curriculum that is intellectually rich, meaningful, and developmentally and individually appropriate results in increased interest, ownership, and accountability in the learner.

# Implementation of transformational curriculum

The implementation phase of curriculum is what goes on every day in classrooms. Implementation involves everything—teachers and children interacting in a learning environment. Just as goals dictate curriculum planning, goals must also be upheld at the implementation stage. At least four elements of curriculum implementation are vital for a transformational curriculum to achieve its potential: the concept of the classroom as community, classroom climate, teacher behaviors, and communication; each is discussed in more detail below.

## Classroom as community

A community is a place where individuals share common values, goals, and activities. It is a place where each member takes on roles to provide sufficient services so that the community's goals are reached. In communities, everyone does not do the same thing at the same time, but groups work together to achieve common goals. A community is a place where social bonds are established and individuals can flourish.

The Curriculum and Assessment Guidelines emphasize the importance of social interaction to the learning process. To meet this and the other curriculum guidelines that address the learning processes requires that the classroom become a community of learners, with

the teacher(s) involved in co-constructing knowledge along with the children.

The classroom can become a small community if teachers choose to make it such. To achieve a sense of community in the classroom, teachers must think of classrooms as part of an even larger community: the school or child care program in which the classroom is nested. Classrooms in many schools, however, have such psychological distance between them that they seem miles apart. Bringing the school together involves teachers working as teams for planning and implementation of curriculum. This does not necessarily mean "team teaching," in which teachers divide the curriculum by area of specialization and actually departmentalize the day and children's experiences. Although children are able to relate to more than one adult quite easily and should establish relationships with a variety of people, young children need a home base, someone who knows the whole child literally. Our notion of "team" expands the sense of continuity within the school and within the child's experience. Such teaming involves planning across age levels and strategies to connect siblings and friends from other classes. If the school or program itself provides an open and accessible model among the classrooms within, it is far easier to include parents and other community members, which is another vital element of the classroom as community.

Much of what we advocate in this book, such as promoting learner dispositions like risk taking or creating a culturally safe climate, depends on the degree to which the classroom is connected to the larger community. The way in which family members are welcomed into the classroom does much to create a sense of cultural and interpersonal safety. Similarly, if the curriculum is going to be meaningful and based on "real-life experience," everything can't be brought into the classroom. Even if programs were enormously wealthy and overly stocked with rich learning materials (which, more often, they are not), classrooms could never include all of the objects, experiences, and people that children need and want to learn about, so the classroom has to be opened up to the world around it. For very young children this world may just be walking distance from the building or the nearest store. For older children the parameters can be expanded. Every age group can welcome parents, other family members, and the "experts" who live and work in the community. The benefits of exposure to different adults and children are countless, but certainly include establishing helping relationships, gaining intergenerational experiences, and fostering feelings of continuity and connectedness. In our view, transformational curriculum not only changes and is changed by the child but transforms the classroom itself into a community of learners. To a large extent the sense of community is influenced by various dimensions of the classroom climate, a discussion of which follows.

## Classroom climate

The classroom climate is not unlike the weather; it changes, and it affects how people feel and behave. A supportive learning climate for young children conveys a sense of "safety" on a number of levels: physical, psychological, interpersonal, cultural, and intellectual.

Ensuring children's physical and psychological safety are two of the most basic points addressed in the curriculum guidelines (Guidelines 17 and 18). All of the equipment and materials must be age appropriate for the children served and in good repair. Adequate levels of adult supervision are necessary, especially for new and/or challenging activities, to which children's responses are less certain. Periods of developmental transition, such as when babies learn to roll over or when 6-year-olds learn to ride a bike, require intense supervision.

Psychologically safe classrooms encourage self-expression and foster a sense of competence. Independence is encouraged, but adults are responsive to children's requests for assistance. In a climate of psychological safety, adults give children feedback designed to help them accept themselves and guide them in the use of strategies that maximize the likelihood of success. Adults listen to children and demonstrate interest in what the child wants to do or understand. Children feel free to share their concerns and ask for assistance without an impending sense of adult disapproval.

The climate of physical and psychological safety is influenced by the degree to which the classroom is interpersonally safe. Interpersonal safety results from adults' providing clear guidance about how children treat each other and what they can expect from others in return. Peer interactions include politeness, ways of inviting or including others, ways of communicating dislike for others' behavior, and how to talk and listen to others.

Interpersonally safe classrooms create a climate in which children feel OK if they are different, whether their differences be in personality, ability, or physical appearance. Such classrooms are also culturally safe. Children need to feel a sense of cultural continuity from the look of the environment (pictures and books that include people who look like them), but more importantly, the feeling of acceptance of cultural differences. Creating a culturally safe climate requires coordinating ways to support other aspects of the climate; for example, the classroom's rules for interpersonal safety may be at variance with the rules for safety that the child has learned at home. For the climate to be safe for all children, teachers must be sensitive to different cultural definitions and understandings (for more on cultural safety, see Section 3 of this book; Derman-Sparks & the A.B.C. Task Force, 1989; and Neugebauer, 1992).

Finally, the classroom should convey a feeling of intellectual safety. Children should find many interesting things to do. Materials and activities should be provided that allow for children at different levels of mental sophistication to engage and actively participate. Providing a good mix of open-ended materials (such as Legos) and self-corrective materials (like puzzles) promotes success. The degree of difficulty should vary so that children experience little frustration in their initial efforts. Intellectual safety is supported when children find many things that seem easy to do, with few trials, and a sufficient number of things that challenge them but are within their capacity.

If the learning climate is safe for children—physically, psychologically, interpersonally, culturally, and intellectually—then it is more likely that children will maintain their sense of competence and develop strong dispositions for learning. A critical determinant of the classroom climate is the behavior and communication style of the teacher, to which we turn now.

## Teacher behaviors

During curriculum implementation teachers engage in the kind of interactive teaching in relation to the learning cycle (moving from awareness to exploration to inquiry to utilization in a recursive cycle) demonstrated by individual children that is described in Chapter 3. What the teacher does in implementing the curriculum is most succinctly described as "orchestrate." The teacher coordinates and facilitates numerous activities: she moves around the environment to ensure appropriate use of materials and objects, monitors social and cognitive needs of children, assists when needed, and encourages children's efforts. The orchestrator also prepares children for transitions as activities change throughout the day.

Certain teacher behaviors are especially important for promoting high levels of the learner dispositions—persistence, focused participation, risk taking, hypothesis testing, and self-regulation. Teachers support these kinds of behaviors throughout the day. Teachers assist children to make their efforts easier, more meaningful, less stressful, and more successful because high rates of success are related to high rates of persistence. Teachers do not allow children to lose a sense of competence but are not overly prescriptive and do not act as the primary agent in activities. Teachers provide authoritative responses when needed or seek additional resources to answer children's inquiries (teachers do not need to be omniscient). The operative balance is for teachers to strive not to do things for children that they can do themselves, while also not allowing children to become frustrated by too many things that they cannot do.

Much of teachers' support is in the form of modeling. Teachers provide children with just enough information to begin a project or process; demonstrate aspects of a skill or an activity (rarely the entire process); provide oral coaching or instruction to help a child in a task; ask helpful questions; and give prompts, clues, or cues.

To perform their many roles, teachers rely on assessment, especially observation-based assessment. Observation gives information for providing appropriate support or modeling, for assessing individual children's needs and interests, and for adapting the curriculum and environment.

## Communication

Teachers talk too much; consequently, each day in schools and child care centers, we ask children to listen—listen to instructions, listen to explanations, listen to admonishments, listen to announcements, listen to stories, listen to show-and-tell, listen while I'm talking. . . . It is not surprising that children cannot sustain the level of interest that we hope for if they are required to participate so passively for so much of the time.

Children need to talk. When children talk, many things happen. They develop verbal skills. They share

*IF THE LEARNING CLIMATE IS SAFE FOR CHILDREN—PHYSICALLY, PSYCHOLOGICALLY, INTERPERSONALLY, CULTURALLY, AND INTELLECTUALLY—THEN IT IS MORE LIKELY THAT CHILDREN WILL MAINTAIN THEIR SENSE OF COMPETENCE AND DEVELOP STRONG DISPOSITIONS FOR LEARNING.*

ideas and engage in reciprocal conversations that present alternative points of view. They share their own feelings and hear about the feelings of others, enabling them to develop empathy. Young children need to think out loud; prior to about age 8, children do not have fully developed "private speech" with which to think their thoughts; they need to articulate their thoughts verbally. In early childhood classrooms, if there isn't much talking going on, there isn't much thinking going on.

Children need to talk to construct working models of concepts, usually during play; for instance, when children take on roles in dramatic play, they test their hypotheses about how adults talk in certain social situations. Children need to talk to other children to solve social problems in socially acceptable ways. If we want children to develop positive, prosocial behaviors for expressing feelings, then they have to have opportunities to interact socially with other children and to talk.

Appropriate classrooms provide opportunities to promote communication both informally and formally. Some informal strategies are dramatic play, gross-motor activity, block building and construction activities, miniature play, games, drawing or writing journals, prewriting discussions, reading with book partners, and working on computers in pairs. Some more formal strategies for promoting language are flannel boards; puppets; short dramas; reading stories; telling and retelling stories; asking questions and interviewing; playing telephone; music; dramatic play of activities for which there are known scripts, such as going to a fast food restaurant; class discussions of books and shared experiences; and book writing and making.

Teachers need to be good listeners for many reasons. Teachers need to be available for informal, interpersonal talks with individual children, conversations that answer the question, What do I know about this child? "We got a new puppy" "My grandma is too sick"—such information is most likely to be learned from informal conversation. Teachers also need to be able to listen to find out what the child already knows in order to start where children are in the curriculum. A good opportunity to listen to children is in the role of dictation taker, acting as the recorder of the child's language. In this role the teacher carefully clarifies without overguiding the child's report, while also extending—"Tell me more." Observing also places teachers in the role of listener.

Having articulated the steps in curriculum planning and important issues to remember in implementation, we offer examples for three different age groups—a young preschool group, a kindergarten, and a second grade—to illustrate this planning process in action (for additional examples of curriculum planning, see Chapters 8 and 11 and Volume 2).

# A visit to a classroom for 2- and 3-year-olds

"I think I need a size 10," says John to the salesperson. The clerk responds, "Let me measure to make sure." Ellen gets a shoe measure and places it under John's right foot. "Yes, that's good. You are a 10. Do you want to see some shoes?" "Yes," says John. "There are red shoes, green shoes, blue shoes. . . ." Two children turn the pages of a class-made big book and "read" the pages. "And what color do you like?" "I like yellow ones," says Sara. "I like pink ones," adds her reading partner, Tuyen. Tom sits on the floor with Kahtra playing "Concentration." The children turn the cards over until they occasionally find a match. Over in a corner four children are listening to a teacher read, "The Elves and the Shoemaker." One child sits with an adult and shows how she can buckle her new shoes. Two other children are painting at the easel. They describe their art work as "fancy shoes" and a "pair of boots." "You can tell they are boots," says Maria, "because they have a long part here." One little one walks around with an old pair of high-top tennis shoes on his feet and a very pleased look on his face.

This classroom for 2-1/2- to 4-year-old children is not just an enjoyable environment for children and adults, it is also an interesting place. Visiting a classroom like the one described above reveals a lot about a teacher's perspective on curriculum, but it does not convey much about the planning that occurred prior to the activities observed. In this section we illustrate the planning process in more detail and provide examples to show how the teachers implement the curriculum. At each phase of planning, we see how the four strands of our theoretical model of transformational curriculum help inform the curriculum. Conceptual information, child development knowledge, knowledge from the disciplines, and a description of the learning continuum provide the core understandings that guide curriculum development (only the basics can be included here).

## Planning for 2s and 3s: Selecting a conceptual organizer

To illustrate the planning process, we turn to the teachers in the classroom for 2- through 3-year-olds, who we observed planning a unit with "shoes" as the conceptual organizer. The teachers' selection of shoes as an organizing topic was not arbitrary; they chose this topic based on their knowledge of the developmental issues of this age group and also on their observation of the children. Many other conceptual organizers would be equally reasonable and could have been chosen for this group, such as faces, babies, going to the doctor, or vehicles (as opposed to "transportation," which would be more appropriate for kindergarten). The topic of shoes meets the guidelines for the selection of curriculum content; for example, the topic

1. acknowledges children's interest—children at this age show great interest in all aspects of shoes;

2. is meaningful and relevant to children's everyday experience—teachers observed that a relatively large part of daily activity focuses on shoes (find your shoes, put your shoes on, take your shoes off, put your boots on, see my new shoes, etc.);

3. encourages social interaction—playing shoe store and other activities promotes conversation and social construction of knowledge;

4. draws on child development knowledge—for example, independence is a major developmental task of this age group, and shoes provide daily opportunities for developing and exercising independence;

5. provides many forms of participation for active engagement by children—for instance, shoes provide many opportunities for play, and a sufficient number of age-appropriate songs, games, and literature exist on the topic; and

6. promotes the acquisition of knowledge and skills—"shoes" is a good topic for exploring attributes, such as color and size, and concepts, such as ownership and use.

## Brainstorming

Having agreed on a conceptual organizer—shoes—the team is ready to generate many ideas about the topic that might be used. The initial brainstormed list looked like this:

---

counting shoes

when you wear shoes

color of shoes

whose shoes

dress shoes

muddy shoes

types of shoes

fastenings (buckles, Velcro, lacing)

story about the "runaway shoes" (we have this on tape)

"1, 2, Buckle My Shoe"

dancing shoes

work shoes

big and little shoes

boys' and girls' shoes

losing a shoe

shoe prints

matching shoes

cleaning shoes

old and new shoes

favorite shoes

Will it fit? (Cinderella)

"Elves and the Shoemaker"

song–"Pass the Shoe"

how shoes sound

measuring feet for shoes

Notes: We need to find some more books. We need to see if a shoe repairperson will visit. Do we want to make a shoebox for old shoes for the dress-up center?

---

## Research and recording

"Shoes" met the criteria as an acceptable conceptual organizer, but this is only one of the perspectives of a transformational model. Curriculum planning must also be informed by child development knowledge and the knowledge base of the disciplines. From the perspective of child development, the teachers determined that this unit of study would contribute to the children's development in the following ways:

• **cognitive:** promotes development of cognitive processes, such as matching, remembering, describing, organizing, estimating, measuring, and categorizing by color, size, and function

• **social:** provides opportunities for sharing, turn taking, social interaction, and understanding roles of family members

• **language:** promotes vocabulary development and conversational turn taking (such as verbal exchanges in the shoe store)

• **emotional:** provides opportunities for sharing information about self and family, distinguishing between self and others, and expressing preferences

• **physical:** provides opportunities for developing large-motor abilities, such as walking, coordination, and balance; and fine-motor skills, such as buckling a shoe

• **moral:** promotes understanding of fair exchange (paying for things in stores) and turn taking

The teachers also analyzed the topic from the perspective of the content of the disciplines. Each discipline does not have to be equally represented. Some units of study may have more of a science/math emphasis or a social studies/language emphasis; all units should also balance fine arts and physical activities. Shoes proved to be a good unifying concept because so many elements of the curriculum could be interwoven—the following, for example:

• **language/literacy:** vocabulary, such as "pair," shoe styles ("dress shoes," "sandals"); parts of shoes ("toe," "heel," "sole"); concepts, such as materials for shoes, ownership, function, color, size, labels; and communication, such as questions and answers

• **social studies:** family members and shoes; occupations and shoes; buying and selling shoes (economics)

• **science:** color; sounds of shoes; weather and shoes

• **mathematics:** matching; sorting; measuring; number (pair); one-to-one correspondence; size; sequencing; patterns

• **health:** shoes that fit and don't fit; shoes appropriate to the weather

• **music:** songs and dance

• **physical education:** coordination; movement

• **art:** painting shoes; cleaning shoes

The shoes unit demonstrated its potential for achieving goals for 2- and 3-year-olds related to content, processes, and skills through several specific activities, such as the Concentration game, cutting or tearing out pictures of shoes from catalogs, trying on shoes, sorting, the which-ones-fit game, developing a shoe store play area, reading stories and rhymes, watching someone repair and polish shoes, showing favorite shoes, and bringing in baby shoes.

Here are some examples of research-and-recording activities for the shoes unit:

• *Box of shoes to match*—Two children are asked to put together the shoes that match. The adult may need to show them a match or two, or hold up one and say, "Can you find me a shoe that looks like this one, one that matches?" Discuss why they match, for example, color, size, or type of shoe.

• *Concentration*—Have children cut (as best they can with safe scissors) or tear out pictures of shoes from magazines, and then paste the pictures on small, blank cards. Starting with cards upright, first ask children to find matching pairs. Later, in sets of three pairs per deck, play the Concentration game.

• *Old and new art work*—Ask several children to bring a pair of old and new shoes. Discuss how shoes get old; paint pictures of new shoes and old shoes.

• *Shoe repair*—Invite a repairperson to visit. Let small groups of children watch and ask questions as he or she fixes and cleans several pairs of shoes.

• *Listening tape*—Record appropriate songs and stories on audio tape for children to listen to in a quiet area.

• *Make a display*—Have children bring old shoes from home with a picture of the owner.

• *Shoe store*—Talk with children about going to buy shoes. Discuss what happens, who you meet, and what you do at the shoe store. Ask children to bring shoes and shoeboxes from home to make a shoe store. Get or make a device for measuring feet, put a mirror on its side on the floor, set up chairs, etc.

## Extending and refining

During this phase of the planning process, each idea is discussed, and if it is viewed as appropriate, then it is written out and included. In some cases ideas will be offered and then discarded, such as tying and lacing shoes, which is too difficult for this age group. At this point plans are refined and teachers develop a continuum of learning and development to guide them. Teachers would not start with the shoe store, for example, because such dramatic play is at the utilization level of the learning cycle; instead, the plan would begin with many opportunities to become aware of and explore shoes. Following are examples of how the teachers extended and refined their plans for the shoes unit for 2s and 3s.

***Extending and refining the shoes matching game.*** In each new activity teachers discuss with the children why shoes match so that the children develop awareness of the various attributes used to sort the shoes. No new dimension is introduced until the children find shoes with the previous attribute with ease. The sequence might look like this:

1. Begin with four pairs of shoes taken from the feet of children in the group, and help the children sort to find matching sets, placing them next to each other. As other shoes are added to the sorting circle, ask children to look at and describe them.

2. Add more shoes, up to 10 pairs.

3. Add shoes of varying colors from other sources.

4. Add shoes of varying sizes.

5. Add shoes of differing functions or types.

6. Have pictures of mothers, fathers, sisters, brothers, and babies. Ask children to find shoes for each person—"Which ones could the baby wear?" "Which ones could Mom wear?"

***Extending and refining the shoe store.*** The overall goal of this activity is to have children play their experiences in a shoe store, recalling more aspects of the experience as their play becomes more complicated. The order of introduction of the events and who does what will vary depending on how much and what the children remember to reconstruct the experience. Here's one sequence of events:

1. Have shoes in boxes and a chair for a child to sit on while trying on shoes.

2. Have someone be the salesperson.

3. Have a customer look at and try on several pairs of shoes.

4. Have the salesperson find certain shoes as requested.

5. Have the customer "pay" for the shoes.

During week one, begin to organize the shoes on a shelf according to size, from smallest to largest. During week two, encourage children who are customers to ask for certain colors of shoes. In week three, encourage them to ask for certain kinds of shoes, such as boots, tennis shoes, or dress shoes.

## Scheduling and arranging

Planning involves determining when and where the numerous activities and projects will occur. Some sequence is hypothetically developed by the teachers to think through and play out the possible progression the activities might take; nevertheless, the actual order (such as size before color) will change depending on the behaviors of the children. The learning cycle provides a good method for generally organizing activities in the classroom. The goal is to have activities that promote learning at each level of the cycle: awareness, exploration, inquiry, and utilization. This increases the likelihood of adapting for individual differences in experience and level of understanding. Activities the teachers plan relevant to the learning cycle for the shoe unit, for example, might look like this:

- **To create awareness:** reading a book about shoes, discussing buying new shoes, having a fashion show of favorite shoes, bringing family members' shoes from home, trying on shoes

- **To encourage exploration:** guessing whose shoes, reading the book *Whose Shoes?*, setting up a play area with lots of shoes to try on to play dress-up

- **To encourage inquiry and investigation:** observing a shoe repairperson, finding shoes that fit and don't fit, matching shoes with weather, matching shoes to family members, sorting shoes by size and color, talking about buying shoes, comparing old and new shoes

- **To utilize learning about shoes:** playing shoe store

Children's behavior will be affected by where they are in the learning cycle relevant to these understandings. If they have never been to a shoe store, much of that activity will build their awareness, while other children who have had many experiences in shoe stores will act out the events with almost adult-like precision. Most 3-year-olds, for instance, may be experienced enough to play the shoe-matching game with pictures or to act out the shoe store experiences, but some will need to become aware and explore by trying on the various shoes and manipulating them in many ways first.

As a friendly observer in a child care center, Teresa Rosegrant (personal communication, September 15, 1992) watched children playing shoe store for about an hour and then asked, "Can I buy some shoes?" The 3-year-old salesclerk asked, "What do you do?" Teresa replied, "I'm a researcher." The clerk thought for a minute and then said, "I don't think we have researcher shoes." "How about teacher shoes?" Teresa suggested. "Sure," he said, "Our teacher says teachers need comfortable shoes." He carefully searched his stock until he returned with a shoebox containing a pair of fuzzy slippers. "Just right," was his conclusion.

# Thoughts from kindergarten

"You go to school to learn to read and write but mostly just to learn about things . . . everything!" This 5-year-old knows a lot about what school should be about—learning. How we transform classrooms into rich learning environments depends in large part on what the curriculum is about and who controls it. If the adult asks all the questions, then the children lose ownership of what is to be studied. Children must take part in the earliest aspects of curriculum planning if their understandings about the world are to be well developed. Curriculum that is totally planned by adults cannot be transformational; children must be planners as well. On the other hand, classrooms in which only

the children are considered learners are not transformational, either; learning is potentially a shared experience if teachers and children can co-construct meanings. For curriculum to be meaningful, it must not originate solely from textbooks or activity books, not even from teachers, but from all of the participants in the learning context, which should be defined broadly enough to include not only teachers and children but also the children's families and the community. Following are some vignettes from Teresa Rosegrant's kindergarten class during the first months of school that illustrate the planning and implementation principles presented earlier in this chapter.

## Establishing a sense of community

On the first day of school, I sit on the floor with the children and ask, "Do you know anybody in this class? Are some of these children already your friends?" As the discussion progresses it is clear that many children live near each other, went to preschool together, or have siblings who play together. "How many children are 4-years-old?," I ask. "How many are 5, how many are 6? And I'm 43 (yes, that is very old!). Now that we know how old we all are, what else can we find out about each other? What other questions can we ask?" As the children generate questions, I write them down and we find out some answers. Some of the questions are not answered because all of the children do not speak English. We think about how we can communicate. Several children are bilingual, and they translate for the others. Sometimes I draw pictures. We manage to generate a good list of questions. I explain that we need to plan how to get to know each other. "Let's talk some more later. Now it's time to look at the centers and decide what everyone wants to do."

The centers in our classroom are filled with basic preschool and kindergarten materials. There are puzzles and books on a number of topics that relate to learning about other people. There are books and materials about the body, about families, and about homes. A dramatic-play area is furnished with items from several rooms of a home, including baby dolls, occupation hats, and dress-up clothes. There are doll houses, paper dolls, Lego sets, occupation toy vehicles, and several maps with village streets on them. In my plan book I have written the following:

In art, the children will depict themselves in many ways this week. In music, we will learn several friendship and body part songs and games. In physical education, we will find out what we like to do outside and what we do well with our arms and legs. At lunch, we will keep a record of what we like to eat and what foods were tried for the first time. After lunch, we will walk around the school and meet and greet people such as the librarian. At the end of each day, we will share what we have learned about someone else and what we liked doing at school today.

## Supporting social development

My goals for the first week of school are very basic. I want everyone to feel secure, to want to come back the next day, to learn more about each other, to make friends, and to learn how to spend many hours each day together, as friends — all 26 of us. Many routines are established during the first days of school, and most of them must be about how to treat each other and the materials in our class. I hear myself say, "We need to get along with each other. How do we do that?" It's only the third day of school, and yet the children have many ideas. Already children who did not speak any English the first day offer ideas: "Don't push," says Tuyen, and "Share," says William. The list they generate is long—many do's and don'ts. "What does it mean if you do all of these kind, friendly behaviors?" I ask. "Everyone will be happy," says Samantha. "That's a good way to think about it." Of course, I know that we cannot always make people happy, so I say aloud, "Can we always make people happy?" "No," "Yes," and "Maybe" are the answers from around the group. "So what can we do every day?" I ask. "We can try to be a good friend, but when we make a mistake or even on purpose do something to someone, then we can say sorry—that's what my mom says—and try to do better next time," offers Winta. "That is a good idea. Do you think we can all try to be a good friend and see if that can be our first class rule? Then our second rule can be, if you make a mistake, or even if it's on purpose, you can say you are sorry. Our third rule can be that if you do make a mistake, you will try harder to do better." Everyone agrees that our three rules are simpler than the long list; however, I remind them that being a good friend means behaving according to our "do's" list and trying not to do any of the "don'ts." We make a simple sign and draw pictures for each of our three rules.

I find that children are more likely to respond to the concept of being a good friend than focus on a long list of things to do and not do. This is not surprising because making friends is a common interest among 5-year-olds, but it is also important to identify what being a *good* friend means. This process sets a standard that children will try to meet.

On the third day of school, someone pinches another child. The child cries, and I spend time comforting her. I ask the aggressor to wait on the opposite side of the room for me. Once I have finished comforting the victim, I talk with the pincher. "I do not permit anyone in this class to hurt other people," I say. He starts to explain, "She . . . " I interrupt, "This is not a discussion. If you want me to listen to a problem, you must not hurt someone first. Next time if you can't solve the problem, come and get me, and we will work on solutions to the problem. What are you going to do next time?"

"Get you." "And then we can work on solutions, right?" "Yup." It takes him two more days to remember to get me, to talk about other solutions, but he does stop hitting on the fourth day, and we work out a solution that he helps create. For a few weeks he continues to seek my help when he encounters social problems until I suggest that the two children try to solve the problem without me. If they can't work it out, then I'll help.

I relate the above incident not only because dealing with misbehavior is an important part of the kindergarten teacher's job but also because supporting children's social development is an integral part of the curriculum plan. Research on social development (Oden & Asher, 1977; Gottman, 1983; Katz & McClellan, 1991) convinces me that coaching children to acquire social problem-solving skills is an essential part of the teacher's role. Children frequently need adults to provide them with the words and actions to use in problem situations. Once children feel in control in social interactions, they can further extend the learning on their own.

## Providing individual help as needed

"I can't write my name," says the small boy near me. "How many times have you tried?" I ask, "three or four?" "Three," he says. "Well, that means you have to practice a bit more. Can you ride a bike?" "Yes," he proudly answers. "Did you learn to ride a bike after three times?" "NO," he grins, "it took lots of times, but I tried real hard even after I hurt my knee." "Well," I say, "the good thing about writing your name is that it just takes a little practice—and you won't need bandages." Then I write his name on a sentence strip and have him cut apart each letter. "First, it helps to know the letters in your name and where they go. It's just like a puzzle, and you are very good at doing puzzles. I'll show you some other ways to practice the letters in your name, and you can decide what you want to do." I show him how to use sand letters, magnetic letters, chalkboards, and magic slates. Then I help him write his name with a marker. Over the next few days, he learns to put the letters in order quickly and to spell his name as he assembles it. He uses the chalkboards most often. In two weeks he can write his name well enough that he is no longer worried.

During the open-ended period for working in learning centers, I observe in the early weeks of school that the children are unfamiliar with the numerous kinds of math manipulatives in our classroom. To familiarize them with the math materials and help them take full advantage of these important learning tools, I select four different materials each week and demonstrate their use to small groups for a few minutes, followed by about 20 minutes of exploration time. Soon the children begin to select these materials on their own, and I select four other materials to explore with them. Throughout the year we will revisit materials in small groups to provide a springboard for new uses.

Reading happens throughout the day. Although we have a group story time most days, this is only one of many reading experiences. Several times a week children from the upper grades visit our class and spend time with their book partners, reading books one-on-one or to small groups of children whose awareness and exploration of print has not been developed by prior experiences. By the end of the year, a few of the children in the kindergarten are able to read a story to a friend.

One of the popular choices in our classroom is the computer center. The classroom computer is helpful because children can learn how to use programs that are appropriate to their skill level and interests. Children usually work in pairs at the computer, and much conversation is exchanged as they try to negotiate a given program. The computer is a powerful teacher, especially if programs are matched to children's individual needs as learners; for instance, if an individual child is way behind the others on counting or one-to-one correspondence, time spent with interesting computer programs can help the child catch up. Later, children will use the computer lab at school, where they can choose from a suite of programs and work on individually determined goals, not as a whole group.

### Conceptually organizing curriculum

The unit of study generally frames about half of the primary day. The rest of the day is spent on other areas of curriculum content that "do not fit" conceptually with the current unit but that are also important to curriculum goals. The day is filled with many interests that may or may not relate to the topic of study. A unit may last a few days or several weeks depending on how interested the children are and what new ideas develop; some groups may spend more time engaged with the topic of study if they are working on a large project. *The unit of study is a path toward understanding something better, not a wall around the curriculum.*

Among the most interesting units to the children in our kindergarten are "foods we eat" and "our five senses." The children seem never to want to stop learning about these two topics. Each of these topics is accessible to young children. One day the children share their favorite cereals. Everyone brings a box or bag with samples. One mom looks worried because she left the cereal at home, so I reassure her that they can bring the cereal any time this week. The children take turns sharing their cereal; some people haven't tried some kinds of cereal, so we share and compare words to describe the taste. We graph our preferences. "'Real sweet' probably means that sugar is the main ingredient." I show the children where to read the label and how to count whether sugar is second or fifth or higher on the list of ingredients. The group divides the boxes into three categories based on amount of sugar, and we make a graph to show the categories: too much, not bad, and good for you. Most of the children admit that they find some of the cereals too sweet. Although the most preferred cereals do fall on the sweeter end of our chart, the children seem to understand that candy is not a good idea for breakfast. Later we watch a filmstrip on eating right with Winnie the Pooh, and during the class discussion everyone remembers the "too-sweet" cereals.

Both of these units encourage children to bring things from home, so frequent communication with parents is a must. We send a monthly newsletter. It doesn't have to be long, but it should share ideas and interests from school so that parents can communicate with their child about classroom events. In kindergarten and early primary grades, homework should be confined to things that parents are best able to help their child with, like joint observations such as watching and drawing the phases of the moon, listing the fruits and vegetables the family eats, keeping a tooth-brushing record, and developing jobs that children can do to help at home. For young children homework should not be fatiguing and should not take the place of play time, especially outdoors.

The local grocery store lets us make many field trips, and children can learn the workings of all the many departments. The children especially like knowing people at the grocery store and finding out what goes on behind many of the mirrored windows and closed doors. Playing store in the classroom becomes very elaborate, as children bring old boxes and containers to stock the shelves each day. We do a lot of cooking, and the children even invent new recipes; they also love to chop and peel various fruits and vegetables. The children make charts and graphs of our daily efforts. They like to learn about bar codes and mystery spices and tasting things that are too sour or too sweet. They like to learn about different things, to get to know the world . . . to learn about everything!

## A visit to a second grade classroom

Classrooms have a buzzing sound that every teacher knows. It's the sound of children working together on a variety of projects and tasks in a harmonious way. In this section Teresa Rosegrant shares her first-hand observations from a visit to a second grade classroom. In her description we clearly see the implementation of transformational curriculum as well as clear evidence of the planning process that occurred prior to her visit.

In this particular classroom the teacher, Mrs. Warner, moves around to see how each group is doing. She hears, "Our bird book is almost finished. Do you want to see my penguin?" "Does anyone eat birds' eggs—not chickens, you know; other kinds, like a robin?" "Humpty, Dumpty...who is going to the king's men?" "The ostrich is definitely the biggest; then, yes, it's the vulture—oh, they are s-o-o-o-o ugly." "Our omelet is going to have green peppers. Is it like egg foo yung?" "If everybody has to have the same, then we each get two eggs, if there are a dozen, see."

The teacher checks the clock and announces that it's time to record or report progress made during project time. Group leaders scurry to find folders or tape recorders to describe their group's progress by drawing, telling, and/or writing. The cooking group asks for help, and the teacher enters their discussion about ways to cook eggs and the cultures that they have selected. It is difficult for the group to figure out how to display their menu, and the teacher offers to take pictures of the various egg dishes. "Look," she says, "here is a box of menus, and some have real pictures. You can look at them and see which one you would like to use as a model." The children empty the box and begin to study the menus. "You'll need more time to discuss this," the teacher says. "I'll come back to your group later." She moves on and assists each group in one way or another.

As I, a visitor, walk around the classroom, I look at stories about birds, a graph comparing birds, several bird games, clay birds, a display of birds' nests with carefully worded signs, and a picture display with text from a bird-watching field trip. There is even a hand-made field guide. A sign on the wall advertises that this afternoon several groups will be acting out fables that include birds. "A few assignments were required, several were optional, and many of these activities resulted from the children themselves as they extended the tasks or projects. Their interests led to many of the projects you see around the room," explains Mrs. Warner. "This looks like a lot to manage," she states, reading my eyes, "but actually the students conference with me to determine how they will communicate their learning and share their studies with the class. My role changes as I move from orchestrating to informing to assisting, depending on the situation. I must say, the day goes by quickly, and everyone stays busy and interested."

The goals for the unit on birds are written above many learning centers and in the personal journals of the children. In the "What is a bird?" center, the goals are evident in the questions asked: What do all birds have in common? What do some birds have in common? What are the parts of a bird? What do birds eat? Where do birds live? How do birds raise their young? Do all birds migrate? Where do birds go to migrate? Why do birds live in some places and not others? How do people help or harm birds? How do birds sound? Do all birds sing and call?

This morning the center is filled with activity. "We just received a birdcall tape in the mail, and one group is listening to the calls and listing the birds," explains the teacher. "I'm not sure what they have in mind yet. Many of the goals for the centers evolve as the children become more interested and informed. The display on what birds eat was a project of two groups that researched and collected the sample jars." (Several rows of jars are filled with tasty bugs and other samples of bird food.) A mural of migrating birds was another idea from a group. A book on eggs was the interest of two children who found nests in their yards. A display of state birds was an activity the teacher planned and worked on with several children.

Mrs. Warner explained how the bird unit began and evolved: "I asked children to pay close attention to things around them as they travel to school. I know that birds are interesting to children once they take time to watch. Once we had listed and identified a few birds, I knew that I needed to do more to build their awareness of the topic. So we went to the library and found many books on birds. One book was on birdwatching. I read parts of it to the class over several days. Then we invited two birdwatchers to class who eventually took small groups on nature walks. We couldn't go as a large group; we would have scared all the birds away! The walks and more reading led to offers to have several parakeets and canaries visit for a while. The observation of the caged birds enabled the children to explore firsthand many aspects of birds but also to see the limitations of observing pet birds. Then we took a field trip to the zoo and participated in a zoo lab on birds. I also checked out a classroom kit about birds from the zoo that includes many beaks and feathers and other objects. This led to more serious investigation about feathers; beaks; ways birds hunt, live, fly, and raise their young. Then it seemed that a dozen or more projects just 'took off.' I have no difficulty following the course of the learning cycle on this topic and can see that there are still children at the awareness level and exploration stage—at the 'What is a bird?' center, examining the zoo kit—while other children are already using what they have learned to draw pictures of large birds of prey."

Another center in this classroom was called "the writer's corner." In this area was a table with every kind of tool a young writer might want, two baskets of books on birds, and many notebooks with photograph album pages inside. "I like to use the photo album pages because children can easily mount pictures and text and then put the plastic cover over them. If they change their minds, they can just pull the plastic back and redo a page," explains Mrs. Warner. I spy an interesting book, called *Funny Facts About Our Feathered Friends*. This book is a favorite of some of the older children in the group who are very much into humor. Children are also making their own books, including some backyard observation record books, books about specific birds, drawings and descriptions, and several beginning drafts of biographies of Audubon. Above the writing center is a simple set of directions: get an idea, write down what you know, find out some more, organize your thoughts, share your thoughts, and stop when your work makes you happy. "That is a 7-year-old's interpretation of the writing process," says Mrs. Warner. On the table are numerous fictional stories about birds. Nearby two girls are drawing pictures for a story about a parakeet that escapes one day at school. I could tell that the account was not entirely fictional.

I wander over to a small area where two children are cleaning several bird cages. On the wall above the cages, a sign says, "Writers are observers. Scientists are observers. Friends are observers." This is clearly the work of the teacher. "I wanted the children to see the relationship between art, science, and social studies, and also that we can have a relationship with animals, with nature. We have had many discussions about the role of observation in our lives, and it is rewarding to see how thoughtful children can be if guided a bit," Mrs. Warner concludes as she once again makes a tour of the room.

Even such a brief visit reveals that this classroom is a collaboration between the teacher and the children. Mrs. Warner has clearly done her share of brainstorming, researching-and-recording, revising-and-extending, and scheduling-and-planning activities, but it is also apparent that the children initiated ideas at every phase of curriculum development. "The children also have a sense of contributing to their class and the school. We select things to share and to display and make sure everyone feels included." Near her desk is a large tablet with dates on each page. "It is a written record about what we learn each day. I call it our daily report," she explains. "At the end of each day, we spend 30 minutes writing down what we have learned that day and identifying any new questions we might have for tomorrow. Each morning we review the entire book. That way we have a chronology and a plan. We also decide who will do which activities, and then the children fill in their own journals with things to do and ideas worth remembering."

As I say goodbye and move toward the door, I hear a group of children wondering aloud how people learned to fly in airplanes and who made planes first. I stop and look back across the room. I already have an idea where the unit of study is probably heading. I can imagine the various forms of air travel hanging from the ceiling, the long timeline of attempts to defy gravity, and the humming sound of children learning and thinking about more to learn.

## References

Christie, J., & Wardle, F. (1992). How much time is needed for play? *Young Children, 47*(3), 28–33.

Derman-Sparks, L., & the A.B.C. Task Force. (1989). *Anti-bias curriculum: Tools for empowering young children*. Washington, DC: NAEYC.

Gottman, J. (1983). How children become friends. *Monographs of the Society for Research in Child Development, 48*(3, Serial no. 291).

Hohmann, C., Banet, B., & Weikart, D. (1979). *Young children in action*. Ypsilanti, MI: High/Scope Press.

Jones, E., & Reynolds, G. (1992). *The play's the thing . . . Teachers' roles in children's play*. New York: Teachers College Press.

Katz, L. (1991). Pedagogical issues in early childhood education. In S.L. Kagan (Ed.), *The care and education of America's young children: Obstacles and opportunities. Ninetieth Yearbook of the National Society for the Study of Education* (pp. 50–68). Chicago: University of Chicago Press.

Katz, L., & Chard, S. (1989). *Engaging children's minds: The project approach*. Norwood, NJ: Ablex.

Katz, L., & McClellan, D. (1991). *The teacher's role in the social development of young children*. Urbana, IL: ERIC Clearinghouse on Elementary and Early Childhood Education.

Kritchevsky, S., Prescott, E., & Walling, L. (1977). *Planning environments for young children: Physical space*. Washington, DC: NAEYC.

Krogh, S. (1990). *The integrated early childhood curriculum*. New York: McGraw-Hill.

Massam, J., & Kulik, A. (1986). *And what else?* Bothell, WA: The Wright Group.

Neugebauer, B. (Ed.). (1992). *Alike and different: Exploring our humanity with young children* (rev. ed.). Washington, DC: NAEYC.

Oden, S., & Asher, S. (1977). Coaching children in social skills for friendship making. *Child Development, 48*, 495–506.

Prescott, E., Jones, E., Kritchevsky, S., Milich, C., & Haselhoe, E. (1975). *Assessment of child rearing environments: An ecological approach*. Pasadena, CA: Pacific Oaks College.

Raines, S., & Canady, R. (1989). *Story s-t-r-e-t-c-h-e-r-s: Activities to expand children's favorite books*. Mt. Rainier, MD: Gryphon House.

Raines, S., & Canady, R. (1991). *More story s-t-r-e-t-c-h-e-r-s: More activities to expand children's favorite books*. Mt. Rainier, MD: Gryphon House.

Raines, S., & Canady, R. (1992). *Story s-t-r-e-t-c-h-e-r-s for the primary grades*. Mt. Rainier, MD: Gryphon House.

Rosegrant, T., & Cooper, R. (1986). *Talking text writer: Professional guide*. New York: Scholastic.

Scales, B., Almy, M., Nicolopoulou, A., & Ervin-Tripp, S. (1991). New York: Teachers College Press.

Shores, E. (1992). *Explorers' classrooms: Good practice for kindergarten and the primary grades*. Little Rock, AR: SACUS.

Wassermann, S. (1991). *Serious players in the primary classroom: Empowering children through active learning experiences*. New York: Teachers College Press.

# Reaching Potentials of Children With Special Needs

*Mark Wolery, Phillip S. Strain, and Donald B. Bailey, Jr.*

---

## Editors' introduction

In the previous chapters we described planning appropriate curriculum, taking into consideration all of the perspectives that inform curriculum, including normative child development knowledge. Throughout the discussion we included the traditional caveats about individual variation and diversity; however, we did not address the specific question of inclusion of children with disabilities and the implications for curriculum. To do so we invited leaders of the Division for Early Childhood of the Council for Exceptional Children to address the applicability of the Curriculum and Assessment Guidelines for children with special needs. In Chapter 7 Mark Wolery, Phillip Strain, and Donald Bailey describe best practices for children with special needs and analyze the applicability of the NAEYC and NAECS/SDE guidelines and the NAEYC guidelines for developmentally appropriate practice.

This discussion could not be more timely. Both political and pedagogical trends are causing the fields of early childhood education and early childhood special education to converge. From a political perspective, national laws now ensure access to services for children with disabilities. Due to the recent passage of the landmark civil rights legislation, the Americans with Disabilities Act (ADA), all early childhood programs must be prepared to serve children with special needs. Full implementation of the ADA, coupled with the Individuals with Disabilities Education Act, means that full inclusion of children with disabilities will become a reality, thus bringing early childhood education and early childhood special education closer together than ever before. Work remains to be done to expand the knowledge base, but the foundation is well laid. As Safford (1989) points out, "The fields of early childhood education and special education have a great deal in common because of their stress on children as individuals, and their recognition of every child's right to an education that is appropriate to individual and developmental needs" (p. xi).

With access to programs theoretically no longer an issue, the most important questions now are pedagogical; these are the questions that Wolery, Strain, and Bailey address. Their conclusion—that the framework of developmentally appropriate practice is necessary but not sufficient for meeting the needs of children with

*Preparation of this chapter was supported in part by cooperative agreement No. H024K90005, Early Childhood Research Institute—Integrated Programs, between the Office of Special Education Programs, the U.S. Department of Education, and the Allegheny-Singer Research Institute. The opinions expressed, however, do not necessarily reflect the positions or policies of the U.S. Department of Education, and no official endorsement should be inferred. The authors acknowledge and appreciate the comments and assistance provided by Dr. Barbara J. Smith on an earlier draft of this chapter.*

disabilities—provides an important springboard for further work to define best practices for all children. Although early childhood education and early childhood special education converge at certain points, differences remain to be negotiated. Solutions are being offered; for example, "One difference frequently noted is use by special educators of direct instructional approaches, congruent with the view of education as intervention. To the degree that providing for young children with handicaps within mainstream settings implies the need for more direct instruction than typical children may require, it is essential to adapt such instruction so that it is congruent with developmentally appropriate practices" (Safford, 1989, p. 71).

It is clear that each field needs to learn from the other as we work closely together to ensure individually appropriate practice for each child. Again quoting from Safford, "Programs that are developmentally appropriate for young children reflect a philosophical orientation and basic pedagogy capable of accommodating the needs of most young children considered exceptional. They need not become special education settings to do so. At the same time, some of the provisions required to ensure individual appropriateness of the program for children with specific handicaps offer the potential to enhance learning experiences for typical children as well" (p. 72). Those program dimensions are described in Chapter 7.

\* \* \* \* \*

The early education of young children with special needs is a challenging task, but a great deal has been learned from research and practice. This chapter has four purposes: (1) to describe "children with special needs" and list goals for their early education; (2) to identify current best practice with such children; (3) to discuss the relevance of the guidelines for developmentally appropriate practice (Bredekamp, 1987) and curriculum and assessment (NAEYC & NAECS/SDE, 1991) to their early education; and (4) to list resources for additional information. This chapter has many limitations. It does not address intervention with infants and toddlers who have special needs (Hanson & Lynch 1989; Meisels & Shonkoff, 1990). It does not provide sufficient information to implement adequate services for young children with special needs; the cited literature includes some of this information as it is understood today. The chapter is not a definitive statement on the adequacy of the guidelines in meeting the needs of children with disabilities; such a statement is not possible at this time because of lack of research (Carta, Schwartz, Atwater, & McConnell, 1991). Despite these limitations the chapter delineates fundamental principles for providing services to families and children who have or are at risk for having developmental delays and disabilities. Our goals will be met if readers gain an appreciation of the special considerations involved in providing such services and if discussions are stimulated about how those services are best provided.

## Children with special needs and goals for their early education

To understand and evaluate the relevance of the NAEYC and NAECS/SDE guidelines to young children with special needs, two questions are pertinent: *Who are children with "special needs"?* and *What are the goals of early education with such children?*

### Who are children with "special needs"?

Describing young children with special needs is similar to describing *Americans*. Because of their diversity, the task defies completion; consider these examples:

**Anthony** is 4 years old and is a beautiful child with a condition called *autism*. From a photograph, you would not know that Anthony has special needs; however, a few minutes of observation quickly dispels that perception. He rarely initiates interactions with his peers; he plays with few toys and rarely uses them as they are intended; he says few words and does not use them consistently; he appears to understand little that is said to him; he seems content to stand and flap his arms up and down rapidly, wander aimlessly about the room, or sit with his head cocked to one side looking out of the corner of his eyes; and he may burst into episodes of screaming and hitting his head furiously if he is upset, but it is difficult to know what will upset him. He rarely sleeps through the night, is not toilet trained, and eats only a few different kinds of foods.

**Rachel** is also 4 years old. She is a typical-looking child who appears bright and eager, but she has a profound hearing loss that cannot be corrected with hearing aides. Her play indicates that she is a very intelligent young girl. Her physical abilities appear to be within normal limits; she has been toilet trained for a couple of years, and she likes and does many of the things that other young children do; however, she does not talk and does not hear what others say. She uses sign language, but none of the children in her class know what she is trying to communicate.

**Latricia** is also 4 years old but looks obviously different from other children; she has developmental delays related to a condition called *Down syndrome*. She plays with toys, but her play is not complex; she feeds herself but only uses a spoon; she speaks, but her speech is frequently difficult to understand; she initiates interactions with other children and responds when they initiate contact with her, but those interactions are usually brief. Although she walks, runs, and rides a trike, she is fearful of climbing on the outdoor equipment, and her movements are awkward.

**Jason** is also 4 years old, and he obviously has special needs; he has cerebral palsy that affects his equilibrium and ability to control his movements. He cannot walk or crawl; his arm movements are stiff and uncoordinated. He speaks, but it is nearly impossible to understand him. He drools excessively when he speaks. He appears to understand everything that is going on around him. He uses a special chair and other special equipment, for example, an electronic device to communicate. He is not toilet trained, but he sometimes indicates when he is wet. He cannot feed himself. He takes medication daily to control a seizure disorder.

These children, whom we will revisit later in this chapter, have special needs, but their example does not capture the range of possible needs. Children with special needs frequently are divided into three broad categories: (a) children with identifiable conditions that interfere with their development and learning, (b) children with developmental delays but no apparent biological impairments, and (c) children who are at risk for developmental delays or disabilities because of a variety of environmental and/or biological factors (Harbin, Gallagher, & Terry, 1991). Under the Education of the Handicapped Act (often referred to as P.L. 94–142, and now called the Individuals with Disabilities Act), preschool children in some states and school-age children can receive special education services through 10 diagnostic categories: mental retardation, serious emotional disturbance, hearing impairments and deafness, visual impairments and blindness, or-

thopedic impairments, speech or language impairments, other health impairments, specific learning disabilities, autism, and traumatic brain injury. (For more information, see Haring and McCormick [1990] and Blackhurst and Berdine [in press]). The 1986 amendments (P.L. 99–457) to the Education of the Handicapped Act established two programs important to young children: services for infants and toddlers (birth to 36 months) and services for 3- through 5-year-old children with disabilities (Smith, 1988; Garwood & Sheehan, 1989). According to the amendments states are allowed to report the number of preschool children with disabilities who are served by using the term *developmental delay* instead of the 10 categories; thus, some states use the term *developmental delay* to determine eligibility for early special education services.

Five comments about these categories are pertinent. First, for each diagnosis, a range of developmental effects occur—from mild, to moderate, to severe/profound. One child may have a mild hearing loss; a second, a moderate hearing loss; and a third, a severe loss; thus, children with the same diagnosis may be very different from one another in the severity of their disability. Second, the diagnosis does not result in specific treatments or educational interventions (Strain, 1988). Two children with mild mental retardation may need very different types of education. Similarly, a child with a visual impairment will not necessarily be helped with glasses; the nature of the impairment will indicate whether glasses will be beneficial. Rather than the diagnosis, their educational programs depend

© Nancy P. Alexander

on their developmental skills; their competence in the classroom and at home; and the goals, values, and priorities of their families to determine necessary forms of intervention. Third, in most cases, the diagnosis does not result in an accurate prediction of later abilities. When many adults with mental retardation who live and work in the community were first diagnosed, the prediction was that they would need long-term care in residential institutions. Unfortunately, for other individuals with identical diagnoses, the prediction was correct. This difference in outcome is related to the lack of accurate initial diagnoses and, more importantly, to what happened after they were diagnosed. Frequently those who surpass the predicted outcome and are able to live in the community had determined families who received assistance and support from many people. The long-term effects of most diagnoses are not known because early intervention is relatively new, and its effects, combined with those of high-quality education throughout the school-age years, are not well understood. Fourth, each condition can occur alone or in combination. One child may have only visual impairment, but another may have mental retardation, physical disabilities, a hearing loss, and a communication disorder. Fifth, the major use of the categories is to determine eligibility for special services, although the criteria vary across states.

In summary, young children with special needs are a tremendously diverse group. To the casual observer, some of them do not appear to have disabilities; others have obvious disabilities. Some disabilities have relatively minor impact on development and learning; others may have major and lasting effects. Two certain facts about children with special needs are *they are all children* and *they all have unique needs*. These comments are not made to state the obvious but to make two fundamental points. First, because children with special needs are children, they have needs shared by all children. These include physical needs for shelter, rest, and nourishment and psychological needs to be nurtured, safe, and accepted. Second, children with developmental delays and disabilities have needs that are *NOT* shared by all other children. They need environments that are specifically organized and adjusted to minimize the effects of their disabilities and to promote learning of a broad range of skills. They need professionals who are competent in meeting the general needs of young children *and* are competent in promoting learning and use of skills important to the specific needs of children with disabilities. Also, they need personnel who value working cooperatively with families to meet family needs and to help families promote their child's development.

*TWO CERTAIN FACTS ABOUT CHILDREN WITH SPECIAL NEEDS ARE THEY ARE ALL CHILDREN AND THEY ALL HAVE UNIQUE NEEDS. FIRST, BECAUSE CHILDREN WITH SPECIAL NEEDS ARE CHILDREN, THEY HAVE NEEDS SHARED BY ALL CHILDREN. THESE INCLUDE PHYSICAL NEEDS FOR SHELTER, REST, AND NOURISHMENT AND PSYCHOLOGICAL NEEDS TO BE NURTURED, SAFE, AND ACCEPTED. SECOND, CHILDREN WITH DEVELOPMENTAL DELAYS AND DISABILITIES HAVE NEEDS THAT ARE NOT SHARED BY ALL OTHER CHILDREN.*

Services to young children with special needs are governed by federal law (e.g., P.L. 94–142 and P.L. 99–457), relevant federal regulations, and state laws and regulations. Unlike other educational programs that are more locally controlled, these federal laws dictate any decisions about curriculum and assessment. Some key provisions of these laws are important (Turnbull, 1990). All children with disabilities are entitled to a free appropriate public education, regardless of their skill levels and the severity of their disabilities. Unbiased testing, classification, and placement procedures must be used and must include parental notification and consent. Children must be placed in the least restrictive (most normalized) appropriate placement, meaning that to the extent possible, they should be educated with children who do not have disabilities. Parents have a right to participate in decisions related to their child's education and the policies of the state and local educational agencies. Parents also have the right to procedural due process, meaning that they can challenge the school's decisions and actions that affect their children. Finally, children have a right to an individualized and appropriate education—an Individualized Educational Program, or IEP. At a minimum, each IEP must include a summary of the child's present levels of functioning; annual goals; short-term instructional objectives; statement of the educational and related services needed, such as speech/language therapy or physical therapy; dates of initiation and expected duration of services; justification for the placement; and identification of individuals responsible for implementing the program (Turnbull, 1990). In addition, P.L. 99–457 encourages the inclusion of family goals on the IEP. The IEP should assume a central role in guiding the services that children receive; it should not be a document that is developed, signed, and rarely consulted.

## What are the goals of early education for children who have special needs?

The goals of early intervention for children with special needs come from many sources: legislation, parent preferences, theoretical perspectives, research, and practical needs. Bailey and Wolery (1992) discuss seven primary goals, which are described briefly below.

### 1. Supporting families in achieving their own goals

Families voluntarily participate in early intervention. Their children often have complex needs, but those needs are best understood through the parents' eyes. Further, some families have needs that extend beyond facilitating their child's development. Because intervention is most likely to be effective if it is consistent with parents' goals and priorities, family support is a key mission of early intervention programs.

### 2. Promoting child engagement and mastery

Young children spend most of their time at home, in child care centers, and in schools, although some children with special needs also spend a lot of time in hospitals. A key goal of early intervention is to help children learn to interact with and be successful in those environments. Several studies have shown that children with special needs interact with toys and materials for shorter periods of time than do normally developing children (Weiner & Weiner, 1974), are less persistent at difficult tasks, are less goal oriented, and give up sooner (Jennings, Connors, Stegman, Sankaranarayan, & Mendelsohn, 1985). Early intervention ought to help children engage actively, strive for mastery of the demands within various environments, and become as independent as possible.

### 3. Promoting development in important areas

A third goal of early intervention is to promote children's developmental progress in a variety of areas, including the traditional areas of cognitive, motor, communication, play, social, and self-care skills (toileting, dressing, and feeding), as well as self-esteem and self-control.

### 4. Building and supporting social competence

One of the most consistent findings in the research literature is that young children with special needs engage in less frequent and less sophisticated social play than their normally developing peers (Guralnik & Groom, 1987). Although the promotion of social competence is an important goal for all children, it is especially important for children with special needs because deficits in social skills may be lifelong, and social skills are needed throughout one's life.

### 5. Facilitating the generalized use of skills

Another common finding in the research literature is that children with special needs often do not *generalize* well (Warren & Kaiser, 1986); that is, information or skills learned in one setting may not be used in another. Because isolated skills are likely to be of little use, a fifth goal is to help children use and apply their skills in a variety of appropriate circumstances.

### 6. Providing and preparing for normalized life experiences

As discussed later, children with disabilities ought to be able to participate in programs provided for children with typical development. In addition, teachers should use normal teaching strategies, such as developmentally appropriate practices, and provide classrooms similar to those for normally abled children; and help children with disabilities learn skills that will promote transition into general classrooms.

### 7. Preventing future problems or disabilities

Many children are at risk for future problems for a variety of biological or environmental reasons, although problems are not currently obvious; for example, a child with Down syndrome may show minor delays during infancy, yet significant delays in the future are likely. Early intervention should prevent or reduce the chance of additional delays and reduce the need for later specialized services.

## Current best practices in early education of children with special needs

Current "best" practices for meeting the goals listed above are described in this section. These practices are derived from research, previous discussions of this issue (e.g., McDonnell & Hardman, 1988; Carta et al., 1991), experience with service systems, and beliefs about how meaningful early education should be provided.

### Assessment activities should be done to make specific decisions

Young children with special needs are assessed to get information to make several different types of decisions. Common decisions are whether to refer the child for additional assessment, whether the child has a developmental delay or disability, whether the child is eligible for special services, what should be taught, where the child should be placed, what services are needed, whether the curriculum should be changed to improve child progress, and whether the early education program was successfully dealing with the child's disability. Each decision requires asking specific questions *and* using different measures and measurement procedures. In Table 1 each decision, type of assessment, relevant questions, measurement procedures, and resources is presented.

Teachers are intimately involved in assessing children to decide what to teach when developing the IEP. To illustrate the characteristics of such assessments, we turn to the example of Scott, who is 5 years old and has moderate mental retardation. He has been in early intervention for a number of years and is enrolled in a developmentally appropriate kindergarten. He has communication disorders, a suspected hearing impairment, and some motor weaknesses. The characteristics of curriculum-planning assessments (IEP planning assessments), a description of each characteristic, and an example of how assessment was done for Scott are shown in Table 2.

Identifying the IEP goals is only the beginning. The team must develop a plan for ensuring that children achieve those objectives. This involves determining whether children need to learn how to do the skills (acquisition), how to do them smoothly and rapidly (fluency building), how to continue to do them after instruction has stopped (maintenance), and/or how to use and apply the skills when and wherever they are needed (generalization) (Horner, Dunlap, & Koegel, 1988; Wolery, Bailey, & Sugai, 1988). Attention to each of these types of learning is critical to providing quality early education. The team must also design the classroom, select materials, and identify instructional procedures that will result in engagement and learning. Also, each IEP should be viewed as a *tentative plan*. The teacher must continually observe the child to decide whether the curriculum should be changed to promote greater progress.

### Services should be family centered

Most educators acknowledge the central role of families in the development of all young children, but attention to family values and priorities is critical when children have disabilities. In part, this is necessary because the law (P.L. 94–142 and P.L. 99–457) requires that parents be participants in decisions related to their children's educational programs (Turnbull, 1990); however, more importantly, the provision of family-centered or family-focused services is a defensible and effective way of delivering early education (Dunst, 1985). This is so because children are members of their family units, which are members of larger social networks and systems (Dunst, Trivette, & Deal, 1988). Also, it is clear that the birth and rearing of children with special needs influence how well families function and the stress they feel (Bailey, 1988; Hanson & Hanline, 1990). Finally, the family's views of their child, their responsiveness to the child, their perceptions of well being, and social support may influence the child's functioning (Silber, 1989; Dunst, Trivette, Hamby, & Pollock, 1990).

*CHILDREN WITH DISABILITIES OUGHT TO BE ABLE TO PARTICIPATE IN PROGRAMS PROVIDED FOR CHILDREN WITH TYPICAL DEVELOPMENT. IN ADDITION, TEACHERS SHOULD USE NORMAL TEACHING STRATEGIES, SUCH AS DEVELOPMENTALLY APPROPRIATE PRACTICES, AND PROVIDE CLASSROOMS SIMILAR TO THOSE FOR NORMALLY ABLED CHILDREN.*

These findings and P.L. 99–457 (requiring a statement of family concerns, priorities, and resources on the Individualized Family Service Plans for families with infants and toddlers) have led us to assess family needs and strengths and develop individualized family intervention plans. Many measures such as written questionnaires and rating scales are used to assess family stress, support and resources, needs, and strengths (Bailey & Simeonsson, 1988). Also, interviews frequently are used in developing these plans (Winton, 1988; Winton & Bailey, 1990). From the assessment a family-centered intervention plan is derived. Bailey, McWilliam, Winton, and Simeonsson (1991) identified seven themes of services that are based on family values and priorities; these appear in Table 3.

To illustrate family-centered services, we turn to Jason, who was described earlier on page 94, The team would interview Jason's parents to identify how well they understand his disability and what issues are particularly stressful to them, for example, feeding him or telling others about his disability. The team also would seek to determine—through rating scales and interviews—what help the family needs in meeting Jason's needs, for example, whether they need help in doing physical therapy, whether they need a sitter for him so that they can have an evening out, whether they need help using his communication device, or whether they need financial assistance in paying for his specialized chair. The team also would help them identify resources available to the family to get these needs met. From these activities, a plan would be developed and implemented based on the priorities, resources, and strengths of Jason's family.

# *Table 1.* ASSESSMENT FOR DECISION MAKING

| Decision | Assessment type | Relevant questions |
|---|---|---|
| Determine whether to refer the child for additional assessment | Screening | Does developmental screening indicate potential for developmental delay or disability? |
| | | Does hearing or visual screening indicate potential sensory impairments or losses? |
| | | Does health screening and physical examination indicate need for medical attention? |
| Determine whether the child has a developmental delay or disability | Diagnostic | Does a developmental delay or disability exist? If so, what is the nature and extent of the delay or disability? |
| Determine whether the child is eligible for special services | Eligibility | Does the child meet the criteria specified for the state to receive specialized services? |
| Determine what the child should be taught | Instructional program planning assessment | What is the child's current level of developmental functioning? |
| | | What does the child need to be independent in the classroom, home, and community? |
| | | What are the effects of adaptations and assistance on child performance? |
| | | What usual patterns of responding and what relationships with environmental variables appear to influence child performance? |
| Determine where the child should receive services and what services are needed | Placement | What does the child need? |
| | | Which of the possible placement options could best meet the child's needs? |
| | | Does the child need specialized services, such as speech/language therapy, physical therapy, occupational therapy, or dietary supervision? |
| Determine whether the child is making adequate progress in learning important skills | Monitoring of instructional program | What is the child's usual performance of important skills? |
| | | Is the child using important skills outside the classroom? |
| Determine whether the desired outcomes were achieved | Program evaluation | Did the child make expected progress? |

## Resources

Bagnato, S.J., Neisworth, J.T., & Munson, S.M. (1989). *Linking developmental assessment and early intervention: Curriculum-based prescription* (2nd ed.). Rockville, MD: Aspen.

Bailey, D.B., & Simeonsson, R.J. (Eds.). (1988). *Family assessment in early intervention*. Columbus, OH: Merrill.

Bailey, D.B., & Wolery, M. (Eds.). (1989). *Assessing infants and preschoolers with handicaps*. Columbus, OH: Charles Merrill.

Fleischer, K.R., Belgredan, J.H., Bagnato, S.J., & Ogonosky, A.B. (1990). An overview of judgement-based assessment. *Topics in Early Childhood Special Education, 10*(3), 13–23.

LeLaurin, K. (1990). Judgment-based assessment: Making the implicit explicit. *Topics in Early Childhood Special Education, 10*(3), 96–110.

## Measurement practices

Use of norm-referenced, developmental screening measures that address multiple domains, are implemented reliably, have concurrent validity with in-depth measures, and are nondiscriminatory.

Use of screening measures that have specific criteria for referral for audiological/visual examinations.

Conducted by nurse, pediatrician, or other health professional.

Measures and procedures depend on the suspected delay or disability but frequently involve standardized measures conducted by professionals who are specifically trained to use them. Frequently are comprehensive and conducted in clinical settings.

Frequently synonymous with diagnostic assessments because children are made eligible for services based on established diagnosis; however, may also include other requirements.

Curriculum-based assessment measures that address multiple developmental domains are used and supplemented with direct observation of children in multiple natural situations, informal testing, and interviews with others, including parents. Frequently conducted by teachers and relevant therapists.

Direct observation in these settings and interviews with family members.

Direct observation, informal assessment with various levels and types of assistance in natural settings.

Direct observation, informal assessment, interviews with others, reinforcement preference assessment, trial use of various instructional procedures, and clinical judgment.

This question is answered by the results of the instructional program planning assessment.

Direct observation, rating scales, and interviews are used to determine the characteristics and potential of each possible placement, and parents are interviewed concerning their preferences.

Based on assessments conducted by registered or licensed therapists in these various disciplines; sometimes norm-referenced measures are used and are supplemented by observation and clinical judgment.

Data collected from unstructured and structured observations of the child in natural contexts; data collected from periodic probes of the child's performance.

Reports by family members of the child's application of important skills.

Measures and measurement procedures vary greatly based on the intended outcomes of the program but frequently include developmental performance and attainment of specified objectives.

Magyary, D., Barnard, K., & Brandt, P. (1988). Biophysical considerations in the assessment of young children with a developmental disability. In T.D. Wachs & R. Wheehan (Eds.), *Assessment of young developmentally disabled children* (pp. 347–370). New York: Plenum.

Meisels, S.J. (1991). Dimensions of early identification. *Journal of Early Intervention, 15*(1), 26–35.

Meisels, S.J., & Provence, S. (1989). *Screening and assessment: Guidelines for identifying young disabled and developmentally vulnerable children and their families.* Washington, DC: National Center for Clinical Infant Programs.

Wachs, T.D., & Sheehan, R. (Eds.). (1988). *Effective teaching: Principles and procedures of applied behavior analysis with exceptional students.* Boston: Allyn & Bacon.

## *Table 2.* ASSESSMENT FOR CURRICULAR PLANNING

### Assessment/Planning

Child's name: *Scott* (see p. 97)

| Characteristic | Description | Example |
|---|---|---|
| Assessment should include a variety of measures in a variety of settings. | The assessment procedures include the use of curriculum-referenced tests, teacher-devised and informal tests, direct observation in natural settings (home and classroom), and interviews with people who know the child. | The teacher uses developmental scales to assess Scott's communication, motor, and cognitive development. She devises some testing situations to determine how he does particular skills. She observes him during play sessions with other children to note his social interaction, play, and language skills. She observes him at lunch and in the bathroom to identify his self-care skills. She interviews his parents, former teachers, and therapists to secure additional information. |
| Assessment results should provide a detailed description of the child's functioning. | The results include a description of (a) the child's developmental skills across all relevant areas, (b) what the child can and cannot do, and (c) what factors influence the child's skills/abilities. | The teacher analyzes the results of her assessment activities, summarizes what Scott can and cannot do in each area, and describes what factors appear to influence his performance (e.g., what toys he appears to like, which children he interacts with, what help he needs on different tasks, and what appears to motivate his behavior). |
| Assessment activities should involve the child's family. | The family should fulfill the following roles: receive information from professionals, observe the assessment activities, provide information about the child's development and needs, gather new information, and validate the assessment results. | The teacher plans the assessment with the family. She asks them about how Scott does different skills, how he spends his time, and what concerns and goals they have for him. She allows them to observe the testing. She asks them to gather information on some skills at home. She reviews the results with them and asks them to confirm, modify, qualify, and—if necessary—refute the findings. |
| Assessment activities should be conducted by professionals from different disciplines. | Frequently assessment from the following disciplines is needed: speech/language therapy, physical therapy, occupational therapy, audiology, social work, health professionals (nurses & physicians), psychology, nutrition, special education, and possibly others. | The teacher coordinates the assessment activities of the team. Because of Scott's communication delays, a speech and language pathologist assesses him. An audiologist assesses his hearing, a physical therapist and an occupational therapist assess his motor skills, and the special education teacher assists the kindergarten teacher in assessing his social and cognitive skills. |
| Assessment activities should result in a list of high-priority objectives. | Assessment activities will identify more skills than are possible to teach; therefore, those of most value are identified. All team members, including the family, are involved in this decision. Skills are selected to be focused on if they are useful to the child, have long-term benefits, and/or are important to the family. | After the results have been analyzed, the team (including the parents) meets to review the findings. They discuss which skills Scott needs to learn, which ones will be most useful, which will result in long-term benefit, and which are most important to his family. The most important skills are listed as goals on his Individualized Educational Program (IEP). |

## Services should focus on outcomes

The goals noted earlier and the objectives on each child's IEP constitute the goals of early education. They are the foundation for planning the curriculum and are the standard against which the success of early education is judged. Services for young children with special needs should be designed to produce specific, measurable, and meaningful changes in children's interactions with their environments and their lifestyles (McDonnell & Hardman, 1988; Carta et al., 1991). This assumption is justified on at least four grounds.

First, *many children with special needs have delays or disabilities that make them dependent upon others.* For example, children who do not feed themselves must be fed by someone; children who are not toilet trained must be changed by someone; children who do not communicate effectively must have their needs anticipated by others. It is fundamentally unfair to allow such children to continue to be dependent upon others if it is possible (and it usually is) to teach them skills needed for independence.

Second, *many children with special needs have delays or disabilities that keep them from learning well on their own.* For example, children who do not interact with their peers are deprived of learning from their peers and from making friendships with them; children who do not play with toys are unable to take

---

*Table 3.* THEMES OF FAMILY-CENTERED SERVICES

| Theme | Potential Implication |
|---|---|
| Services are focused on the entire family and the child as a member of the family unit. | • Services include assessment of and attention to family needs and priorities; and<br>• professionals must have competencies in working with families as well as with children. |
| Services assist families in making their own decisions, finding their own resources, and becoming independent of professionals. | • Professionals should not make family decisions;<br>• services should not duplicate currently available resources;<br>• professionals should help families find their own sources of support; and<br>• professionals should encourage family independence rather than dependence. |
| Families' needs for information, social support, explaining their child's disabilities to others, community services, financial assistance, and help in general family functioning should determine the nature and amount of services. | • Professionals should help families identify their needs;<br>• professionals should structure services based on the families' views of needs; and<br>• professionals should recognize that the needs may change rapidly, which will mean that changes are required in the service plan. |
| Services should help families achieve a normalized lifestyle (i.e., a lifestyle similar to what they would have if the child did not have disabilities). | • Professionals need to assist families in identifying what constitutes a normalized lifestyle for them; and<br>• professionals may need to help families achieve the identified lifestyle. |
| Services should be sensitive to the cultural diversity of families. | • Professionals should allow families to define their needs, goals, and aspirations based on their own culture; and<br>• professionals should avoid preconceived ideas of family roles, behaviors, and goals. |
| Services should be individualized. | • Professionals should assess family needs, strengths, and aspirations; and<br>• professionals should assist families in developing plans based on identified needs. |
| Services for families should be coordinated across agencies. | • Professionals must communicate with other agencies; and<br>• professionals must assist families in interacting with other agencies. |

---

advantage of this important way of learning; and children who do not imitate are unable to learn by watching peers. Failing to address these problems leaves children to learn in less normal, less useful, and more dependent ways.

Third, *many children with special needs develop more slowly than their typically developing peers.* Allowing them to continue in slow paths of development results in greater and greater differences in their abilities from those of their peers. As a result they have less access to community activities and are placed in more restrictive educational settings. Allowing them to continue in paths that limit their opportunities and ensure expensive restrictive placements is inhumane and economically unwise.

Fourth, *many children with special needs have disabilities that interfere with how they interact, and, as*

*a result, they often acquire additional handicaps.* Children who cannot communicate their needs and desires often use problem behaviors to meet their needs (Donnellan, Mirenda, Mesaros, & Fassbender, 1984). For example, a child who cannot ask for toys may use grabbing and aggression to obtain them. If allowed to continue, these behaviors may become the child's primary means for meeting a wide range of needs. Children with weak muscle tone often move in ways that cause physical deformities (Campbell, 1987; Smith, 1989). Allowing them to engage in behaviors that produce further disabilities is ethically indefensible. These realities require purposeful planning of children's early education experiences and the use of carefully designed teaching procedures to promote learning of needed skills (Odom & Karnes, 1988; Bricker, 1989; Bailey & Wolery, 1992).

---

*Table 4.* **EXAMPLES OF RESTRICTIVE PRACTICES FOR VARIOUS ENVIRONMENTAL DOMAINS THAT SHOULD BE AVOIDED**

|  | Availability | Accessibility | Organization | Scheduling & Use |
|---|---|---|---|---|
| Space | No outdoor play space for gross-motor and movement activities | Book area located in a loft that is not independently accessible by motorically impaired children | Boundaries for activity areas not clearly specified, resulting in frequent shifts from area to area and toys and materials distributed across the room | No scheduled time for use of outdoor play space |
| Materials/ Equipment | Inadequate number of blocks in play area to encourage complex constructions or play by more than one child | Housekeeping materials are stored in high cabinets accessible only to teachers and not visible to children | Blocks, fine-motor materials, and dolls all placed on the same set of shelves, with no organizational pattern or cues for proper storage | Sand- and water-play equipment available, but either no designated time for use or no teacher support to promote appropriate engagement with sand and water materials |
| Persons | No nonhandicapped peers available | Nonhandicapped peers in building, but cared for in separate classes | Nonhandicapped peers in same classroom, but grouping children by ability for instructional activities results in infrequent opportunities for interaction | Nonhandicapped peers present, but no systematic strategies employed to foster social-communicative exchanges between handicapped and nonhandicapped children |

*Taken from Bailey, D.B., & McWilliams, R.A. (1990). Normalizing early intervention.* Topics in Early Childhood Special Education, 10(2), 33–47.

To illustrate how services should focus on outcomes, we turn to Latricia, whose disability is described on page 94. For Latricia, the intervention team would purposefully teach skills that would make her more independent, for example, help her learn to eat with a fork; design a classroom environment that would increase the length of her interactions with peers and help her learn from her peers, probably by using structured play activities with peers; design educational experiences that would increase her developmental skills; and use specific language training to ensure that her difficulties in communication do not lead to problem behaviors and additional handicaps.

### Services should use normalized but effective and efficient interventions

Designing classroom services for young children with special needs involves many decisions, including how to organize the physical space of the classroom, design activity areas, devise daily schedules, use appropriate teacher behaviors and roles, select and use appropriate teaching strategies, implement activities, observe children's behavior, and make changes in activities to help children learn. Four standards are used to judge how well these decisions are made for children with special needs (Carta et al., 1991).

First, the curriculum should be *appropriate and normalized*. This means that it should be individualized, developed with input from families, and involve contact with typically developing peers. The curriculum also should be similar to that found in high-quality programs for children with typical development, such as those programs that follow the NAEYC and NAECS/SDE guidelines. Bailey and McWilliam (1990) identified a number of restrictive practices (shown in Table 4) that should be avoided. Several sources discuss how to organize and structure classrooms for children with disabilities (Odom & Strain, 1984; Bricker, 1989; Safford, 1989; Bailey & Wolery, 1992). Also, sources exist for evaluating classrooms (Wachs, 1988; Bailey, 1989).

Second, the practices should be *effective*. This means that the curriculum should result in children learning *and* using the skills listed on their IEPs and the skills involved in the goals listed above. Many effective curriculum strategies have been developed through research and experience, and some of them are listed later in this section.

Third, the curriculum should result in *efficient learning*. Efficiency refers to curricular strategies that are effective *and* are "better" than other strategies. Specifically, the curriculum should not waste children's time, should allow them to learn many skills at once, and should help them use and apply those skills.

Fourth, *parents should be satisfied* with the curriculum. Parents should be pleased with how their children

*THE CURRICULUM SHOULD BE APPROPRIATE AND NORMALIZED. THIS MEANS THAT IT SHOULD BE INDIVIDUALIZED, DEVELOPED WITH INPUT FROM FAMILIES, AND INVOLVE CONTACT WITH TYPICALLY DEVELOPING PEERS. THE CURRICULUM ALSO SHOULD BE SIMILAR TO THAT FOUND IN HIGH-QUALITY PROGRAMS FOR CHILDREN WITH TYPICAL DEVELOPMENT, SUCH AS THOSE PROGRAMS THAT FOLLOW THE NAEYC AND NAECS/SDE GUIDELINES.*

spend time, what they do during the day, the methods used to teach them, and the interactions their child has with his or her peers and the adults in the program. Furthermore, parents should be satisfied with the skills their children are learning. Parental satisfaction can be determined from regular surveys of their views and by determining whether children achieve the IEP objectives.

Because the curriculum for young children with special needs should result in learning specific skills (the IEP goals), it is necessary to ensure that children have enough opportunities to learn them. Bricker (1989) recommends analyzing the child's entire daily schedule (home and classroom) and identifying times when each skill could be taught, practiced, and reinforced. Ideally several opportunities would occur each day for the child to learn and use important skills; sometimes the daily schedule must be changed to make this happen.

Many intervention strategies exist for teaching young children with special needs, including being responsive to children's interactions with materials and people (Dunst, Lesko, Holbert, Wilson, Sharpe, & Liles, 1987); reinforcing desirable and more complex skills (Cooper, Heron, & Heward, 1987); using peers to facilitate social play and interactions (called *peer-mediated strategies*) (Strain, 1981; Kohler & Strain, 1990) and communicative skills (Goldstein & Wickstrom, 1986); providing opportunities and prompting more complex language skills (called *naturalistic language strategies*) (Halle, Alpert, & Anderson, 1984; Warren & Kaiser, 1988); and using teacher assistance and reinforcing children's responses (called *response-prompting strategies*) (Wolery, Ault, & Doyle, 1992). Many variations of these general types of procedures exist and have been used effectively in mainstreamed programs. Most of these procedures can be used during low-structure activities, such as free play, snack time, housekeeping play, and block play; during transitions between activities; and during more structured activities, such as circle time, music, story time, and small-group instruction (Bailey & Wolery, 1992; Odom & Karnes, 1988; Peck, Odom, & Bricker, in press). Below are three examples of effective and efficient intervention strategies.

*Example of using peers.* Anthony (described on page 93) rarely responds to peers who interact with him. Given the importance of good social-interaction skills, his teacher decides to use peer social-initiation training to teach him to interact. Through models, direct teaching, and role playing, she teaches three of his nonhandicapped classmates to get him to play and keep him playing. She then provides times for these peers and Anthony to play together. She reminds the peers to use the skills she has taught them and praises them after each play period. The teacher measures the amount of time Anthony spends in social interactions during the play periods.

*Example of using a naturalistic language strategy.* Ashley is a 3-year-old girl with several communication disorders. Her intervention team has selected putting two words together as an instrumental goal. During play time Ashley's teacher gives her a wand for blowing bubbles and a small amount of bubble fluid. Ashley loves blowing bubbles and quickly uses up all of the fluid. Her teacher looks at her. Ashley says, "Bubble." The teacher reaches for the bubble fluid; says, "Tell me more"; and looks at Ashley. If Ashley says, "More bubbles" or "Bubble, please," the teacher gives her more bubbles; if she does not answer, he says, "Say, 'More bubbles,'" and gives her a chance to repeat his statement.

*Example of using teacher assistance.* Kisha is a 6-year-old girl with mild mental retardation and physical disabilities. Her intervention team has selected naming body parts as an instructional goal. As a result, her teacher places dolls and dress-up clothes in the dramatic play area. When Kisha is in this area, he moves near her. He pretends to need help dressing a doll and uses constant time delay to teach her names of the body parts as he manipulates them. This is done using the following steps. He points to an elbow and says, "What's this?," and before she can answer he says, "This is an elbow." He repeats this several times over the next day or two. Later he says, "What's this?" and waits a few seconds for her to answer. If she does not answer, he tells her. Each time she is correct, he praises her and they continue playing.

These examples show how teachers purposefully use a procedure to teach children selected skills. The examples also show that these procedures can be used during regular, ongoing activities. With children who have disabilities, *their day should be full of usual activities* that are adapted by using effective teaching procedures that are embedded within them.

## Services should be monitored regularly and adjusted as needed

As noted above, services for children with special needs are designed to teach skills that address their needs; however, few intervention teams can plan a curriculum that will work all of the time for all children with special needs because development and needs are complex, and assessment and teaching procedures are imperfect. The curriculum thus may not work or may work slowly; this requires teachers to monitor its effects regularly (Bricker, 1989; Bricker & Veltman, 1990). Monitoring asks, *Are the curricular strategies being used, are they used correctly, are children engaged in the activities, are they learning the important skills, are they using and applying those skills, and are parents pleased with the program's procedures and results?* (Wolery & Fleming, in press). The answers to these questions are used to make adjustments in the curriculum. To answer these questions teachers must observe children regularly. Numerous data collection systems have been used to understand the effects of the curriculum (Cooper et al., 1987; Wolery et al., 1988). Also, guidelines have been developed to analyze the results of the observations and make decisions based on the results (Liberty, 1988; Haring, Liberty, & White, 1990). These guidelines allow the teacher to determine whether adequate progress is being made and suggest changes when progress is not as expected.

*Example of monitoring progress toward goals.* A goal for Rachel (described on p. 94) is for her to learn to use manual sign language to label what and with whom she is going to play; however, she does not know the signs for the names of children in her class or for different toys or activities that are available. Her teacher therefore asks (verbally and with manual signs) what she is going to do and allows her to point to the children and toys or activities with which she will play. After she points, the teacher shows her the correct signs. As Rachel learns the signs, he will expect her to use them. He keeps a record of each sign he has shown her and which ones she uses spontaneously. This record will be used to decide whether he needs to provide more direct instruction on the names of her peers and toys.

## Services should be provided in mainstreamed settings

Mainstreaming refers to serving children with special needs in programs designed for children without disabilities. Integration is a more general term and refers to any mixing of children with and without special needs (Odom & McEvoy, 1988). Providing early education to both groups of children in the same program has been practiced and studied for 20 years.

The rationale for mainstreaming and its benefits are enumerated elsewhere (Bricker, 1978; Peck & Cooke, 1983) and are summarized in Table 5.

## Transition to other programs should be planned

The movement of young children with special needs from one program to another or from the early education to the elementary program requires careful and early planning (Salisbury & Vincent, 1990). This planning should occur 6 to 12 months before the transition and should address several issues. The concerns of the family—such as the child's safety— and the nature of services should be addressed by having families meet with the staff in the receiving program, talk with other parents from that program, and observe the new program. Procedures for communicating with staff in the new placement and the transition procedures should be identified. The skills needed by the child in the new program should be identified; the manner in which the new classroom operates should be discussed; and the resources available, such as the presence of a teaching assistant or speech and language services, should be

evaluated. The staff in the new program should be invited to observe the child in his or her current program, and they should receive a clear description of the child's goals and of procedures that work with the child. Finally procedures should be established to follow up on whether the new placement is effective. Issues related to transitions are described in detail in several sources (see Noonan & Kilgo, 1987; Fowler, Chandler, Johnson, & Stella, 1988; Carta, Atwater, Schwartz, & Miller, 1990).

## Services should involve members of several disciplines

Given the complexity of development and the subtle effects of delays and disabilities on it, assistance from a number of disciplines is necessary for children with special needs. Clearly no single discipline prepares its members to adequately address all of the needs of children with disabilities and their families. Few programs can employ the range of professionals needed to adequately assess children with special needs, plan the curriculum, and implement and monitor its effects. In practice few programs need all of the professionals on a full-time basis; thus, securing consultation services from members of these disciplines may be the most reasonable practice (McCollum & Hughes, 1988). Having the necessary team members is only part of the task, however. The team also must be a cohesive unit that works together. This is accomplished by promoting family involvement and decision making on the team, developing and using communication skills, establishing a team philosophy, developing and implementing a structure for decision making, learning to disagree effectively, and ensuring team leadership (Bailey & Wolery, 1992). It should be noted that the inclusion of multiple disciplines in the early education of children with special needs does not mean that each member of the team works with the child in isolated therapy sessions; rather, the knowledge and methods of team members are shared and integrated into a plan that is used by all adults who interact with the child.

## Services should be based on research

Providing services to young children with special needs is a relatively new enterprise. Much has been learned, but much remains to be learned; thus, teachers and program leaders must apply what is known from research, make decisions based on sound logic and experience when research is lacking, and conduct and assist others in conducting meaningful research. When instructional practices have a research base showing that they work, little justification exists for ignoring that information and using practices that do not have supporting evidence; thus, teachers must be aware of the research literature and must apply it to their practice. The literature cited in this chapter serves as a beginning for understanding the existing research.

# Relevance of the NAEYC and NAECS/SDE guidelines to children with special needs

It is fair to ask, Can the guidelines for developmentally appropriate practice and appropriate curriculum be applied to children with special needs? Our answer is, Yes, but children probably will not benefit as much as they should unless modifications and expansions are made. This prompts another question, Are the expansions so drastic that we should abandon efforts to apply the guidelines and evaluate their effects? Our answer is a resounding, No! In part we provide this answer because the guidelines for developmentally appropriate practice (Bredekamp, 1987) and the Curriculum and Assessment Guidelines of NAEYC and NAECS/SDE (1991) clearly recognize the importance of individual differences and the need to adapt the

curriculum to those differences. Clearly the expansions are issues that deserve careful and intense study, but they are not so great that we should shrink from the task. In fact, investigation of these expansions is likely to change our knowledge of young children *with and without disabilities*. Experiences with mainstreaming over the past two decades suggest a conclusion that probably will be made concerning the guidelines and children with special needs 20 years from now: *The guidelines are the context in which appropriate early education of children with special needs should occur; however, a program based on the guidelines alone is not likely to be sufficient for many children with special needs*. That is, programs that use the guidelines may be good places for children with special needs to receive their early education, but those programs must be adjusted to be maximally beneficial to those children and their families. These statements cause us to ask, "What modifications are necessary?" The precise answer to this question awaits further research—much research; but based on the best practices listed above, some suggestions can be made.

**First,** services for young children with special needs must focus on achieving specific goals. This statement is based on the four grounds listed earlier (p. 101–102) and the assumption that the special needs of children with developmental delays and disabilities are not likely to be addressed without purposeful planning, implementation, and adjustment of the early educational curriculum. In terms of the NAEYC guidelines, an explanation is necessary. The guidelines for developmentally appropriate practice (Bredekamp, 1987) were developed, in part, to correct the inappropriate practices and structure of many programs for young children. As is well known, many programs focus heavily on academic skills and use instructional arrangements and procedures employed with older children. These inappropriate practices have produced the inaccurate view that planning instruction to cause learning of specific skills is harmful (in fact the need to correct this misperception was one precipitating factor in the development of the Curriculum and Assessment Guidelines presented in this book). This misperception may lead some to believe that the goal-driven instruction necessary for young children with

*P*ROGRAMS THAT USE THE GUIDELINES MAY BE GOOD PLACES FOR CHILDREN WITH SPECIAL NEEDS TO RECEIVE THEIR EARLY EDUCATION, BUT THOSE PROGRAMS MUST BE ADJUSTED TO BE MAXIMALLY BENEFICIAL TO THOSE CHILDREN AND THEIR FAMILIES.

## *Table 5.* SUMMARY OF RESEARCH ON MAINSTREAMING

| Statement | Reference |
|---|---|
| • Placement in mainstreamed classrooms is appropriate for most children with special needs. | Guralnick (1990) |
| • Many programs for typically developing children report enrolling children with special needs. | Wolery, Fleming, & Venn (1990) |
| • Several models of programs for mainstreaming young children with special needs have been developed, used, and tested. | Hoyson, Jamieson, & Strain (1984); Peck, Killen, & Baumgart (1989); Templeman, Fredericks, & Udell (1989) |
| • A variety of effective teaching procedures have been developed and tested in mainstreamed classrooms. | Safford (1989); Peck, Odom, & Bricker (in press) |
| • Mainstreaming seems to have the largest impact on the social skills of young children with special needs. | Buysse & Bailey (1991) |
| • Mainstreaming appears to facilitate developmental progress for children with special needs and children without disabilities as well as nonmainstreamed programs do. | Odom & McEvoy (1988); Buysse & Bailey (1991) |
| • Typically developing children do not appear to learn inappropriate behaviors as a result of their mainstreaming experience. | Odom & McEvoy (1990) |
| • Barriers to effective mainstreaming include lack of adequately prepared staff; philosophic differences; staff attitudes; lack of specialized services (e.g., speech and physical therapy); and broad societal forces, such as limited fiscal resources, emphasis on competitive outcomes for children in the educational reform movement, and unclear policy directives and guidance. | Odom & McEvoy (1990); Strain and Smith (in press) |
| • The curriculum within the mainstreamed program influences the extent to which children with special needs benefit from that experience; mainstreaming alone is not enough. | Fewell & Oelwein (1990); McLean & Hanline (1990); Strain (1990) |

special needs is another example of inappropriate practice. On the contrary, a clear focus on specific goals does not logically or automatically result in using inappropriate methods.

To guard against inappropriate practices, the assessment activities with children who have special needs must be more comprehensive, focused, and precise than is usual with typically developing children. The assessment activities must describe (a) children's development in detail, (b) their needs in various environments, (c) the influences of the social and physical environment on their behavior, (d) their preferences, (e) their usual styles of responding and patterns of engagement, and (f) factors that motivate their learning. Further, knowledge of child development must be applied to both the assessment practices and the design of the curriculum. Similarly, curricular strategies are used more purposefully than is common with typically

developing children. Children's interactions, routines, and activities must be structured more intentionally, and effective instructional strategies should be embedded within them. This may involve use of more direct teacher assistance, peers to influence their behavior, and systematic reinforcement. Clear evidence exists that some children with special needs will not learn or will learn slowly unless teacher assistance and systematic reinforcement are used carefully (Cooper et al., 1987; Wolery et al., 1992). Further, the monitoring of children's progress may require more focus, more systematic data collection. In addition, decisions concerning necessary changes in the curriculum must be based on data collected on child performance (Bailey & Wolery, 1992). These extensions of the NAEYC guidelines are seen as defensible, appropriate, and necessary to ensure that children's "special" needs are addressed and that they benefit from enrollment in the program.

*To guard against inappropriate practices, the assessment activities with children who have special needs must be more comprehensive, focused, and precise than is usual with typically developing children.*

**Second,** to adequately meet the needs of children with developmental delays and disabilities, a more family-centered approach is needed. Multiple sources exist for implementing this recommendation (Fewell & Vadasy, 1986; Bailey & Simeonsson, 1988; Dunst et al., 1988, Seligman & Darling, 1989). Two areas require particular attention. Personnel need competencies related to identifying and addressing the needs, goals, and priorities of families. These competencies must address the needs of the child as well as those of the family. In addition, families must participate in making decisions about how early education is conducted and about the goals it attempts to achieve. Families must be active members on the team that makes decisions and carries out the intervention plan for the child.

**Third,** the involvement of professionals from many disciplines is necessary for assessing, planning, implementing, and adjusting the educational plans of young children with special needs. This shifts the application of the NAEYC and NAECS/SDE guidelines from primarily an educational service to an educational service embedded within an interdisciplinary context. This extension requires a new set of skills for early educators including—but not limited to—shared decision making, communicating with other professionals, learning the languages of other disciplines, and integrating therapy goals into the curriculum. Fortunately models and strategies exist for making this expansion a reality. The primary barriers, however, are the lack of fiscal resources to secure the services of needed professionals and the shortage of personnel in some of the disciplines, particularly personnel who have expertise in working with families and young children.

**Fourth,** transition practices need to be expanded and implemented earlier and with more purposeful planning. This expansion must include consideration of family concerns and goals for the transition. Models and procedures exist for implementing this change, however, and the expansion does not constitute a drastic departure from currently recommended practices.

**Fifth,** to understand the relevance of the NAEYC and NAECS/SDE guidelines to the early education of young children with special needs, considerable information is needed, which, in our view, is best obtained through careful and systematic research. This research probably should be conducted in programs using the guidelines and likely requires collaboration between early educators who have training in regular and special education. Without such research, the relevance of the guidelines will continue to be ill-understood and open to debate.

# Summary

In this chapter we stated that children with special needs are a tremendously diverse group who share needs with all other children but also have unique needs. We listed goals for their early education and described practices that are seen as necessary for addressing their needs. We concluded that young children with special needs should receive their early education in programs adhering to the NAEYC and NAECS/SDE guidelines for developmentally appropriate practice and appropriate curriculum; however, we also concluded that those programs must be adjusted to provide the best possible education to children with special needs. It is important to note that this chapter does not provide sufficient information to implement services for young children with special needs; the sources included in the reference list are the starting place for getting that information. Finally, we concluded that additional research is needed to understand the relevance of the NAEYC and NAECS/SDE guidelines to young children with special needs.

## References

Bailey, D.B. (1988). Assessing family stress and needs. In D.B. Bailey & R.J. Simeonsson (Eds.), *Family assessment in early intervention* (pp. 95–118). Columbus, OH: Merrill.

Bailey, D.B. (1989). Assessing environments. In D.B. Bailey & M. Wolery (Eds.), *Assessing infants and preschoolers with handicaps* (pp. 97–118). Columbus, OH: Merrill.

Bailey, D.B., & McWilliam, R.A. (1990). Normalizing early intervention. *Topics in Early Childhood Special Education, 10*(2), 33–47.

Bailey, D.B., & Simeonsson, R.J. (Eds.). (1988). *Family assessment in early intervention.* Columbus, OH: Merrill.

Bailey, D.B., & Wolery, M. (1992). *Teaching infants and preschoolers with disabilities* (2nd ed.). Columbus, OH: Merrill.

Bailey, D.B., McWilliam, R.A., Winton, P.J., & Simeonsson, R.J. (1991). *Implementing family-centered services in early intervention: A team-based model for change.* Chapel Hill, NC: Frank Porter Graham Child Development Center.

Blackhurst, A.E., & Berdine, W.H. (in press). *An introduction to special education.* Glenview, IL: HarperCollins.

Bredekamp, S. (1987). *Developmentally appropriate practice in early childhood programs serving children from birth through age 8* (rev. ed.). Washington, DC: NAEYC.

Bricker, D. (1978). A rationale for the integration of handicapped and non-handicapped children. In M.J. Guralnick (Ed.), *Early intervention and integration of handicapped and non-handicapped children* (pp. 3–26). Baltimore: University Park Press.

Bricker, D. (1989). *Early intervention for at-risk and handicapped infants, toddlers, and preschool children.* Palo Alto, CA: VORT.

Bricker, D., & Veltman, M. (1990). Early intervention programs: Child focused approaches. In S.J. Meisels & J.P. Shonkoff (Eds.), *Handbook of early childhood intervention* (pp. 373–399). New York: Cambridge University Press.

Buysse, V., & Bailey, D.B. (1991). *Mainstreamed versus specialized settings: Behavioral and developmental effects on young children with handicaps.* Manuscript submitted for publication.

Campbell, P.H. (1987). Programming for students with dysfunction in posture and movement. In M.E. Snell (Ed.), *Systematic instruction of persons with severe handicaps* (pp. 188–211). Columbus, OH: Merrill.

Carta, J.J., Atwater, J.B., Schwartz, J.S., & Miller, P.A. (1990). Application of ecobehavioral analysis to the study of transitions across early education. *Education and Treatment of Children, 13*(4), 298–311.

Carta, J.J., Schwartz, I.S., Atwater, J.B., & McConnell, S.R. (1991). Developmentally appropriate practice: Appraising its usefulness for young children with disabilities. *Topics in Early Childhood Special Education, 11*(1), 1–20.

Cooper, J.O., Heron, T.E., & Heward, W.L. (1987). *Applied behavior analysis.* Columbus, OH: Merrill.

Donnellan, A.M., Mirenda, P.L., Mesaros, R.A., & Fassbender, L.L. (1984). Analyzing with communicative functions of aberrant behavior. *Journal of the Association for Persons with Severe Handicaps, 9*(3), 201–212.

Dunst, C.J. (1985). Rethinking early intervention. *Analysis and Intervention in Developmental Disabilities, 5*, 165–201.

Dunst, C.J., Trivette, C., & Deal, A. (1988). *Enabling and empowering families: Principles and guidelines for practice.* Cambridge, MA: Brookline Books.

Dunst, C.J., Trivette, C., Hamby, D.M., & Pollock B. (1990). Family systems correlates of the behavior of young children with handicaps. *Journal of Early Intervention, 14*, 204–218.

Dunst, C.J., Lesko, J.J., Holbert, K.A., Wilson, L.L., Sharpe, K.L., & Liles, R.F. (1987). A systematic approach to infant intervention. *Topics in Early Childhood Special Education, 7*(2), 19–37.

Fewell, R.R., & Oelwein, P.L. (1990). The relationship between time in integrated environments and developmental gain in young children with special needs. *Topics in Early Childhood Special Education, 10*(2), 104–116.

Fewell, R.R., & Vadasy, P.F. (1986). *Families of handicapped children: Needs and supports across the life span.* Austin, TX: PRO-ED.

Fowler, S.A., Chandler, L.K., Johnson, T.E., & Stella, M.E. (1988). Individualizing family involvement in school transitions: Gathering information and choosing the next program. *Journal of the Division for Early Childhood, 12*(2), 208–216.

Garwood, S.G., & Sheehan, R. (1989). *Designing a comprehensive early intervention system: The challenge of PL 99–457.* Austin, TX: PRO-ED.

Goldstein, H., & Wickstrom, S. (1986). Peer intervention effects on communicative interaction among handicapped and non-handicapped preschoolers. *Journal of Applied Behavior Analysis, 19*, 209–214.

Guralnick, M.J. (1990). Major accomplishments and future directions in early childhood mainstreaming. *Topics in Early Childhood Special Education, 10*(2), 1–17.

Guralnick, M.J., & Groom, J.M. (1987). The peer relations of mildly delayed and non-handicapped preschool children in mainstreamed play groups. *Child Development, 58*, 1556–1572.

Halle, J.W., Alpert, C.L., & Anderson, S.R. (1984). Natural environment language assessment and intervention with severely impaired preschoolers. *Topics in Early Childhood Special Education, 4*(2), 36–56.

Hanson, M.J., & Hanline, M.F. (1990). Parenting a child with a disability: A longitudinal study of parental stress and adaption. *Journal of Early Intervention, 14*, 234–248.

Hanson, M.J., & Lynch, E.W. (1989). *Early intervention: Implementing child and family services for infants and toddlers who are at risk or disabled.* Austin, TX: PRO-ED.

Harbin, G.L., Gallagher, J.J., & Terry, D.V. (1991). Defining the eligible population: Policy issues and challenges. *Journal of Early Intervention, 15*, 13–20.

Haring, N.G., & McCormick, L. (Eds.). (1990). *Exceptional children and youth* (5th ed.). Columbus, OH: Merrill.

Haring, N.G., Liberty, K.A., & White, O.R. (1990). Rules for data-based strategy decisions in instructional programs. In W. Sailor, B.Wilcox, & L. Brown (Eds.), *Methods of instruction for severely handicapped students* (pp. 159–192). Baltimore: Paul H. Brookes.

Horner, R.H., Dunlap, G., & Koegel, R.L. (Eds.). (1988). *Generalization and maintenance: Life-style changes in applied settings.* Baltimore: Paul H. Brookes.

Hoyson, M., Jamieson, B., & Strain, P.S. (1984). Individualized group instruction of normally developing and autistic-like children: The LEAP curriculum model. *Journal of the Division for Early Childhood, 8*, 157–172.

Jennings, K.D., Connors, R.E., Stegman, C.E., Sankaranarayan, P., & Mendelsohn, S. (1985). Mastery motivation in youth preschoolers: Effect of a physical handicap and implication for educational programming. *Journal of the Division for Early Childhood, 9*, 162–169.

Kohler, F.W., & Strain, P.S. (1990). Peer-assisted interventions: Early promises, notable achievements, and future aspirations. *Clinical Psychology Review, 10*(4), 441–452.

Liberty, K. (1988). Decision rules and procedures for generalization. In N.G. Haring (Ed.), *Generalization for students with severe handicaps: Strategies and solutions* (pp. 177–204). Seattle: University of Washington Press.

McCollum, J.A., & Hughes, M. (1988). Staffing patterns and team models in infancy programs. In J.B. Jordan, J.J. Gallagher, P.L. Hutinger, & M.B. Karnes (Eds.), *Early childhood special education: Birth to three* (pp. 129–146). Reston, VA: Council for Exceptional Children.

McDonnell, A., & Hardman, M. (1988). A synthesis of "best practice" guidelines in early childhood services. *Journal of the Division for Early Childhood, 12*, 328–341.

McLean, M., & Hanline, M.F. (1990). Providing early intervention services in integrated environments: Challenges and opportunities for the future. *Topics in Early Childhood Special Education, 10*(2), 62–77.

Meisels, S.J., & Shonkoff, J.P. (Eds.). (1990). *Handbook of early childhood intervention.* New York: Cambridge University Press.

National Association for the Education of Young Children & National Association of Early Childhood Specialists in State Departments of Education. (1991). Guidelines for appropriate curriculum content and assessment in programs serving children ages 3 through 8. *Young Children, 46*(3), 21–38.

Nonnan, M.J., & Kilgo, J.L. (1987). Transition services for early age individuals with severe mental retardation. In R.N. Ianacone & R.A. Stodden (Eds.), *Transition issues and directions* (pp. 25–37). Reston, VA: Council for Exceptional Children.

Odom, S.L., & Karnes, M.B. (1988). *Early intervention for infants and children with handicaps: An empirical base.* Baltimore: Paul H. Brookes.

Odom, S.L., & McEvoy, M.A. (1988). Integration of young children with handicaps and normally developing children. In S.L. Odom & M.B. Karnes (Eds.), *Early intervention for infants and children with handicaps: An empirical base* (pp. 241–267). Baltimore: Paul H. Brookes.

Odom, S.L., & McEvoy, M.A. (1990). Mainstreaming at the preschool level: Potential barriers and tasks for the field. *Topics in Early Childhood Special Education, 10*(1), 48–61.

Odom, S.L., & Strain, P.S. (1984). Classroom-based social skills instruction for severely handicapped preschool children. *Topics in Early Childhood Special Education, 4*(3), 97–116.

Peck, C.A., & Cooke, T.P. (1983). Benefits of mainstreaming at the early childhood level: How much can we expect? *Analysis and Intervention in Developmental Disabilities, 3*(1), 1–22.

Peck, C.A., Killen, C.C., & Baumgart, D. (1989). Increasing implementation of special education instruction on mainstreamed preschools: Direct and generalized effects of non-directive consultation. *Journal of Applied Behavior Analysis, 22*, 197–210.

Peck, C.P., Odom, S.L., & Bricker, D. (Eds.). (in press). *Integrating young children with disabilities into community programs: From research to implementation.* Baltimore: Paul H. Brookes.

Safford, P.L. (1989). *Integrated teaching in early childhood: Starting in the mainstream.* White Plains, NY: Longman.

Salisbury, C.L., & Vincent, L.J. (1990). Criterion of the next environment and best practices: Mainstreaming and integration 10 years later. *Topics in Early Childhood Special Education, 10*(2), 78–89.

Seligman, M., & Darling, R.B. (1989). *Ordinary families, special children: A systems approach to childhood disability.* New York: Guilford.

Silber, S. (1989). Family influences on early development. *Topics in Early Childhood Special Education, 8*(4), 1–23.

Smith, B.J. (1988). Early intervention public policy: Past, present, and future. In J.B. Jordan, J.J. Gallangher, P.L. Huntinger, & M.B. Karnes (Eds.), *Early childhood special education: Birth to three* (pp. 213–228). Reston, VA: Council for Exceptional Children.

Smith, P.D. (1989). Assessing motor skills. In D.B. Bailey & M. Wolery (Eds.), *Assessing infants and preschoolers with handicaps* (pp. 301–338). Columbus, OH: Merrill.

Strain, P.S. (1981). *The utilization of classroom peers as behavior change agents.* New York: Plenum.

Strain, P.S. (1988). The evaluation of early intervention research: Separating the winners from the losers. *Journal of the Division for Early Childhood, 12*, 182–190.

Strain, P.S. (1990). LRE for preschool children with handicaps: What we know, what we should be doing. *Journal of Early Intervention, 14*, 291–296.

Strain, P.S., & Smith, B. (in press). Global education, social, and policy forces affecting preschool mainstreaming. In C.A. Peck, S.L. Odom, & D. Bricker (Eds.), *Integrating young children with disabilities into community programs: From research to implementation.* Baltimore: Paul H. Brookes.

Templeman, T.P., Fredericks, H.D., & Udell, T. (1989). Integration of children with moderate and severe handicaps into a day care center. *Journal of Early Intervention, 13*, 315–328.

Turnbull, H.R. (1990). *Free appropriate public education: The law and children with disabilities* (3rd. ed) Denver: Love.

Wachs, T.D. (1988). Environmental assessment of developmentally disabled infants and preschoolers. In T.D. Wachs & R. Sheehan (Eds.), *Assessment of young developmentally disabled children* (pp. 321–346). New York: Plenum.

Warren, S.F., & Kaiser, A.P. (1986). Generalization of treatment effects by young language-delayed children: A longitudinal analysis. *Journal of Speech and Hearing Disorders, 51*, 239–251.

Warren, S.F., & Kaiser, A.P. (1988). Research in early language intervention. In S.L. Odom & M.B. Karnes (Eds.), *Early intervention for infants and children with handicaps: An empirical base* (89–108). Baltimore: Paul H. Brookes.

Weiner, E.A., & Weiner, B.J. (1974). Differentiation of retarded and normal children through toy-play analysis. *Multivariate Behavioral Research, 9*, 245–257.

Winton, P.J. (1988). The family-focused interview: An assessment measure and goal-setting mechanism. In D.B. Bailey & R.J. Simeonsson (Eds.), *Family assessment in early intervention* (pp. 185–205). Columbus, OH: Merrill.

Winton, P.J., & Bailey, D.B. (1990). Early intervention training related to family interviewing. *Topics in Early Childhood Special Education, 10*(1), 50–62.

Wolery, M., & Fleming, L.A. (in press). Implementing individualized curriculum in integrated settings. In C.A. Peck, S.L. Odom, & D. Bricker (Eds.), *Integrating young children with disabilities in community programs: From research to implementation.* Baltimore: Paul H. Brookes.

Wolery, M., Ault, M.J., & Doyle, P.M. (1992). *Teaching students with moderate and severe handicaps: Use of response prompting procedures.* White Plains, NY: Longman.

Wolery, M., Bailey, D.B., & Sugai, G.M. (1988). *Effective teaching: Principles and procedures of applied behavior analysis with exceptional students.* Boston: Allyn & Bacon.

Wolery, M., Fleming, L.A., & Venn, M. (1990). *Year 01 report: Curriculum modification component of the Research Institute on Preschool Mainstreaming.* (Grant No. H024K90005). Allegheny-Singer Research Institute, Pittsburgh, PA.

# Appendix A

## *Publications related to young children with special needs*

### General issues in special education

Blackhurst, A.E., & Berdine, W.H. (in press). *An introduction to special education.* Glenview, IL: HarperCollins.

Haring, N.G., & McCormick, L. (Eds.). (1990). *Exceptional children and youth* (5th ed.). Columbus, OH: Merrill.

Turnbull, H.R. (1990). *Free appropriate public education: The law and children with disabilities* (3rd ed.). Denver: Love.

### General issues in early education with young children who have special needs

Fallen, N., & Umansky, W. (1985). *Young children with special needs* (2nd ed.). Columbus, OH: Merrill.

Gallagher, J.J., Trohonis, P.L., & Clifford, R.M. (1989). *Policy implementation and P.L. 99–457: Planning for young children with special needs.* Baltimore: Paul H. Brookes.

Garwood, S.G., & Sheehan, R. (1989). *Designing a comprehensive early intervention system: The challenge of P.L. 99–457.* Austin, TX: PRO-ED.

Jordan, J.B., Gallagher, J.J., Huntinger, P.L., & Karnes, M.B. (Eds.). (1988). *Early childhood special education: Birth to three.* Reston, VA: Council for Exceptional Children.

Lynch, E.W., & Hanson, M.J. (1992). *Developing cross-cultural competence: A guide for working with young children and their families.* Baltimore: Paul H. Brookes.

Meisels, S.J., & Shonkoff, J.P. (Eds.). (1990). *Handbook of early childhood intervention.* New York: Cambridge University Press.

Neisworth, J.T., & Bagnato, S.J. (1987). *The young exceptional child: Early development and education.* New York: Macmillan.

Odom, S.L., & Karnes, M.B. (1988). *Early intervention for infants and children with handicaps: An empirical base.* Baltimore: Paul H. Brookes.

### Assessment of young children with special needs

Bagnato, S.J., Neisworth, J.T., & Munson, S.M. (1989). *Linking development assessment and early intervention: Curriculum-based prescriptions* (2nd ed.). Rockville, MD: Aspen.

Bailey, D.B., & Wolery, M. (Eds.). (1989). *Assessing infants and preschoolers with disabilities* (2nd ed.). Columbus, OH: Charles Merrill.

Benner, S.M. (1992). *Assessing young children with special needs: An ecological perspective.* White Plains, NY: Longman.

Gibbs, E.D., & Teti, D.M. (1990). *Interdisciplinary assessment of infants: A guide for early intervention professionals.* Baltimore: Paul H. Brookes.

Lindner, T. (1990). *Transdisciplinary play-based assessment: A functional approach to working with young children.* Baltimore: Paul H. Brookes.

Simeonsson, R.J. (1986). *Psychological and developmental assessment of special children.* Boston: Allyn & Bacon.

Wachs, T.D., & Sheehan, R. (Eds.). (1988). *Assessment of young developmentally disabled children.* New York: Plenum.

### Teaching young children with special needs

Bailey, D.B., & Wolery, M. (1984). *Teaching infants and preschoolers with handicaps.* Columbus, OH: Merrill.

Bailey, D.B., & Wolery, M. (1992). *Teaching infants and preschoolers with disabilities* (2nd ed.). Columbus, OH: Merrill.

Bricker, D. (1989). *Early intervention for at-risk and handicapped infants, toddlers, and preschool children.* Palo Alto, CA: VORT.

Hanson, M.J., & Lynch, E.W. (1989). *Early intervention: Implementing child and family services for infants and toddlers who are at risk or disabled.* Austin, TX: PRO-ED.

Horner, R.H., Dunlap, G., & Koegel, R.L. (Eds.). (1988). *Generalization and maintenance: Life-style changes in applied settings.* Baltimore: Paul H. Brookes.

Musselwhite, C.R. (1986). *Adaptive play for special needs children: Strategies to enhance communication and learning.* Boston: College Hill Press.

Odom, S.L., McConnel, S.R., & McEvoy, M.A. (1992). *Social competence of young children with disabilities: Issues and strategies for intervention.* Baltimore: Paul H. Brookes.

Peck, C.P., Odom, S.L., & Bricker, D. (Eds.). (in press). *Integrating young children with disabilities into community programs: From research to implementation.* Baltimore: Paul H. Brookes.

Pennsylvania Department of Education, Bureau of Special Education. (1991). *Early intervention guidelines.* Harrisburg, PA: Pennsylvania Department of Education.

Safford, P.L. (1989). *Integrated teaching in early childhood: Starting in the mainstream.* White Plains, NY: Longman.

Strain, P.S. (Ed). (1981). *The utilization of classroom peers as behavior change agents.* New York: Plenum.

Thurman, S.K., & Wilderstrom, A.H. (1990). *Infants and young children with special needs: A developmental and ecological approach* (2nd ed.). Baltimore: Paul H. Brookes.

Warren, S.F., & Rogers-Warren, A. (Eds.). (1985). *Teaching functional language: Language intervention series.* Austin, TX: PRO-ED.

Wolery, M., Ault, M.J., & Doyle, P.M. (1992). *Teaching students with moderate and severe disabilities: Use of response prompting strategies.* White Plains, NY: Longman.

Wolery, M., Bailey, D.B., & Sugai, G.M. (1988). *Effective teaching: Principles and procedures of applied behavior analysis with exceptional students.* Boston: Allyn & Bacon.

### Family issues with young children who have special needs

Bailey, D.B., & Simeonsson, R.J. (Eds.). (1988). *Family assessment in early intervention.* Columbus, OH: Merrill.

Dunst, C.J., Trivette, C., & Deal, A. (1988). *Enabling and empowering families: Principles, guidelines and practices.* Cambridge, MA: Brookline Books.

Fewell, R.R., & Vadasy, P.F. (1986). *Families of handicapped children: Needs and supports across the life span.* Austin, TX: PRO-ED.

Gallagher, J.J., & Vietze, P.M. (1986). *Families of handicapped persons: Research, programs, and policy issues.* Baltimore: Paul H. Brookes.

Seligman, M., & Darling, R.B. (1989). *Ordinary families, special children: A systems approach to childhood disability.* New York: Guilford.

### Journals that address young children with special needs

*Infants and Young Children.* Published quarterly by Aspen Publishers, 7201 McKinney Circle, Frederick, MD 21701.

*Journal of Early Intervention* (Formerly *Journal of the Division for Early Childhood*). Published quarterly by the Division for Early Childhood of the Council for Exceptional Children, 1920 Association Drive, Reston, VA 22091.

*Topics in Early Childhood Special Education.* Published quarterly by PRO-ED, 8700 Shoal Creek Boulevard, Austin, TX 78758.

# Appendix B

## Resources related to young children with special needs

Clearinghouse on Handicapped and Gifted Children
The Council for Exceptional Children
1920 Association Drive
Reston, VA 22091–1589

The Division for Early Childhood (DEC)
The Council for Exceptional Children
1920 Association Drive
Reston, VA 22091
Phone: (703) 620–3660

National Center for Clinical Infant Programs (NCCIP)
2000 14th Street, North
Suite 380
Arlington, VA 22201–2500
(703) 528–4300

National Early Childhood Technical Assistance System (NEC–TAS)
Suite 500
NCBC Plaza
Chapel Hill, NC 27514
(919) 962–2001

National Head Start Resource Access Program
Administration for Children, Youth, and Families
Office of Human Development Services
P.O. Box 1182
Washington, DC 20013

U.S. Office of Special Education Programs
Early Childhood Branch
330 C Street, S.W.
Washington, DC 20202
(202) 205–9084

# SECTION III

# Reaching Potentials of All Children

*The Curriculum and Assessment Guidelines strongly emphasize the need for cultural relevance and respect for cultural and linguistic diversity. In this section the issue of culturally appropriate curriculum and practice is explored in depth. Louise Derman-Sparks draws on the curriculum guidelines to expand on her previous work on antibias, multicultural curriculum. Barbara Bowman reflects on her experience attempting to implement developmentally appropriate practice in programs for minority children and expands the concept to include attention to culturally appropriate practices. Liz Wolfe and Teresa Rosegrant address the timely issue of providing appropriate programs for bilingual and multilingual groups of children.*

# Reaching Potentials Through Antibias, Multicultural Curriculum

*Louise Derman-Sparks*

Young children use the same cognitive organizing principles for grappling with the realities of human diversity as they do for understanding other aspects of their physical and social world. Consider, for example, the following conversation at my family's 1991 Passover Seder (the seder honors the ancient Jewish Exodus from slavery in Egypt).

> My niece announced, "I'm half Jewish." (One parent is Jewish.) "Uh huh," I replied. "The Jewish people went through the water and they didn't get wet. They got to the other side. The people who weren't Jewish got drowned," she continued. "That is what the Passover story tells us, that the Egyptian soldiers drowned," I confirmed, but her expression remained quizzical. So I decided to ask her, "What do you think happened to the people who were half Jewish?" "They got to the other side too," she replied, paused, and then concluded, "but they got a little bit wet."

Afterward, a cousin wondered, "How did you ever think of that question?" (The Passover story does not mention people being "half Jewish.") I don't know if my question was "right" in any absolute sense, but trying to follow my niece's line of thinking, I sensed that the issue was important to her. She seemed emotionally satisfied with her solution; moreover, it was a cognitively clever one. She got to the other side safely, and she acknowledged her identity as she understands it at 4-1/2 years old.

This chapter is about the core issues involved in creating developmentally appropriate curriculum that can nurture children's healthy, positive self-identity and their dispositions and skills to interact comfort-

ably and respectfully with the wide range of human diversity. In this chapter four important issues are addressed. First, a critique is offered of current curriculum approaches to diversity in light of the NAEYC and NAECS/SDE Curriculum and Assessment Guidelines (1991; pp. 9–27, this volume). Second, goals are identified for antibias, multicultural curriculum and developmental expectations for children at various ages. Third, developmentally and contextually appropriate decision making in different settings is analyzed. Finally, suggestions are provided of ways to integrate antibias, multicultural activities into the more general early childhood curriculum. The ideas in this chapter are exploratory. As educators gain more experience in implementing an antibias, multicultural approach, it will become possible to extend, deepen, and refine our understanding of developmentally and contextually appropriate teaching and learning about diversity.

## Applying the curriculum guidelines to current practices

The most common approaches to addressing diversity in early childhood programs have been curriculum grounded in three different philosophical perspectives: European American culture–centered, difference denial (the colorblind approach), and multicultural education. The first approach assumes that one culture is superior to others; the second approach denies the importance of cultural differences; and the third approach frequently deteriorates into "tourist" curriculum that visits non–European American cultures from time to time. None of these approaches make cultural or other aspects of human diversity a central component of education. In addition, all of these approaches reflect and reinforce societal racist messages. In numerous ways they also do not meet many of the guidelines for appropriate curriculum (NAEYC & NAECS/SDE, 1991) delineated in this book (pp. 19–22).

In a European American culture–centered classroom (a perspective that historically dominated early childhood education and still continues to be practiced in many programs), all aspects of the curriculum, including materials, aesthetic environment, space organization, teaching style, and activity content, are organized solely from a European American perspective. This approach does not meet at least half of the curriculum guidelines. The European American culture–centered approach is not based on a theoretical base consistent with prevailing research on how children learn about diversity (Guideline 1); cannot adequately achieve social, emotional, and cognitive goals for all children (Guideline 2); does not encourage development of positive feelings and dispositions toward diversity (Guideline 3); is not meaningful for an increasingly growing proportion of American children (Guideline 4); neither reflects the needs and interests of individual children nor incorporates a wide variety of learning experiences, materials, and instructional strategies (Guideline 6); is not sensitive to and respectful of cultural and linguistic diversity and does not promote positive relationships with families who do not fit the ideological norm of mainstream European American culture (Guideline 7); and does not build on and elaborate all children's current knowledge and abilities (Guideline 8). Information and images about groups that are not part of mainstream European American culture are neither accurate nor credible according to either the recognized standards of several disciplines, such as anthropology and history, or reality (Guideline 11); do not promote feelings of safety, security, and belonging for all children (Guideline 18); do not provide experiences that promote feelings of success and competence for all children (Guideline 19); and are not flexible in relation to children's cultural and individual needs (Guideline 20).

The difference-denial, or "colorblind" approach—a progressive attempt to counter the beliefs of bigotry—argues, rightfully so, that we are all human beings sharing a common biological heritage and therefore are all fundamentally the same "under the skin." By insisting on recognizing only the similarities among different people, however, curriculum cannot acknowledge the realities of children's various cultural heri-

*TOURIST CURRICULUM TOO OFTEN DOES NOT HAVE INTELLECTUAL INTEGRITY. TO MAKE ACTIVITIES ABOUT CULTURE (A COMPLEX SUBJECT) MANAGEABLE FOR YOUNG CHILDREN, DISCRETE, SMALL "PIECES OF CULTURE" ARE DISCONNECTED FROM THEIR OVERALL CONTEXT. IN THE PROCESS, ACTIVITIES MISREPRESENT, TRIVIALIZE, AND STEREOTYPE THE CULTURES THEY ARE DESIGNED TO "TEACH" ABOUT.*

tages, history, and experiences with racism, the impact of dominant-culture gender norms on young children's development, or the adaptation needs of children with disabilities. In practice, a colorblind or difference-denial approach typically results in a European American–centered curriculum because conscious attention is not paid to either group cultural variations or individual differences resulting from cultural and other forms of diversity. Consequently, this approach violates the same guidelines as does the European American–centered curriculum, even though the intent behind the colorblind perspective is to create a nurturing environment for all children.

The philosophy of multicultural curriculum was an important step forward in its recognition that children grow up in diverse cultural contexts that must be brought into and respected in the classroom and in its intention to teach children to appreciate different ways of living. Multicultural curriculum often becomes "tourist" curriculum, however, where cultures other than mainstream European American are brought into the classroom from time to time—as additions to the "regular" curriculum. Examples of such curriculum may be a special bulletin board, an occasional holiday celebration or parent visit, or even a week's unit, while the materials, content, and methods of the daily program remain essentially European American culture–centered. "Tourist" multicultural curriculum is inappropriate in several ways. First, activities are frequently not consistent with research on how children learn about their identity or construct attitudes toward people different from themselves (Guideline 1). Consider, for example, typical activities used to teach children about "Indian" culture: making "fry bread," playing in a tepee, reading a folktale with illustrations of life in the past, and dressing up at Thanksgiving as Indians with feather "headdresses." These activities reinforce the misconception held by preschool children all over the United States that "all Indians are the same" (for example, they all live in tepees, wear feathers, eat the same foods, and lived in the past). Moreover, none of these activities directly challenges the even more insidious belief held by preschoolers that "Indians go around shooting people with arrows."

Second, tourist curriculum too often does not have intellectual integrity (Guideline 11). To make activities about culture (a complex subject) manageable for young children, discrete, small "pieces of culture" are disconnected from their overall context. In the process, activities misrepresent, trivialize, and stereotype the cultures they are designed to "teach" about. For example, having preschoolers do sand painting to learn about "Indian" culture, an activity suggested in several curriculum guides, makes all three mistakes. Sand painting is part of a serious healing ritual practiced by learned adults, not a "fun," sensory art activity; moreover, it is not practiced by all Native American peoples. Disconnecting pieces of culture from their overall context results in curriculum that does not respect and support diversity within a culture (Guideline 7) or the needs and interests of individual children within a group (Guideline 6). An example is adding a sombrero to the dramatic play area as the way to teach about Mexican American culture, even though sombreros are not part of the daily life of most urban Mexican Americans today except, perhaps, for people who sing in a mariachi band or belong to a traditional dance group.

Third, tourist curriculum tends to focus on the process of the activity while ignoring the appropriateness of the content—one of "the three most common fallacies that mark curriculum debate" (p. 12, this volume). Consequently, numerous activities may appear "developmentally appropriate" because they are hands-on and use materials that children like, while the content is inappropriate. The activity of sand painting, mentioned above, is a case in point. While the material engages children actively (Guideline 13) and is enjoyable (Guideline 19), the content does not meet other key guidelines (6, 7, and 11).

Focusing on the process of teaching without sufficient attention to the appropriateness of content also frequently leads to activities that do not set realistic goals related to a designated age group (Guideline 5). One common example—having children make simplified, trivialized versions of an ethnic group's crafts—contradicts the emphasis on young children's engaging with art materials experimentally and with freedom to express their own ideas in whatever symbolic forms they choose. This activity also violates the guideline of intellectual integrity (11). Using folktales to teach young children about various ethnic groups is another example. These wonderful stories enrich imagination and emotional development and therefore have a place in early childhood education, but the stories can

be confusing as tools for fostering preschoolers' and kindergartners' awareness of diversity because folktales that are set in the far past of a culture are confused with the lives of people in the present. By the time children are 7 or 8 years old, folktales can be studied for the rules of behavior and the spiritual beliefs of the people who created them.

Focusing only on the process of an activity also runs the danger of ignoring the contextual appropriateness of content *for a specific group of children,* thereby violating many guidelines (2, 4, 5, 6, 7, 8, 9, 12, 15). The children in preschool X, for example, live in a city that is predominately European American, with a small Chinese American population. The teacher's multicultural guidebook lists the "Dragon Festival" as a Chinese cultural activity, so the children make a dragon and have a parade, like Chinese people do. The children go along; many even enjoy it. This activity in no way fosters their ability to caringly and fairly interact with people who are Chinese American, however. If the preschoolers have any idea at all about "Chinese people," it is probably influenced by prevailing stereotypes (such as "They have slanty eyes"). Preschoolers may have some of their own ideas about dragons, which probably have little relationship to the meaning of the dragon in the festival, which they are not yet cognitively ready to understand, in any case. In this context, the activity is developmentally inappropriate because it is *contextually inappropriate.* On the other hand, if the children in preschool X live in a city where there are many Chinese Americans, if some of the children are Chinese Americans, and if their community actively celebrates the Dragon Festival, then it becomes contextually appropriate to integrate Dragon Festival activities into a developmentally appropriate study of how each of the children's families live and of the community surrounding the preschool.

Finally, tourist curriculum neither integrates content about diversity across other subject areas (Guideline 10) nor provides conceptual frameworks for children so that their mental constructions based on prior knowledge and experience become more complex over time (Guideline 9).

By the 1980s some conceptualizations of multicultural education marked a significant improvement over "tourist" curriculum. Banks (1981); Derman-Sparks (1989); Kendall (1983); Ramsey (1987); and Williams, DeGaetano, Sutherland, and Harrington (1985) argue for the integration of a multicultural perspective into all aspects of the environment and for curriculum that uses research about the development of identity and attitudes and incorporates basic principles of sound early childhood education. Banks (1988) and Derman-Sparks and the A.B.C. Task Force (1989) also assert the need for activities that foster

*SOME OF THE ACTIVITIES BEING IMPLEMENTED IN THE NAME OF ANTIBIAS CURRICULUM DO NOT ALWAYS RESPECT KEY GUIDELINES. CONTENT MUST BE ADAPTED TO SPECIFIC GROUPS OF CHILDREN, TAKING INTO ACCOUNT CULTURAL AND INDIVIDUAL VARIATIONS, IN ORDER TO REFLECT AND BE GENERATED BY THE NEEDS AND INTERESTS OF THE CHILDREN, RESPECT AND SUPPORT DIVERSITY, AND BE REALISTIC FOR MOST CHILDREN IN THE AGE RANGE FOR WHICH IT IS DESIGNED.*

children's awareness of social justice, beginning in preschool and continuing throughout schooling. The curricula that these writers propose have the potential for meeting the majority of the Curriculum and Assessment Guidelines identified in this book; however, teachers must be vigilant that their practice does, in fact, carry out this potential. For example, based on my experiences, some of the activities being implemented in the name of antibias curriculum do not always respect key guidelines. Content *must be adapted to specific groups of children, taking into account cultural and individual variations,* in order to reflect and be generated by the needs and interests of the children (Guideline 6), respect and support diversity (Guideline 7), and be realistic for most children in the age range for which it is designed (Guideline 5).

## Goals and developmental expectations for learning about diversity/antibias content

Before identifying curriculum goals and appropriate developmental expectations, it is important to understand how children develop a sense of their own identity and their attitudes toward diversity. Young children do not arrive in early childhood programs as "blank slates" on the subject of diversity; rather, they bring along a personalized data bank that includes observations of various aspects of people's characteristics, experiences with comfortable adults' responses to their questions about human differences, exposure to socially prevailing biases and learned positive or negative responses to various aspects of people's identities, and self-constructed "theories" about what causes diversity. In general, a body of research about children's development of identity and attitudes reveals several key points.

By 2 years of age, children have already embarked on their lifelong task of figuring out "who I am." They are aware of and curious about differences and simi-

larities among people, ask questions, organize the "data" they gather, and construct "theories" about diversity congruent with their general cognitive stages of development as well as their life experiences. Adult verbal and nonverbal responses to children's questions and feelings about various aspects of people's identities teach either comfort or discomfort with human differences. Not only overtly bigoted or prejudiced responses lead to children's discomfort with diversity. Adult reactions that reflect the common misconception that by simply noticing and asking about human differences, children are either demonstrating or learning prejudice also teach discomfort. Statements such as "It's not polite to ask" or "I'll tell you later" or "It doesn't matter" do not give children the help they need to form positive ideas about themselves or positive dispositions toward others and their diversity.

Between 2-1/2 and 3-1/2 years of age, children also become aware of and begin absorbing socially prevailing negative stereotypes, feelings, and ideas about people based on gender, race, ethnicity, class, and disabilities. All children are exposed to biases in one form or another, and usually a combination of forms (parents, extended family, neighbors, teachers, friends, television, children's books, movies), whether or not they have actual contact with people from various backgrounds. For example, every year, from the last week in October through the end of November, inaccurate, stereotypic, insulting images of Native Americans permeate children's lives, on television specials and ads, on store decorations, on greeting cards, in children's books, and on school dittos about Thanksgiving. Even children whose parents do not hold prejudiced or stereotypic beliefs about Native Americans, and Native American children themselves, absorb this misinformation unless adults actively intervene.

Based on previous research and their own observational and anecdotal data about children's construction of identity and attitudes, Derman-Sparks and the A.B.C. Task Force (1989) formulated four overall objectives for teaching about diversity that apply to children of all ages. Each objective includes knowledge, attitudes, and skills components. Achievement in each goal area builds on and reinforces achievement in the other three and occurs in an ever-widening spiral beginning in toddlerhood and continuing into adulthood. The following framework (see pp. 118–121) identifies developmental expectations or tasks for 2-1/2- to 8-year-old children within these four curriculum goals. In general, 2- through 5-year-olds' learning is at the awareness-and-exploration stage, while 6- through 8-year-old children begin to engage in inquiry and utilization of knowledge and skills. Keep in mind that a framework such as this only describes general developmental trends. Variation in children's group cultural

# Goals and Developmental Expectations of Antibias, Multicultural Curriculum for Young Children

## Goal 1: To foster each child's construction of a knowledgeable, confident self-identity

This goal includes both personal and group identity, for many children a bicultural identity. It means fostering confidence, not superiority.

| 2- and 3-year-olds | 4-year-olds | 5-year-olds | 6-year-olds | 7- and 8-year-olds |
|---|---|---|---|---|
| • are intrigued with their physical characteristics, including gender; anatomy; skin, eye, and hair color and texture; and physical abledness.<br><br>• see themselves as single, unique individuals; for example, 3s typically consider their name as a part of themselves and are therefore puzzled when another child has the same name as theirs. They also consider skin color, gender, anatomy, and other characteristics as part of their individuality.<br><br>• begin naming their gender identity but are not yet clear which biological or social attributes determine it.<br><br>• do not yet have gender or racial constancy; they think that their gender identification can change by dress or play preferences and that they can change their skin color and eye color. | • continue strong interest in their physical characteristics and what names describe them and begin constructing gender, race, and ethnic identity constancy.<br><br>• begin to see themselves (including their ethnic group name) as part of their family, while still focused on themselves as individuals and not yet as members of larger groups.<br><br>• are rapidly absorbing the rules of behavior and the language of their home culture, not from formal lessons but from their daily life experiences. In general, their "egocentrism" includes thinking that their family's way of life is how everyone else lives.<br><br>• are vulnerable to the influence of societal norms and socially prevailing biases. Questions related to identity may reflect not only confusion about identity constancy but also awareness of negative societal messages about themselves. | • have established a rudimentary sense of gender and race identity that includes constancy.<br><br>• have a heightened interest in the meaning of each component of identity in relation to other children's ideas.<br><br>• experience heightened possibilities of receiving teasing or rejection from other children based on an aspect of identity.<br><br>• experience heightened possibilities of absorbing socially prevailing norms or negative stereotypes about themselves. | • have constructed a core sense of identity that includes their gender, race and ethnicity, physical abledness, and beginning awareness of class.<br><br>• become increasingly interested in "hanging out" with and identifying with classmates who are alike, for example, girls with girls, boys with boys.<br><br>• begin to identify themselves and their families as members of larger racial or ethnic groups.<br><br>• can suffer serious damage both to personal self-esteem and to a positive sense of racial or ethnic group identity if they experience the impact of societal biases. | • are constructing or have constructed the cognitive ability of "class inclusion" that makes possible children's understanding of how they can have many different aspects of identity and still be one person, and of how people who are not exactly the same as them can belong to the same ethnic group as they do.<br><br>• begin to weave the various aspects of identity into a whole (I am a boy, am Mexican American, speak English and Spanish, like rap, am Catholic, am middle class).<br><br>• demonstrate heightened interest in learning about their ethnic group in their community, city, and country, especially through oral histories and written autobiographies and biographies, although learning still must be concrete.<br><br>• grapple with where they fit as an individual into their group identities—their gender, their ethnicity. |

## Goal 2: To foster each child's comfortable, empathetic interaction with diversity among people

This goal includes developing the *disposition* as well as the knowledge to understand and appreciate similarities and differences among people, to respectfully and effectively ask and learn about differences, and to comfortably negotiate and adapt to differences.

| 2- and 3-year-olds | 4-year-olds | 5-year-olds | 6-year-olds | 7- and 8-year-olds |
|---|---|---|---|---|
| • notice and ask about other children's and adult's physical characteristics, although they are still more interested in their own.<br><br>• notice other children's specific cultural acts, for example, Elena speaks differently from me; Mei eats with chopsticks; Jamal's grandpa, not his mother, brings him to school.<br><br>• may exhibit discomfort and fears about skin color differences and physical disabilities. | • are increasingly interested in how they are alike and different from other children; construct "theories" that reflect "preoperational thinking" about what causes physical and apparent cultural differences among the children and adults they know, societal stereotypes, and discomforts.<br><br>• although still focused on themselves and others as individuals, begin to classify people into groups by physical characteristics (same gender, same color, same eye shape) using the general classification schemes they apply to inanimate objects (for example, lack of class inclusion).<br><br>• are often confused about the meaning of adult categories for what "goes together." For example, how can a light-skinned child | have a dark skinned parent? Why are children called Black when their skin isn't black? Mexican people speak Spanish, so if I don't speak Spanish, then I am not Mexican. Girls are supposed to have girl names, so how can "Sam" be a girl? How can you be an "Indian" if you aren't wearing feathers?<br><br>• begin to become aware of and interested in cultural differences as they relate to the daily lives of children and adults they know (for example, who makes up their family, who lives in their house, what languages they speak, what jobs family members do).<br><br>• show influence of societal norms in their interactions with others ("Girls can't do this; boys can") and learned discomforts with specific differences in their interactions with others ("You can't play; your skin is too dark"). | • demonstrate continued interest in gender, racial, ethnic, and ability differences and similarities, as well as an awareness of additional characteristics such as socioeconomic class, age, and aging.<br><br>• demonstrate heightened awareness of themselves and others as members of a family and curiosity about how families of other children and teachers live, for example, can Sara have two mommies?<br><br>• continue to construct theories to classify or explain differences among classmates.<br><br>• continue to absorb and use stereotypes to define others, and to tease or reject other children. | • have absorbed much of their family's classification systems for people, but still get confused about why specific people are put into one or another category by adults.<br><br>• use prevailing biases, based on aspects of identity, against other children.<br><br>• are beginning to understand that others also have an ethnic identity and various lifestyles as they understand their own emerging group identity. | • demonstrate heightened curiosity about other people's lifestyles, religion, and traditions, including people with whom they do not have direct contact.<br><br>• can begin to appreciate the deeper structural aspects of a culture, such as beliefs about humans' relationship to the land and the impact of different historical environments on people's ways of life.<br><br>• understand, through new cognitive tools, that there are different ways to meet common human needs.<br><br>• can begin to appreciate the past if history is presented concretely through stories about real people.<br><br>• may experience heightened in-group solidarity and tension or conflict between children based on gender, race, ethnic identity, and socioeconomic class, and exclusion of children with disabilities because of interest in their own groups and because of the impact of societal biases on them. |

## Goal 3: To foster each child's critical thinking about bias

Thinking seriously about bias means developing the cognitive skills to identify unfair and untrue images (stereotypes), comments (teasing, name calling), and behaviors (discrimination) directed at one's own or another's identity—whether gender, race, ethnicity, disability, class, age, weight, or other characteristics— *and* the emotional empathy to know that bias hurts.

| *2- and 3-year-olds* | *4-year-olds* | *5-year-olds* | *6-year-olds* | *7- and 8-year-olds* |
|---|---|---|---|---|
| • are learning to be comfortable with various differences through repeated, supportive experience. These experiences lay a foundation for later understanding of "fair"/ "unfair" images and behaviors. | • can begin to use concrete experiences and verbal feedback from adults to explore the reality of their "theories" or misconceptions about human differences.<br><br>• can begin to develop the foundation for critical thinking by comparing a fair and an unfair image.<br><br>• can begin to learn to distinguish between a person's action that is not positive and a person's identity.<br><br>• can accept the limits of not teasing a person because of who they are and develop emotional understanding (empathy) that teasing or rejection because of identity hurts, just as hitting does. | • can begin to think critically about stereotypes, comparing reality to stereotyped images and determining what is fair or unfair<br><br>• can begin engaging in critical thinking about unfair or hurtful behaviors (name calling, teasing) in specific, real situations.<br><br>• can begin problem solving, caring ways to respond to differences.<br><br>• can begin engaging in critical thinking about specific societal norms, but only on an individual basis. For example, "Some people say that a person who uses a wheelchair can't be a teacher, but I know that Martha is a teacher." | In addition to what 5-year-olds can do,<br><br>• can also begin to engage in comparisons about correct and incorrect beliefs about various groups (not just individuals) by gathering and using concrete data relevant to them (for example, "Some people say men can't be nurses/take care of children, but we have gathered evidence that says otherwise"; "Girls can't do science, but we have learned . . ."; "People who are visually impaired can't work, but we have learned . . ."). | • have the cognitive tools to think about their own ideas and begin to understand about the influence of socially prevailing stereotypes on them, although they have absorbed and internalized many stereotypes and prejudices.<br><br>• can use emerging reading and writing skills to help them gather data that challenges stereotypes and erroneous ideas about people based on gender, race, ethnicity, disabilities, class, or other characteristics. |

# Goals and Developmental Expectations of Antibias, Multicultural Curriculum for Young Children (continued)

## Goal 4: To foster each child's ability to stand up for herself or himself and for others in the face of bias

Confronting bias means helping each child learn and practice a variety of ways to speak up (a) when another child acts in a biased manner toward her or him, (b) when a child acts in a biased manner toward another child, and (c) when an adult acts in a biased manner. Goal 4 builds upon Goal 3; critical thinking and empathy are necessary components of acting for oneself or for others in the face of bias.

| *2- and 3-year-olds* | *4-year-olds* | *5-year-olds* | *6-, 7-, and 8-year-olds* |
|---|---|---|---|
| • are learning acceptable ways to express their feelings when they want something or when others hurt them. | • engage in simple problem-solving and conflict-resolution techniques for dealing with incidents of teasing or rejection directed at their own and others' identity. | • problem-solve and use ways to handle specific unfair comments and behaviors that arise in their school or home lives.<br><br>• gain emotional food-for-thought from stories about adults who have worked for social justice, especially adults they know.<br><br>• with adult help, create and engage in simple group actions based on a concrete, meaningful experience in their daily lives, for example, working to get a handicapped parking space at their child care center. | • develop fair classroom behavior rules for identity issues with greater understanding, more autonomy, and more depth.<br><br>• identify respectful ways to ask about cultural behaviors and ideas different from their own.<br><br>• learn about people who work for social justice in their communities.<br><br>• problem-solve conflict situations involving bias.<br><br>• problem-solve specific group actions related to a concrete discriminatory situation in their school or immediate community. |

experiences, as well as individual differences, affect when and how specific developmental expectations or tasks appear in and are demonstrated by a particular child. Only continual observations of and talking with children enable a teacher to clothe the framework with living reality.

## Planning developmentally and contextually appropriate antibias, multicultural curriculum

Deciding what specific content will best foster multicultural, antibias goals with a particular child or group of children requires a combination of developmental and contextual analysis. In this section developmental issues will be discussed first; followed by a discussion of the sources of multicultural, antibias curriculum necessary for ensuring that curriculum choices are individually appropriate; and finally, the implications of implementing such curriculum in various contexts will be described.

### Applying a developmental framework

The simplest and most effective way to apply a developmental framework to making choices about diversity content is to think of the child as the center of a series of concentric circles. Start with a child's experiences of self, and then move outward in concentric circles to family, neighborhood, city, country, and other countries. Simultaneously, move in a time continuum that begins with current experiences, to learning about the immediate past and future, and then to learning about the more distant past and future. This paradigm of development in terms of concentric circles of experience is the best way to ensure developmentally appropriate curriculum content. The question of what constitutes real experiences within each concentric circle is vital, however.

Teachers who explain a lack of diversity content in their curriculum by insisting that young children do not notice or "care" about differences among people seriously *underestimate* developmental realities. All children, including those growing up in racially or ethnically homogeneous communities, are aware of

© Subjects & Predicates

differences among themselves, including gender, physical characteristics, family styles, traditions, religious beliefs, and disabilities, and do have contact with both positive and negative images and messages about various people. Integrating antibias, multicultural curriculum goals into the educational program of all children is therefore relevant (Guideline 4), reflects the needs and interests of the children (Guideline 6), and builds upon what children already know (Guideline 8). The key is first choosing content that enables young children to explore their own direct experiences of diversity and then introducing new forms of diversity in ways that connect to the children's learning about themselves and their classmates (Guidelines 8 and 9).

On the other hand, it is equally important not to *overestimate* what young children can learn efficiently and effectively and what they need to function capably in their world (Guideline 12). Examples of overestimation are including activities that attempt to teach 3- and 4-year-olds about "ethnic groups" before the preschoolers have constructed the concept of *group* beyond their family, introducing content about countries from which their families emigrated in the far

---

*DECIDING WHAT SPECIFIC CONTENT WILL BEST FOSTER MULTICULTURAL, ANTIBIAS GOALS WITH A PARTICULAR CHILD OR GROUP OF CHILDREN REQUIRES A COMBINATION OF DEVELOPMENTAL AND CONTEXTUAL ANALYSIS.*

---

past, or expecting that a few activities in one "unit" about a culture are sufficient to foster a disposition of respect for and comfort with diversity in the face of pervasive societal biases.

Antibias curriculum choices must also carefully explore and evaluate what are meaningful critical thinking and activism activities at various ages. If content is unrelated to children's interests and current level of reasoning, then the activities can defeat their purpose, which is to foster problem-solving and decision-making abilities (Guideline 15).

Achieving the four goals of antibias curriculum cannot occur in one year of preschool exposure. Activities related to each goal will have to be repeated in many different ways for several years as children construct increasingly complex understandings about themselves and about others (Guideline 9).

Implementing antibias, multicultural curriculum means facing the challenge presented by Guideline 14: "Curriculum values children's constructive errors and does not prematurely limit exploration and experimentation for the sake of ensuring 'right' answers." Clearly, young children make many constructive errors as they grapple with figuring out the assorted components of their identity and as they crystalize attitudes toward others. Some of their "errors" reflect developmental ways of thinking; others represent the influence of socially prevailing biases; yet others are a mixture of both. Moreover, some of the "constructive errors" are potentially seriously damaging to a child's self-esteem or positive attitudes toward aspects of human diversity. When a 4-year-old thinks that a spread-out line of 10 checkers is more than a pushed-together line of 10 checkers, no harm occurs to that child's sense of self and her ability to function in the world at that point in her life, or to other children. Within a year or so, the 4-year-old will construct the principle of conservation that 10 checkers are still 10 checkers no matter how much space they take up. On the other hand, if the same 4-year-old thinks that brown skin is dirty because of lack of experience with dark-skinned people and therefore will not hold the hand of a brown-skinned classmate, harm *does happen* to her classmate and to her own socioemotional growth and ability to function in the world. Furthermore, while adult society will foster and reinforce the child's eventual discovery that 10 equals 10, society may neither encourage nor support the discovery that brown skin is *not* dirty and that refusing to hold a brown-skinned classmate's hand is hurtful, unfair, and unacceptable. In fact, adult society may actually reinforce the child's "constructive error" so that it becomes prejudice.

Effectively handling "constructive errors" about diversity requires thoughtful balancing between respect and understanding of a child's level of reasoning and informed sensitivity to the error's potential for damage to children's socioemotional and cognitive development. Identifying a range of potential damage can help in decision making about which of the following strategies constitutes an appropriate response: (A) let the "error" stand; (B) find developmentally or culturally appropriate ways to involve the child in concrete experiences that contradict her theory and that can lead to new concepts; or (C) directly communicate why the idea is not acceptable and set limits on its expression. If a 5-year-old draws a picture of herself as a surgeon operating on a patient and wearing a pink gown and tiara (K. Taus, personal communication, February 20, 1990), then strategy A is most appropriate because this belief does no present harm, and later knowledge of reality will change the belief. On the other hand, if the same child insists that girls can't play with blocks, then a combination of strategies B and C is necessary because this belief is presently harmful to both the child's and other classmates' developing cognitive abilities. If a 4-year old is afraid to sit in a wheelchair because he thinks he will lose the ability to walk, strategy B seems best—finding the constructive error that underlies the fear and gradually helping the child overcome it. On the other hand, if a preschooler tells another child who uses a wheelchair, "You can't play with us. You're a baby because you can't walk," then it is essential to employ strategy C first, followed by strategy B. If a 3-year-old thinks that people get their skin color from paint, then strategy B seems most effective; if another 3-year-old refuses to hold a classmate's hand because of her skin color, then strategy C followed by strategy B must be used.

Teachers can learn a great deal about children's thinking and reasoning by attending to their "wrong answers" (Guideline 14). At the same time, every teacher must also attend to the potential harm of societal biases to the children for whom she is responsible and, when necessary, set limits of psychological and emotional safety (Guideline 18). This is no different from setting rules about physical safety while encouraging children's large-motor exploration or setting limits on hitting as a way to solve problems while promoting young children's conflict-resolution skills.

## Sources of antibias, multicultural curriculum

For curriculum to be developmentally appropriate, it must also be individually and culturally appropriate to each child; therefore, the children, their families, society, and teachers provide important sources of antibias, multicultural curriculum. Following is a discussion of each of these sources.

*MULTICULTURAL CURRICULUM CONTENT MUST BE ADAPTED TO THE CULTURAL AND INDIVIDUAL VARIATIONS OF EACH NEW GROUP OF CHILDREN IF IT IS TO BE DEVELOPMENTALLY AND CONTEXTUALLY APPROPRIATE. ACTIVITIES THAT APPEAR IN PRINT OR THAT OTHER TEACHERS FIND EFFECTIVE ARE NOT RECIPES TO BE STRICTLY COPIED, BUT ONLY POSSIBILITIES.*

*Children's culturally relevant needs, experiences, interests, questions, feelings, and behaviors.* Children are the starting place of curriculum planning. Teachers must be familiar with research about children's construction of identity and attitudes and have a developmental perspective based on the research. Moreover, it is crucial that teachers regularly gather data throughout the year from the children with whom they work about their ideas, feelings, and skills for handling diversity. Data comes from observing children's interactions; listening to and noting questions and comments; and interviewing the children on their ideas about dimensions of diversity, such as gender, race, ethnicity, and disabilities.

*Families' beliefs, concerns, and desires for their children.* Over the school year teachers must gather information from parents about (a) what they want their children to know about various aspects of their identity, what name the parents use for their ethnic identity, what they believe to be important, how gender roles fit in, and how the parents want their children to handle bias directed against them; (b) what experiences their children have with various aspects of diversity at home and in their community; (c) where families fit on the continuum of assimilation to the dominant culture versus biculturalism; and (d) concerns and disagreements about antibias, multicultural curriculum topics.

*Societal events, messages, and expectations that permeate children's environment.* Teachers must continually be alert to the visual, verbal, and behavioral messages about human diversity—both positive and negative—that children absorb from TV, radio, movies, books, toys, greeting cards, lunchboxes, other children, extended family, religious or spiritual leaders, and teachers. This means watching children's television, visiting the toy stores and bookstores in children's neighborhoods, and paying critical attention to the images in children's clothing and toys as well as to all the materials placed in the classroom. It is important to remember that children's ideas about themselves and others do not just come from their families, a misconception that many teachers continue to have.

*Teachers' knowledge, beliefs, values, and interests.* Teachers design daily curriculum by weaving together threads from these four curriculum sources. What issues teachers see and hear from children, parents, and society, and what they choose to act on or ignore, are strongly influenced by their own cultural beliefs, unexamined attitudes, discomforts, and prejudices, as well as by their knowledge of children's development and learning and of societal biases. An essential component of creating appropriate antibias, multicultural curriculum, therefore, is the teacher's increasing self-awareness about her own identity, cultural beliefs, and behaviors and attitudes toward various aspects of other people's identities.

## Contextually appropriate content: Making curriculum decisions in different contexts

Having addressed developmental appropriateness by describing a developmental framework, and having examined the sources of curriculum that influence decisions about what is individually appropriate, we now turn to contextual appropriateness. To look at how curriculum choices might work in practice, let us examine three different classroom configurations: classroom A, which is ethnically diverse; classroom B, which is composed of all White European Americans; and classroom C, which is composed of all children of color. For the sake of brevity, this discussion will be limited to content for the four goals of antibias, multicultural curriculum related to race and cultural issues for 3- and 4-year-olds; however, the same procedure would apply to other content areas, such as gender, disabilities, or class, and to other age groups.

*Classroom setting A: Ethnically diverse children.* In this setting the background of each child provides the content for the teacher to initiate and fuel children's year-long awareness and exploration learning about themselves and each other. This includes activities that enable children to keep developing within their home culture while also beginning to learn how to participate in the dominant European American culture. It is essential to ensure equitable representation of each child's background in the environment and in all activities. If the majority of children come from one racial or ethnic group, with a few children from other groups, it is important to ensure that the "minority" children are not just tokenly represented. Parents may also be concerned that their child will be singled out and become the target of bias if the teacher only highlights their child's differences from the "majority" group.

SECTION III—REACHING POTENTIALS OF ALL CHILDREN

Once learning about differences and similarities within the group of children has become an ongoing "thread" of the class, much of the content for working on critical thinking and activism will emerge from the comments and interactions of the children as they engage in learning about themselves and each other. In addition, the teacher initiates exploration of key stereotypes coming from the larger society to which preschoolers are exposed, such as Native American stereotypes surrounding Thanksgiving. Content from the children's caregivers that is especially essential in an ethnically diverse setting includes (1) what ethnic identity terms families use (being sensitive to issues that are faced by children in interracial families and children who have been adopted into racially or ethnically different families); (2) what families want their children to know about their culture; and (3) family socialization values and methods. The challenge of creating a classroom environment and teaching styles that are culturally relevant to all of the children is heightened in an ethnically diverse setting. Teachers must be prepared to engage in problem solving with families and with other staff to meet both the children's and the families' cultural needs and the teacher's beliefs about curriculum.

### Classroom setting B: All White European American children.

In this setting the first step remains children's learning about themselves and each other. The physical and cultural differences among European American families will provide sufficient content for this step. The challenge, however, is to use these activities as a context for the next key step—introducing and weaving learning about further physical and cultural diversity into the ongoing daily curriculum. Once awareness of and comfort with differences within the group of children has become an ongoing "thread" of the class, then it is time to enter step two.

What new information regarding cultural diversity to introduce is determined by what other ethnic groups live in the children's wider community, city, or state. For example, if the city has recently gained a sizable Hmong population, learning about Hmong people becomes appropriate. Just as activities based on the children in the class do not talk about "all European Americans" or about Europe of the past, but about Becky and her family now or Jim and his family now, so, too, must these activities focus on individual people and families in the present. For example, using the persona doll technique (Derman-Sparks & the A.B.C. Task Force, 1989), a teacher can introduce two dolls—one girl and one boy—who "are" Hmong. Telling stories about the dolls and their "families," supplemented by children's books, pictures, and objects "brought" by the dolls, offers numerous opportunities to explore physical and cultural learning about kinds of people who are new to the children's experiences, for example, grandparents, a new baby, or teachers and children encountered on the first day of school.

Some content for working on antibias critical thinking and activism skills will arise out of the children's interactions with each other; however, the bulk of content will come from the teacher's initiating exploration of the misconcepts and discomforts children are absorbing from socially prevailing biases in their environment. Potential parental issues in an all-White setting may include parents' objections to children exploring differences (a colorblind view is that "it will teach them prejudice") or objections from parents who hold strong prejudices against specific ethnic groups. Preparing oneself to discuss with and educate parents who hold either of these views is part of contextually appropriate curriculum.

### Classroom setting C: All children of color.

This kind of classroom may consist of children from one ethnic group, such as all African American; all Chinese American; or mixed ethnic groupings, such as African American and Mexican American or combinations of various Latino groups. Since racism makes the task of constructing a knowledgeable, confident self- and group identity much more difficult for children of color, nurturing each child's positive identity and appreciation of other members of his ethnic group constitutes a primary goal of the curriculum. Activities that teach children ways to identify and resist negative images and messages about themselves and that counter intragroup biases are directly tied to self- and group-concept activities. If the group is ethnically diverse (although still all non–European Americans), then learning about each other becomes the content for goal two—developing comfortable, empathetic interaction with diversity. If the group is ethnically homogeneous, then learning about other "ethnic minorities" proceeds as described for Classroom B. Critical thinking activi-

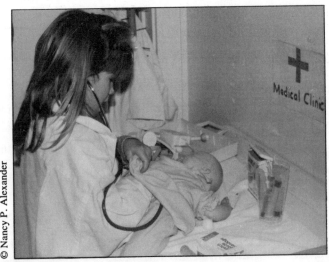

© Nancy P. Alexander

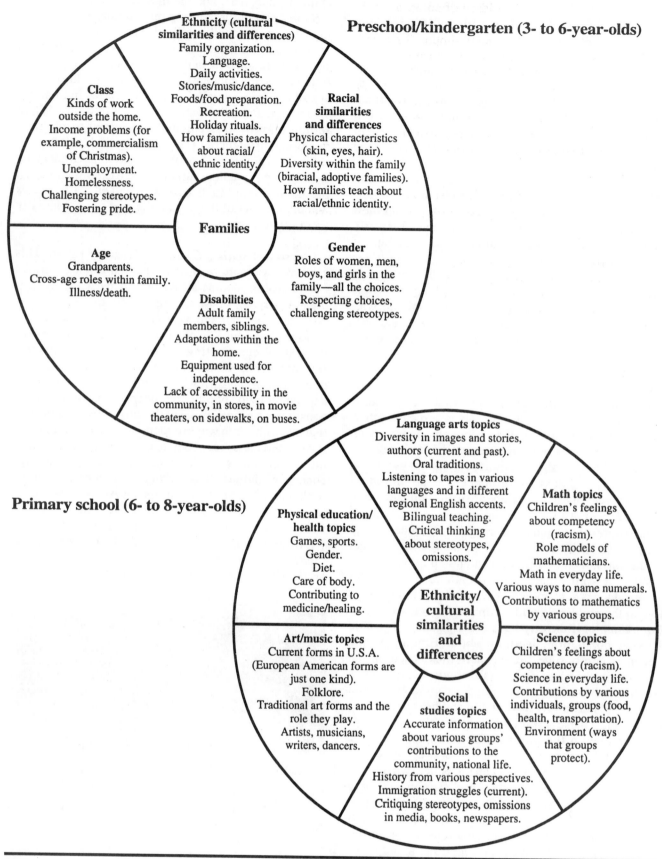

**Preschool/kindergarten (3- to 6-year-olds)**

**Ethnicity (cultural similarities and differences)**
Family organization.
Language.
Daily activities.
Stories/music/dance.
Foods/food preparation.
Recreation.
Holiday rituals.
How families teach about racial/ethnic identity.

**Class**
Kinds of work outside the home.
Income problems (for example, commercialism of Christmas).
Unemployment.
Homelessness.
Challenging stereotypes.
Fostering pride.

**Racial similarities and differences**
Physical characteristics (skin, eyes, hair).
Diversity within the family (biracial, adoptive families).
How families teach about racial/ethnic identity.

**Families**

**Age**
Grandparents.
Cross-age roles within family.
Illness/death.

**Gender**
Roles of women, men, boys, and girls in the family—all the choices.
Respecting choices, challenging stereotypes.

**Disabilities**
Adult family members, siblings.
Adaptations within the home.
Equipment used for independence.
Lack of accessibility in the community, in stores, in movie theaters, on sidewalks, on buses.

**Primary school (6- to 8-year-olds)**

**Language arts topics**
Diversity in images and stories, authors (current and past).
Oral traditions.
Listening to tapes in various languages and in different regional English accents.
Bilingual teaching.
Critical thinking about stereotypes, omissions.

**Physical education/ health topics**
Games, sports.
Gender.
Diet.
Care of body.
Contributing to medicine/healing.

**Math topics**
Children's feelings about competency (racism).
Role models of mathematicians.
Math in everyday life.
Various ways to name numerals.
Contributions to mathematics by various groups.

**Ethnicity/ cultural similarities and differences**

**Art/music topics**
Current forms in U.S.A. (European American forms are just one kind).
Folklore.
Traditional art forms and the role they play.
Artists, musicians, writers, dancers.

**Science topics**
Children's feelings about competency (racism).
Science in everyday life.
Contributions by various individuals, groups (food, health, transportation).
Environment (ways that groups protect).

**Social studies topics**
Accurate information about various groups' contributions to the community, national life.
History from various perspectives.
Immigration struggles (current).
Critiquing stereotypes, omissions in media, books, newspapers.

ties address the socially prevailing biases directed at all "minority" groups.

In settings that serve all children of color, a bicultural approach is another aspect of antibias, multicultural curriculum, balancing support for development within the home culture with awareness and exploration about how to act in the dominant European American culture—for example, learning behavioral rules or learning English while continuing to learn the home language. Close collaboration with the children's families is an integral part of this work, using methods such as those described for Classroom A.

## Integrating antibias, multicultural planning into the total curriculum

In addition to choosing developmentally appropriate and contextually relevant content for a particular group of children, it is essential to integrate learning about diversity into all aspects of the program; otherwise, activities still run the risk of falling into the traps of "tourist curriculum." Antibias, multicultural topics are integral to all of the other subjects that comprise early childhood curricula. One practical brainstorming technique for identifying the numerous topic possibilities is "webbing," which takes its name from a spider web image.

The center of the web is the starting point for planning. This can be any number of traditional topics, such as "my body," "families," "the world of work," or an on-going theme in social studies, science, math, language arts, physical, or health curriculum; a societal event, such as honoring Dr. Martin Luther King, Jr., Day; or an issue raised by the children, such as their insistence that a person who is visually impaired cannot work. The next step is brainstorming the many possible antibias, multicultural issues that stem from the subject at the web's center and seeing how the various issues interconnect. The third step is identifying specific content for a particular classroom. This requires doing contextual/developmental analysis: what is meaningful to this group of children, what resources and knowledge the teacher has, and what family issues might arise. Step four is listing possible activities that are developmentally or culturally appropriate for the particular group. The webs on page 126 illustrate steps one and two. The first is for preschool/kindergarten themes, and the second relates to primary school subjects.

Integrating diversity content into the whole curriculum requires breaking down the false dichotomy between the teacher's launching a specific subject versus waiting for the subject to emerge from the children and never mentioning the subject if the children don't.

Developmentally/contextually appropriate teaching is a continuous interaction between adults and children, not a one-sided contribution from one or the other. Teachers are responsible for brainstorming, planning, and initiating diversity topics based on their analysis of the children's needs. Teachers create awareness through many methods, such as bringing new materials into the environment and observing children's responses before creating more activities, or reading a book to children and conducting a discussion to uncover their ideas. The teacher's careful attention to children's thinking and behavior leads to modifications and additions to plans. These become new lines on an already existing web or the center of a new web, and the cycle of brainstorming and planning begins anew. If the teacher does not create a material and emotional environment that clearly communicates that diversity is important, valued, and safe in the classroom, then children will not raise issues. Conversely, if the teacher does not pay attention to children's ideas, interests, and learning styles, then specific diversity content may not be meaningful to them.

To summarize, antibias, multicultural curriculum content must be adapted to the cultural and individual variations of each new group of children if it is to be developmentally and contextually appropriate. Activities that appear in print or that other teachers find effective are not recipes to be strictly copied, but only possibilities. Educators' thoughtful articulation of the reasoning underlying their content choices is nowhere more urgent than in antibias, multicultural curriculum. Fostering children's healthy, positive self-identity and the desire and skills to live comfortably, effectively, and respectfully with the wide range of human diversity is vital to our nation's survival.

## References

Banks, J. (1981). *Multiethnic education: Theory and practice.* Boston: Allyn & Bacon.

Banks, J. (1988). *Multiethnic education: Theory and practice* (2nd ed.). Boston: Allyn & Bacon.

Derman-Sparks, L., & the A.B.C. Task Force. (1989). *Anti-bias curriculum: Tools for empowering young children.* Washington, DC: NAEYC.

Kendall, F. (1983). *Diversity in the classroom: A multicultural approach to the education of young children.* New York: Teachers College Press.

National Association for the Education of Young Children and National Association of Early Childhood Specialists in State Departments of Education. (1991). Guidelines for appropriate curriculum content and assessment in programs serving children ages 3 through 8. *Young Children, 46*(3), 21–38.

Ramsey, P. (1987). *Teaching and learning in a diverse world.* New York: Teachers College Press.

U.S. Department of Health and Human Services, Head Start Bureau. (1991). *Multicultural principles for Head Start programs.* Washington, DC: Author.

Williams, L., De Gaetano, Y., Sutherland, I., & Harrington C. (1985). *Alerta: A multicultural-bilingual approach to teaching young children.* Reading, MA: Addison-Wesley.

9

# Reaching Potentials of Minority Children Through Developmentally and Culturally Appropriate Programs

*Barbara T. Bowman*

The National Association for the Education of Young Children (NAEYC) published two documents that have become reference points for evaluating programs for young children, *Developmentally Appropriate Practice in Early Childhood Programs Serving Children From Birth through Age 8* (Bredekamp, 1987) and Guidelines for Appropriate Curriculum Content and Assessment in Programs Serving Children Ages 3 Through 8 (National Association for the Education of Young Children & National Association of Early Childhood Specialists in State Departments of Education, 1991; pp. 9–27, this volume). These documents outline an approach to the education of young children that brings together developmental research, widely accepted curricula goals, and the accumulated practical wisdom of teachers. These guidelines contain examples of practices that exemplify developmentally appropriate educational principles and are intended as a guide, rather than a rigid methodology. Indeed, an essential element of developmentally appropriate practice is individual appropriateness; flexibility is necessary, and practices must be adapted to individual differences in children's learning rates and styles.

Nevertheless, developmentally appropriate practice has been criticized as inconsistent with the background, experience, cultural style, and family values of many low-income and minority people (Delpit, 1988; Jipson, 1991). Critics contend that NAEYC–recommended practices may not be the most effective practices to promote school learning for children who are not White, who do not live in mainstream communities, who do not speak standard English, and who are in the low-income bracket. Critics are concerned that imposing developmentally appropriate practice may cause alienation, frustration, and failure for children, families, and teachers.

For the past 24 years, the Erikson Institute in Chicago has provided technical assistance to public schools, child care centers, and Head Start programs serving low-income African American, Asian American, Native American, Hispanic, and White children and families. The purpose of these projects is to help teachers use developmental principles in programs for low-income and racial- and linguistic-minority children. All of the projects grapple with ways to arrange education and care so that children will not continue the trajectory of school failure that is characteristic of older members of their communities. From these projects we at the Erikson Institute have observed positive improvements for both children and teachers; for example, we have seen classrooms become more interesting and productive places for children to learn,

128

and teachers have gained renewed energy for their work. We have also encountered some difficulties, however, that must be overcome if developmentally appropriate programs are to be successfully implemented for all children.

Discussions of cultural and developmental issues are ongoing at the Erikson Institute; however, this chapter describes my own attempt to understand some of the problems and to find solutions. Although most of the examples cited here describe miscommunication between schools and centers and the children and families in low-income African American communities, the principles apply to all "culturally different" groups as they interact with mainstream institutions.

This chapter discusses three major areas of concern that must be addressed if developmentally appropriate practices are to facilitate—rather than impede—the development of minority children. These areas of concern are (1) ways that teachers and students together mutually construct understandings—ways of making meaning, (2) family expectations, and (3) classroom management and teaching practices. Before discussing what I have learned about each of these issues in trying to implement developmentally appropriate practice with minority children, I will first present several important caveats about group identity that are relevant to any discussion of cultural groups.

# Group identity

Discussing characteristics of minority groups in this country is complex for a number of reasons. First, while every child is deeply rooted in his or her own community and culture, all children who live in the same community and share a culture are not identical. Group markers—whether of race, social class, or gender—do not completely describe any one individual belonging to that group. Children's behavior results from the integration of group mores with their own individual (genetic/temperamental) characteristics; the pacing of cultural expectations with their developmental (age/stage) capabilities; and the syntheses of the conflicting roles, beliefs, and attitudes of various members of the childrearing community. Whenever we discuss culture, therefore, we are in danger of stereotyping individuals.

This discussion must include the caveat that different communities and the individuals within those communities may have quite different beliefs and behaviors. My purpose in discussing group behavior is not to describe invariant behavior of children from such groups but to point out how different assumptions about the nature of the world, different ways of encoding thought in speech, and different understanding about the meaning of behavior cause conflict between children, families, and teachers that undermines meaningful education.

Another obstacle to the discussion of culture is the confounding effect of poverty: social class has overarching effects on racial and ethnic identity (Laosa, 1980; Wilson, 1987). To what extent particular characteristics represent a group's adaptation to limited resources and to what extent they represent critical aspects of cultural heritage is difficult to disentangle. School achievement is based, more or less, on the acquisition of middle-class, White values and behaviors. For low-income minority children, this means two layers of potential conflict as the issues of class and racial, linguistic, and ethnic identity merge.

Another difficulty in discussing the behavior of various groups in America is separating individual responsibility from cultural embeddedness. In many ways the conflicts between children, families, and teachers are not the fault of individuals; yet most conflicts are attributable to the intractable racism and classism endemic in our society. Even when people want to break out of their ethnocentric perspective and avoid pejorative comparisons between groups, they have a problem doing so. Such problems are testimony to the fact that people from the many groups represented in the United States live their lives in different worlds from each other, creating differences between them that make it difficult to understand and communicate with one another.

Culture forms a prism through which members of a group see—a prism created from "shared meanings." These meanings are implicit, almost unconscious, definitions of what is normal human behavior. Groups "see" the world from different perspectives and "make sense" of their experience in different ways. Teachers working with children and families who live outside the mainstream of American life must recognize these differences and respond to them. My point is not to conclude that developmentally appropriate classrooms cannot be established when teachers and children come from different worlds, rather that the definition

*CULTURE FORMS A PRISM THROUGH WHICH MEMBERS OF A GROUP SEE—A PRISM CREATED FROM "SHARED MEANINGS." THESE MEANINGS ARE IMPLICIT, ALMOST UNCONSCIOUS, DEFINITIONS OF WHAT IS NORMAL HUMAN BEHAVIOR. GROUPS "SEE" THE WORLD FROM DIFFERENT PERSPECTIVES AND "MAKE SENSE" OF THEIR EXPERIENCE IN DIFFERENT WAYS.*

of developmentally appropriate must pay greater attention to cultural differences and build an understanding of culture's subtleties into teacher preparation and classroom management. By definition, developmentally appropriate programs must be responsive to individual and cultural variation (Bredekamp, 1987), and there is evidence that programs can be successful in this goal (Burts, Hart, Charlesworth, Fleege, Mosley, & Thomasson, 1992). The challenge for teachers is to overcome the tendency to see their own individual and cultural perspectives as the norm and others' cultural perspectives as deviations. The appropriateness of a program is determined by the experience of the children in the program, not by conformity to a teacher's own cultural definition of what is appropriate.

© BmPorter/Don Franklin

## Making meaning

Central to our current understanding of the teaching/learning process is the concept that adults and children "make meaning" together through their interactions with one another (Vygotsky, 1978). According to this perspective, children internalize (reconstruct) knowledge and skills as a consequence of social interactions with adults and older peers, as well as through their own actions. Children learn in an ongoing process of mutual social engagement in which adults help them organize knowledge in ways that "make sense" to both the children and the adults. Adults lead children (scaffold knowledge) into a shared reality.

Through social interaction children learn to act, believe, and feel in ways that are consistent with others in their community. A group's goals and objectives and the relationships, behavior, and practices recommended by family and friends are internalized and contribute to a child's definition of self. Gradually children internalize the adult rules for "making meaning" as they participate together in activities. Vygotsky (1978) stated that knowledge is first created between an adult and a child (interpsychic) and gradually becomes a part of what and who the child is (intrapsychic); what is learned from social interaction becomes part of the personality structure and personal identity of the child. As Erikson (1950) said, "No ego can develop outside of social processes which offer workable prototypes and roles" (p. 366).

One dimension of making meaning is encompassed in a group's world view—their perspective on life, their philosophy for living. According to Shade (1982), the African American "perspective" is that "the people within one's environment should be approached with caution, wariness, and a sense of distrust" (p. 220). This world view affects children's behavior in school. Reflecting feelings of vulnerability and mistrust may

deter African American children from sharing their views and opinions in school, where they feel unsure of the reception their ideas may get. Teachers trying to establish language-rich classrooms may feel frustrated at the children's reluctance to talk freely and their use of a restricted language code. Teachers may assume that the children's language development is inadequate, unaware that many of the children have a full, rich command of language in informal settings and that language proficiency (particularly telling stories, playing word games, and attending to the sound of speech) is highly valued in the African American community.

Children acquire "scripts" (mutually understood ways of thinking and behaving) through their interactions with others in their families and communities, in which behavior and meanings are coordinated. Unfortunately when children and teachers come from different cultures, the meaning of their scripts may be mutually unintelligible. Even more puzzling for them, they may be unaware of their different understanding because cultural knowledge is so tacit. For example, Delpit (1988) points out that there are rules of power enacted in classrooms that African American children often do not know—discourse patterns, interacting styles, and spoken and written language codes that may be quite different from their own.

Script differences between teachers and children in developmentally appropriate classrooms may be reflected in a variety of ways. For instance, teachers in a developmentally appropriate classroom are usually anxious to maintain an atmosphere of self-direction and have scripts for implementing this objective. They may use indirect forms of address ("Do you want to come sit over here?") to children who are accustomed to scripts in which adults give clear directions about the behavior they want ("Sit here!"). Teachers may ask children to "choose an activity" and expect them to stick with it, while the children's scripts call for changing activities whenever they feel like it. Teachers may tell children to "think for yourself," but the children's script says, "do what everyone else is doing." Children who are used to authoritarian disciplinarians are confused when teachers are indirect; children who are accustomed to a great deal of personal freedom may feel hampered and constrained by the nagging attention of teachers; young children, whose very lives depend on obedience, may be unsure of the meaning of "think for yourself." Children and teachers have trouble making sense out of each others' scripts.

Young children's learning is context bound, meaning that it is tied to specific settings (see Rogoff, 1990, for a discussion of situated cognition). To learn something new, children must retrieve old knowledge and build upon it. Before entering school, all children have already learned a great deal: for instance, a child may know how to count, add, subtract, and solve word problems that occur in the context of daily life (Lawson, 1986). To evoke this knowledge in a classroom setting, however, children must see the connection between what they have already learned and the more formal school contexts (Ginsburg, 1982). Adults must help children see the similarities between contexts so that they can apply what they know and add to their knowledge.

Teachers of young children in developmentally appropriate classrooms often try to join informal knowledge to formal knowledge through reference to such activities as setting tables, assuming that children have had experience allocating items in this way. Many children's home experience, though, does not include such distributive activities. In their homes, people do not regularly mete out goods and services all at once; instead, each person draws on the common supply as needed. For them, the context (setting tables) that is meant to elicit knowledge of one-to-one relationships does not evoke what the teacher expects. This does not mean that the children have no informal knowledge to draw on; it does mean that the activities traditionally used may not be the best points of reference. The same children who never set a table may have sophisticated knowledge of one-to-one relationships in jumping rope to rhymes and in basketball scoring. It is only as teachers understand when, by whom, and under what conditions different knowledge and skills are embedded that they can make appropriate context referents for children.

Another dimension of group difference is cultural style. In recent years considerable research has been done on the perceptual, cognitive, and linguistic styles of various cultural communities (Cole & Bruner, 1972; Hilliard & Vaughn-Scott, 1982; McGoldrick, 1982; Shade, 1982; Hale-Benson, 1986). Results demonstrate that groups vary on a number of characteristics. One of these differences is the extent of field sensitivity as opposed to field independence among members of different groups. Field-dependent people are said to

prefer a global view of the world, rather than focusing on the parts or pieces of a visual field. Rameriz and Price-Williams found that both African American and Mexican American children "prefer the field-dependent approach while European Americans demonstrated a field-independent preference" (Shade, 1982, p. 227). Children belonging to field-dependent groups are described as finding "wholes" the more salient aspects of the environment. Unfortunately for field-dependent children, schools tend to reward those children who are more field independent and prone to breaking down problems, rather than responding more intuitively and holistically.

One of the core values of developmentally appropriate practice is that children's natural talents and ways of organizing the world be accepted and validated; however, children who prefer approaches not valued by schools are at a disadvantage. Lawson (1986), for example, noted that the question-answering pattern characteristic of African American children is different from that of White children. African American children's responses are more likely to be analogical (answers that relate objects or events to themselves or their experience) rather than referential (ones that name the object or event). Children of each group have the ability to make both analogic and referential answers, but they select the type of answer that in their past experience is appropriate in the context in which they are being questioned. When only referential answers are judged correct, African American children fail the test. Children whose cultural styles are different from those of the mainstream may need help extending the range of their response patterns so that they can succeed in two worlds, not just in their own.

Teaching children to live in separate worlds is not easy. Such children must become bicultural, able to switch culturally encoded behavior depending on the context in which they find themselves. The goal is to help them retain their primary identity and at the same time function effectively in the larger society. Biculturalism, however, may carry the seeds of bitter conflict when the social groups involved have beliefs and practices that cannot be reconciled. This is what happens when African American children feel that they must give up their identification with family and friends to find acceptance in other worlds. Many young African American children think that they must deny their own perceptions and say that they are White to identify with the more prestigious majority. Even if such children do better in school by transferring their identification model, the cost in self-denial is too high for the children's long-term mental health and adaptive capacities. Low-income and minority children need an enormous amount of support to maintain a positive identity in several worlds. They must enlarge

*ONE OF THE CORE VALUES OF DEVELOPMEN-TALLY APPROPRIATE PRACTICE IS THAT CHILD-REN'S NATURAL TALENTS AND WAYS OF ORGANIZ-ING THE WORLD BE ACCEPTED AND VALIDATED; HOWEVER, CHILDREN WHO PREFER APPROACHES NOT VALUED BY SCHOOLS ARE AT A DISADVANTAGE.*

their sense of self—not create two separate identities, one good and one bad. Teachers who assume that because a classroom is developmentally appropriate, it does not constitute an identity challenge for many children fail to appreciate the conflicts in behavior, values, beliefs, and expectations that such classrooms may represent for low-income and minority children.

# Family expectations

The challenge of making meaning is also seen in examining the differing expectations of minority families and schools. The emphasis on process over content in developmentally appropriate classrooms, for example, creates a conflict with family expectations and belief systems. For instance, people of color are not usually rewarded for the same attributes that others are rewarded for in our society (Ogbu, 1978; Ellwood, 1988), thus they honor strategies to deal with the reality they know.

Many families believe that prejudice and discrimination prevent their achievement and that they have fewer options than do White, middle-class people. As a consequence, low-income and minority parents and middle-class-oriented teachers often have quite different pictures of what children need from the other. For example, low-income and minority parents often do not see the value of developmental curriculum. Many parents view the nondidactic and child-initiated activity characteristic of a developmentally appropriate classroom as inimical to their children's success; these parents believe that worksheets and other evidence of information and skills are more appropriate than the "messing around" characteristic of informal classrooms. They hear that their children are not learning what they need to know—information derived from test scores and teacher conferences—and they want evidence that children are learning to do well on the gatekeeping tests that determine personal achievement. Parents understand that the real world works according to rules, and they worry whether their children will learn the rules in less structured classrooms.

Some parents, defeated themselves by school, easily accept the notion that their children will not learn well, and these parents lower their expectations for their children's performance. They communicate to their children through their own lowered investment that school is not important and achievement is not expected. Because these parents are fatalistic about their children's chances for school success, they are often unwilling to volunteer their time to classroom activities. Visiting the school or center simply reinforces the parents' feelings of inadequacy and hopelessness.

Other parents, hurt by their interactions with the larger society, send their children the message, "Obey the rules, but don't become engaged." It is often less painful to not try than to try and fail. Their advice is designed to help their children defend themselves in a hostile world. Unfortunately, such uninvolved behavior conflicts with the hopes and aspirations of the teacher for a developmentally appropriate classroom in which children are intensely engaged, where parents participate, and where parents and teachers share a common vision for the future.

Teachers also find it easy to blame parents for their own failures. Often, teachers do not understand why children do not learn from the "developmental" curriculum they provide and conclude that there must be something wrong with the child's family life. The teachers do not understand why parents do not provide the support systems that the teachers think necessary for children to learn: orderly households, regular habits, and environments rich in school-related experiences, such as trips to the zoo, measuring cooking ingredients, and describing the attributes of everything from peas to dinosaurs.

When there is a misfit between home and school, often neither parents nor teachers mediate for children. Parents are unable to help children because they do not know what their children need to know and do to meet teacher expectations; teachers are not effective mediators because they do not know how to attach new knowledge to what children already know.

# Problems in classroom management and teaching practices

When teachers and children share lifestyles and world views, when the same contexts evoke in them similar knowledge and understanding, they have a relatively easy time "making meaning" together. Teachers are familiar with the common experiences that children of a particular age have had. They understand what children value and what is relevant in their lives and can tie new learning to these things. They know the styles and various learning characteristics of children and can use these to encourage learning. They know family and community expectations and can arrange for home and school to reinforce one another.

Today, in our schools and centers, many teachers do not share a personal backlog of common experience with children and families. They do not know what experiences children have had that teachers can draw upon to teach their curriculum. An example of how subtle and pervasive the gap is between school expectations and the experiences of children is exemplified by a test given to inner-city children, in which the stimulus picture was of a boy on a bike with a bag of newspapers. The question was, "Is this boy playing or working?" For inner-city children who have never seen a paper boy on a bicycle, the answer the children gave—"playing"—*is* right, but not according to the testers.

Following are some examples drawn from everyday classroom life that illustrate how the breakdown in communication between children and teachers occurs in developmentally appropriate programs. These challenges must be confronted if minority children are to reach their potentials in developmentally appropriate classrooms and if such practices are to be well implemented.

## Background information and experiences

Using children's everyday experience as a way to make formal learning relevant and meaningful is an important aspect of developmentally appropriate practice. Many teachers, however, find that they know so little about how children live their daily lives that they have little to draw upon. For instance, many teachers are drawn to whole language approaches to teaching reading but fail to appreciate the time needed to move from rich literacy experiences to reading achievement. They are disappointed when children who do not come from literacy-enriched homes do not achieve on the same grade-level schedule as those who do. Children from inner-city communities, for example, often do not come to schools or centers having had the experiential background that ties easily to the reading materials considered most appropriate for young children. Books focus on baby animals, zoo animals, pets, milkmen, kind policemen, grass, and flowers—ideas and concepts not frequently encountered in the children's daily lives. When children do not have the relevant background, they do not learn "naturally" in the seamless and organic way that teachers have been led to expect.

For other teachers the life experiences of many low-income and minority children and their families are so frightening that the teachers are unable to bridge the gap between home and school. Teachers whose own lives are more ordered, less violent, and include fewer obvious illegal activities may feel frightened and uncertain when confronting children whose lives are so different; thus, teachers' sense of competence and control is lost, and the quality of their interaction with children is skewed. Teachers also may feel shocked and helpless when they hear about the events that occur in children's lives. As one sensitive teacher cried, "How do you help a child edit an essay on incest, or respond to disclosures about stolen goods, or hold class discussions on the mores of drug dealers instead of community helpers?" Vast areas of the daily lives of some low-income and minority children are cut off from those of their teachers, leaving teachers unable to nurture ties between school-related skills and knowledge and children's daily lives.

## Developmental assessment

To determine what children are ready to learn and what processing capabilities the children can draw on to understand and respond to new experiences, teachers need to be able to assess children's potential for learning. When children fail to perform in ways that teachers expect, the teachers must understand why. Does the child not have the developmental competence for a task, or has he simply not had experience with the particular context in which the task is embedded?

Developmental achievements look quite different from one community to another. This difference is obvious when children speak an altogether different language from that of the teacher. It is easy to understand why English-only teachers are not able to judge the linguistic competence of Spanish-only or Chinese-only children, but in school this is rarely the case for very long. Most young foreign-language-speaking children are between a beginning knowledge of English and fluency. Teachers must try to decide whether a child's understanding is impeded by poor English, developmental immaturity or delay, or socioemotional problems that affect linguistic performance.

Assessment of children who speak dialects of English is equally difficult. Black English-speaking children's pronunciation is often difficult for standard English-speaking teachers to understand, and its usage, standard at home, may be considered incorrect at school. Teachers must decide whether the expression of ideas in nonstandard English represents "mistakes" or an alternative form. When a Black English-speaking child says "Bear bees tired," is she describing the temporary sleepiness of one bear (the correct answer) or making a generic statement regarding all bears (an incorrect understanding of the story)?

Linguistic communication is not just grammar. Rules are social, facial, and corporeal, and they are derived from the data bank of the child's own world. Social rules encompass what things are talked about, with whom, under what circumstances, for what purpose, and with what intonation and gesticulation. How the eyes are used (docile or combative), the shape of the mouth (sullen, disapproving, pleased, or ecstatic), and posture (head up or down) all carry messages that reinforce, clarify, or deny the words used. Further, in many African American communities, the exact meaning of the word is less important than its sound, and meaning may have to be derived from context and intonation rather than from definition.

Many African American children use standard or almost-standard grammar but use other rules of Black English, such as speaking loudly or aggressively and using lots of body language. They may seem angry, aggressive, and induce fear in teachers. Indeed, teachers of quite young children may express concern for their own personal safety. Fear stems from the teachers' misinterpretation of the meaning of children's behavior as well as from the highly vulnerable feeling-state in which many teachers approach low-income minority communities.

Other developmental milestones present equally difficult problems. For instance, "self-control," an important developmental accomplishment, may seem quite different for an African American boy from a community that tolerates high levels of physical aggression and a child from a middle-class, White home, who has been taught to wound with words. Self-help skills are also highly regarded by schools and centers,

yet what children are supposed to do for themselves may vary widely. Teachers, particularly in kindergarten, tend to base their assessment on the children's ability to tie shoes and put on boots rather than on the ability to cross an intersection safely or to keep one's clothes clean. In many communities children use sophisticated categorization skills in daily life (identifying car logos and gang symbols) but do not apply these skills to letters and numbers.

Most children in low-income and minority communities have mastered developmentally similar tasks, but their mastery may be displayed in unfamiliar dress. For instance, teachers often criticize African American children's poor physical control when they will not sit quietly in chairs, yet it is not unusual for the same children to have highly developed physical skills when playing ball or jumping rope. Children may control their bodies for athletics or for peer appreciation but not for the teacher or her lessons. Unless teachers are familiar with how various developmental capabilities look in a given community, they are unable to distinguish one cause of poor achievement from another. As a consequence, low-income minority children are frequently assessed as developmentally delayed or as having emotional difficulties. Screening tests and standardized achievement tests simply compound the problem because they do not help teachers determine the cause of children's difficulty and lead the teachers to assume that there is something wrong with the child, his family, or his community.

### Autonomy in thinking

One of the goals of developmentally appropriate programs is to encourage children to be active constructors of their own knowledge. Piagetians believe that by providing opportunities for children to construct knowledge for themselves from the data bank of their experience, they will become more capable and autonomous thinkers. Teachers want to prepare children to think clearly for themselves rather than depend upon adults for right answers. To support this goal, teachers encourage risk taking in thought and action ("Try it out. It's okay to be wrong."), self-confidence ("What do you think we should do?"), and self-direction ("You decide what you want to do.").

Being an "active learner," however, does not mean "anything goes." Teachers expect children to continue to use many of the social rules that define acceptable behavior, but many children have not learned at home what is "acceptable" to teachers. These children do not understand the implicit social system that is the context for the teachers' intention. Such system variables as time (being places at specific times), preparation (doing homework, having pencils), usefulness of vari-

ous skills (reading and writing), and adult-child interactive patterns (whether verbal instructions are direct or indirect) may be quite different at home and at school. When encouraged to think and act for themselves, children come up with ideas, language, and behaviors outside the range expected by teachers or permitted by schools and centers. Instead of teaching children to handle the challenges they design, teachers often respond by saying, "You can't give these kinds of children freedom," without understanding that "freedom" is meaningful only within the context of a mutually known social system.

Implicit in the type of curriculum that provides more opportunities for autonomy is the understanding that the adult will protect children from taking too-great risks, from placing too much trust in their own assessment of a situation, and from having too much confidence in their own ability to know the relevant facts. For children to be free to be independent, adults must provide appropriate protection.

Many children who live in low-income communities do not have the luxury of protection. Their world is often dangerous, resources are too limited to take chances, and adults are too tired and stressed to create an artificial world just for children. Some responsible parents try to protect their children by limiting freedom, constricting choices, and stressing obedience to adult strictures. Other parents either do not understand why children need protection or are unable to provide it for them, so many children learn through the "school of hard knocks" to distrust risk taking and trial-and-error discovery. Defining active learning for children who do not have a protected environment, who do not share a common pattern of social interaction with teachers, and whose very lives may depend on *not* taking chances is certainly a challenge.

# An expanded definition of appropriate practice

A central tenet of developmentally appropriate practice is that pedagogy should vary in response to individual differences. Developmentally appropriate programs must also adapt the program structure and interactions among adults and children in response to differences in the expectations and demands of different cultures and groups. To implement developmentally appropriate practice in classrooms for low-income and minority children, the following guidelines should be added to the guidelines for appropriate practice:

**1.** Teachers need to know more about the relationship of child development and culture. The behavioral markers teachers use to guide their understanding of

*RAISING QUESTIONS ABOUT THE APPLICABILITY OF DEVELOPMENTALLY APPROPRIATE PRACTICE TO PROGRAMS FOR LOW-INCOME AND MINORITY CHILDREN SHOULD NOT CAST DOUBT ON THE PRINCIPLES ON WHICH THE GUIDELINES ARE BASED. LOW-INCOME AND MINORITY CHILDREN NEED MANY OF THE SAME THINGS THAT OTHER CHILDREN NEED.*

children in their own community are not sufficient when working with culturally different populations.

Teachers need preservice and in-service training to help them recognize developmental milestones and equivalences in behavior across cultural difference. By recognizing that such equivalences exist, teachers can begin the search for a better match between their and the child's understanding of situations and tasks.

**2.** It is essential to teach teachers not to value some ways of achieving developmental milestones over others since young children are particularly sensitive to how adults value them and are vulnerable to lowered self-esteem and self-confidence.

This does not mean that teachers should not teach children to speak, read, and write in standard English, or to process information in the formal idiom of school, or to gather information that is not immediately useful in their lives. It does mean that teachers need to think about how to accomplish these goals with young low-income and minority children whose experiences in life validate other realities.

**3.** Learning mediated by teachers who are personally important is more likely to stick than is learning when the adult is socially distant.

Responsive adults are essential in programs for all young children, particularly for children finding their way in strange terrain. Developmentally appropriate programs require that teachers and children engage in joint activities, give each other emotional gratification, and have mutually intelligible ways of showing that they care about each other. Multiyear placements of the same teachers and children is one way such relationships can be sponsored. These arrangements give teachers and children time to engage one another personally and to build a classroom culture in which children and adults learn from one another how to make meaning together. Parents can also gain a sense of stability and trust through personal knowledge of teachers.

**4.** The assessment of learning outcomes presents a formidable problem for teachers of children outside the economic and cultural mainstream.

Teachers need to develop appropriate ways to assess children's knowledge and skills and to use their assessments to drive curriculum. The inappropriateness of standardized tests is well known among early childhood practitioners, but these tests are particularly inappropriate for use with young children who come from low-income and minority communities. Because their prior experiences do not mirror those of middle-class children, children from low-income families may not learn the same material on exactly the same timetable, although they will have learned a great many other things by the time they start school, and there should be no question about their ability to learn. Teachers using developmentally appropriate practices must recognize their obligation to provide the content that children need to know to function within the developmental framework. Process without content will not move these children toward school achievement.

**5.** Schools and centers need people who can mediate between cultures.

Program mentors who can act as role models, consultants, and sources of information are sorely needed. Unfortunately, in many schools and centers, teachers have little time for reflection, for consultation, and for sharing their insights and problems.

**6.** School learning is most likely to occur when family values reinforce school expectations.

This does not mean that parents must teach the same things at home that teachers teach in school; however, parents and the community must project school achievement as a desirable and attainable ego ideal if children are to build it into their own sense of self. Parents who are afraid of the power of school, who are defensive about their own shortcomings in relation to school, and who do not trust schools and centers to meet their and their children's needs are not likely to send their children to school with the explicit message, "Learn." Interpretation of the school's agenda to parents is as important as—perhaps more important than—many of the other tasks at which teachers spend their time. Only if parents and teachers can collaborate are children free to learn from both.

Raising questions about the applicability of developmentally appropriate practice to programs for low-income and minority children should not cast doubt on the principles on which the guidelines are based. Low-income and minority children need many of the same things that other children need: responsive and thoughtful teachers and caregivers, opportunities to learn with emotional support, and consistency and continuity of

people and of methods. Thoughtful teachers can use developmental principles to

• help young children create meaning in the new context of school;

• help young children attach new learning to what they already know; and

• safeguard children's self-image and self-confidence while the children expand their knowledge and skills.

Standardized curriculum, standardized pedagogy, and standardized assessment strategies, however, are not useful in a multicultural community—nor are they developmentally appropriate.

## References

Bredekamp, S. (1987). *Developmentally appropriate practice in early childhood programs serving children from birth through age 8* (rev. ed.). Washington, DC: NAEYC.

Burts, D., Hart, C., Charlesworth, R., Fleege, P., Mosley, J., & Thomasson, R. (1992). Observed activities and stress behaviors of children in developmentally appropriate and inappropriate kindergarten classrooms. *Early Childhood Research Quarterly, 7*(2), 297–318.

Cole, M., & Bruner, J. (1972). Cultural differences and inferences about psychological processes. *American Psychologist, 26,* 867–876.

Delpit, L. (1988). The silenced dialogue: Power and pedagogy in educating other people's children. *Harvard Educational Review, 58*(3), 280–298.

Ellwood, D. (1988). *Poor support.* New York: Basic Books.

Erikson, E. (1950). *Childhood and society.* New York: Basic Books.

Ginsburg, H. (1982). The development of addition in the contexts of culture, social class, and race. In T.P. Carpenter, J.M. Moser, & T.A. Romberg (Eds.), *Addition and subtraction: A cognitive perspective.* (pp. 191–210). Hillsdale, NJ: Erlbaum.

Hale-Benson, J. (1986). *Black children: Their roots, culture and learning styles.* Baltimore: Johns Hopkins University Press.

Hilliard, A., & Vaughn-Scott, M. (1982). The quest for the minority child. In S. Moore & C. Cooper (Eds.), *The young child: Reviews of research, Vol. 3* (pp. 175–189). Washington, DC: NAEYC.

Jipson, J. (1991). Developmentally appropriate practice: Culture, curriculum, connections. *Early Education and Development, 2*(2), 120–136.

Laosa, L. (1980). Maternal teaching strategies in Chicano and Anglo-American families. *Child Development, 51,* 759–765.

Lawson, J. (1986). A study of the frequency of analogical responses to questions in black and white preschool-age children. *Early Childhood Research Quarterly, 1*(4), 379.

McGoldrick, M. (1982). Ethnicity and family therapy: An overview. In M. McGoldrick, J. Pearce, & J. Giordano (Eds.), *Ethnicity and family therapy* (pp. 3–30). New York: Guilford Press.

National Association for the Education of Young Children & National Association of Early Childhood Specialists in State Departments of Education. (1991). Guidelines for appropriate curriculum content and assessment in programs serving children ages 3 through 8. *Young Children, 46*(3), 21–38.

Ogbu, J. (1978). *Minority education and caste.* New York: Academic Press.

Ramirez, M., & Price-Williams, D. (1974). Cognitive styles of children of three ethnic groups in the United States. *Journal of Cross-Cultural Psychology, 5,* 212–219.

Rogoff, B. (1990). *Apprenticeship in thinking.* New York: Oxford University Press.

Shade, B. (1982). Afro-American cognitive style: A variable in school success. *Review of Educational Research, 52,* 219–244.

Vygotsky, L.S. (1978). *Mind in society.* Cambridge, MA: Harvard University Press.

Wilson, W. (1987). *The truly disadvantaged: The inner city, the underclass, and public policy.* Chicago: University of Chicago Press.

# Reaching Potentials of Linguistically Diverse Children

---

## 10

## *Editors' introduction*

*The United States has traditionally been seen as a culturally diverse society, but only recently has there been recognition that this country is also linguistically diverse. Data from the 1990 census of the U.S. population vividly illustrate this diversity. Almost 14% of Americans between the ages of 5 and 17 speak a language other than English at home. (Data are not available for children younger than age 5, but presumably the statistics are comparable.) In addition, some states have much higher percentages of school-age children whose primary language is not English. For example, 35% of school-age children in California speak a language other than English at home, while 29.5% of children in New Mexico and 28.2% of children in Texas do not speak English at home. (All data are from the U.S. Bureau of the Census, 1990). All states report some percentage of linguistically diverse school children, and 17 states have more than 10%. These percentages are anticipated to increase in the future due to trends in immigration and population. Over the next decade language-minority children will become the majority in many school districts—especially large urban districts—in this nation. Perhaps of even greater interest is*

*the amount of diversity among the spoken languages reported by the Census Bureau; the Census reported 25 language categories, most of which represent numerous different languages or dialects. In New York City alone, public schools report enrolling children from 167 different countries (Vobejda, 1992).*

*The linguistic diversity of our nation's children presents an opportunity as well as a challenge for our schools. The opportunity is, of course, for this country to become a multilingual society like so many other countries in the world. The presence of diverse language speakers in our schools and the existence of bilingual education programs provide the potential for creating a multilingual America. All children who speak a language other than English at home have the potential to become bilingual, biliterate individuals; yet this potential is not being achieved. More importantly, many speakers of other languages are failing to succeed at all, as evidenced by unacceptably high drop-out rates for Hispanic children and other linguistic minorities. As the NAEYC and NAECS/SDE guidelines point out, "A major contributor to early school failure is submersion of non-English-speaking children into classrooms where the children's own* culture and language background are neither incorporated nor valued" (p. 14).

Our purpose in this discussion is to explore the applicability of the Curriculum and Assessment Guidelines to programs serving linguistically diverse young children. Several approaches exist for serving language-minority children. The first approach, bilingual education, is described by Liz Wolfe, Director of Bilingual Education for the Redwood City School District in California. Wolfe supports bilingual education as the preferred learning environment for meeting the needs of second-language learners. Bilingual education programs support the development of the native language while also developing proficiency in English. Wolfe also presents a case for emphasizing primary-language instruction for preschool-age children.

Another approach for second-language learners is English as a Second Language (ESL). This approach is most practical in situations where multiple languages are spoken in a classroom or community, and a bilingual program is therefore not feasible. Teresa Rosegrant, coeditor of this book, teaches kindergarten in a public school that serves 33 different language groups; her kindergarten class of 26 this year included speakers of 14 languages and only one native English speaker. This language diversity makes bilingual education impossible; there simply are not adult role models available for all of these linguistic groups. Bilin-

gual education, as discussed by Wolfe and others, is most feasible when sufficient numbers of children speak the same language other than English. For example, in California, Texas, and Florida, as well as many other states, the numbers of children in school who speak Spanish at home make a bilingual Spanish/English program not only desirable but practical. Similarly, in schools serving Native American children, a bilingual approach supporting the native language, as well as English acquisition, is reasonable.

Another bilingual strategy is the dual-language, or two-way bilingual, approach (Soto, 1991). In these programs the goal is for both language-majority and language-minority children to become bilingual and biliterate. This approach is increasingly being adopted by magnet schools in communities where parents want their children to know two languages.

Regardless of whether a bilingual, ESL, dual-language, or other approach is used, for the program to be effective it must be congruent with sound pedagogical and developmental approaches to second-language acquisition, as well as demonstrate respect and support for the cultures of the children and their families. Wolfe's views are presented first, followed by commentary by Rosegrant from the point of view of a kindergarten teacher in a multilingual school, operating from the English as a Second Language perspective.

# Reaching Potentials Through Bilingual Education

*Liz Wolfe*

In my view, bilingual education is the most effective way of providing early childhood education for linguistically diverse children, and it is the strategy most in keeping with the spirit of the NAEYC and NAECS/SDE Curriculum and Assessment Guidelines (pp. 9–27). In this chapter, research in support of bilingual education is presented, as well as research in support of primary-language instruction in programs for very young children. Issues raised by a multilingual classroom are identified, with suggestions for effective program implementation based on current research findings on second-language acquisition. The importance of involving parents as collaborators with the school program is discussed, and ideas for fostering this collaboration are offered.

One overarching principle informs this discussion: Early childhood programs should be designed with the understanding that, contrary to popular belief, young children develop proficiency—which is not the same as fluency—in a second language slowly. Young children need several years of schooling before reaching an academic par in English with their English-only counterparts. Early childhood programs must make every effort to incorporate the language and culture of the diverse minority groups in the classroom while the children are developing proficiency in English.

## What is bilingual education?

Bilingual education is the instruction of students in two languages. Effective bilingual programs instruct children in all of the academic subjects in their primary languages while they are developing proficiency in English. Throughout the program, the English language skills are developed through comprehensible instruction appropriate to the proficiency level of the children.

Bilingual programs are controversial and continue to be met with strong opposition. Admittedly, this opposition is often politically motivated, but it also results from misinformation. Two common misconceptions about bilingual programs are that children in bilingual programs never learn English and that children in bilingual programs never do well enough in academic subjects to join the mainstream (Krashen & Biber, 1988). Opponents of bilingual programs contend that language-minority children need maximum exposure to English to ever succeed in English. These opinions have raised barriers to bilingual education and have led to the institution of English-submersion education programs for younger and younger children. For example, several states fund prekindergarten pro-

*EARLY CHILDHOOD PROGRAMS SHOULD BE DESIGNED WITH THE UNDERSTANDING THAT, CONTRARY TO POPULAR BELIEF, YOUNG CHILDREN DEVELOP PROFICIENCY—WHICH IS NOT THE SAME AS FLUENCY—IN A SECOND LANGUAGE SLOWLY. EARLY CHILDHOOD PROGRAMS MUST MAKE EVERY EFFORT TO INCORPORATE THE LANGUAGE AND CULTURE OF THE DIVERSE MINORITY GROUPS IN THE CLASSROOM WHILE THE CHILDREN ARE DEVELOPING PROFICIENCY IN ENGLISH.*

grams in public schools to serve children identified as at-risk for school failure; limited-English-speaking children are often identified for these services, which are often provided in English only. An examination of the research on bilingual education and second-language acquisition reveals evidence that contradicts widely held misconceptions about bilingual education and also raises serious questions about the advisability of English-submersion programs for preschool-age children. A discussion of these issues follows.

## The effects of bilingual education

Learning that takes place in the child's primary language does not slow down the child's acquisition of English; rather, instruction by means of the primary language in preschool through the early grades promotes and develops the deeper cognitive and academic skills that predict future success in the mainstream. There is abundant evidence (Cummins, 1981a, b) that many language-minority children develop academic language in English as a result of academic language that has been first developed in their primary languages. ("Academic language" is the language of the subject-matter disciplines; for example, mathematics abounds with terminology such as *addition, subtraction, minus,* and *dividend.*)

How can time spent in instruction in another language increase English proficiency? Children who have had high-quality education in their primary language have had the opportunity to "use language to communicate effectively and to facilitate thinking and learning; to become literate individuals who gain satisfaction, as well as information, from reading and writing, and to think critically, reason, and solve problems" (NAEYC & NAECS/SDE, 1991; p. 18, this volume). Once children have developed these abilities in their native language, they can transfer these skills to any new language.

A common misconception is that language-minority children who appear to quickly acquire English fluency have developed sufficient language proficiency to operate in academic contexts in English. It is important to understand, however, that language used by children for conversational purposes and playground talk is quite different from language necessary for academic achievement in school. Language-minority children may become conversationally fluent in English before they develop the ability to understand or use English in academic situations. Research (Cummins, 1981a, b) demonstrates that it can take approximately two years for children to develop this conversational fluency in a second language. Academic proficiency, however, may take an additional

five years. Second-language learners therefore need five to seven years to develop the academic English that is needed to participate fully and on an equal par with native English speakers in a classroom.

Bilingual programs are often criticized for keeping second-language learners after they have become "fluent." Again, this criticism is based on inaccurate perceptions about the speed with which children become fluent in a second language. A child's skill in English may be judged as fluent, but that does not mean her skills are sufficient for understanding verbal explanations from the teacher, comprehending difficult stories, following oral directions, or understanding other decontextualized language. Children who are diagnosed inaccurately as fluent run the risk of being labeled as slow, disabled, or even retarded on the basis of their limited understanding of academic language (Cummins, 1981a, b; Hakuta, 1986). The question of when to "graduate" children from bilingual education is only part of the dilemma; perhaps a more difficult question is when to begin bilingual education and/or instruction in English and how best to proceed. This leads to the controversial issue of preschool practices for linguistically diverse children.

## The effects of primary-language instruction in preschool

As mentioned earlier, concerns about readiness for school have led to the implementation of prekindergarten programs for limited-English-speaking children in many areas of this country. More research is needed on programs for very young children, but it is clear that preschool programs should be designed with the expectation that young children develop academic proficiency in second languages slowly and will need several years before their English is up to par with that of children who have been speaking English since birth. Currently there is sufficient research to raise concerns about English-submersion programs with preschool children. Wong Fillmore (1991a, b) and others have found that submersing children in English-only preschools can lead to children's losing their ability to communicate effectively in their primary language. When the native language is the only language that the children's parents speak, the ability to communicate and therefore develop a relationship with their child can be seriously undermined. Also of concern is the fact that language constitutes the building blocks of thought, and preschool children are not only developing verbal language at a rapid pace but are also using this language for conceptual development. If the language itself is confused, it is likely that conceptual development will also be adversely affected.

There is evidence to show that supporting primary-language development in preschool has positive effects on academic achievement as well as English-language acquisition. The experimental Spanish-only preschool program of the Carpinteria School District near Santa Barbara, California, is one of the few early childhood programs in the United States to have actually tested this hypothesis. The Carpinteria preschool program used effective early childhood teaching strategies using Spanish as the exclusive language of instruction and emphasized strong parent/community involvement through meaningful linguistic interaction.

The decision to implement an intensive Spanish-only preschool program in Carpinteria was based on the teachers' observations that a large majority of Spanish-speaking children entered kindergarten without adequate skills. Many Spanish-speaking children had been enrolled in the existing bilingual programs provided by Head Start or community child care centers. Both English and Spanish were used concurrently in these programs but with emphasis on developing English. Kindergarten teachers reported that children who had attended these programs often mixed both English and Spanish into "Spanglish."

The major goal of the experimental Spanish-only program was to bring Spanish-dominant children up to a level of readiness comparable to that of the English-speaking children in the community. The project worked in collaboration with the parents of these children, encouraging parents to see themselves as the children's first teachers and providing parents with strategies for providing appropriate learning experiences for their children at home.

The program was designed to integrate language with numerous concrete activities and literacy-related experiences. The evaluation report stated, "The development of language skills in Spanish was foremost in the planning and attention given to every facet of the preschool day.

Language was used constantly for conversing, learning new ideas, concepts and vocabulary, thinking creatively, and problem-solving to give the children the opportunity to develop their language skills in Spanish to as high a degree as possible within the structure of the preschool day" (Campos & Keatings in Cummins, 1986, p. 31).

Participation in this program was voluntary. Children were screened only for age and Spanish-language dominance. The majority of the children were of low socioeconomic status. Most of their parents worked in agriculture and had an average education of about sixth-grade level.

Evaluation of the program demonstrated that it was highly successful in developing readiness skills and English proficiency. The Spanish-dominant children tested at a level of readiness comparable to that of the English-speaking children in the community, as measured by standardized tests. Another outcome of the program was that despite the fact that the children had experienced a Spanish-only program, they performed better on their English proficiency tests than did the other Spanish-speaking children who had been in the bilingual classrooms. The evaluation report explained this finding: "Although project participants were exposed to less *total* English, they, because of their enhanced first language skill and concept knowledge, were better able to comprehend the English they were exposed to" (Campos & Keatings in Cummins, 1986, p. 32). Undoubtedly, the strong emphasis on parent involvement and respect for the culture of the family were also important factors in the success of the Carpinteria program. Parent involvement and cultural sensitivity are acknowledged as elements of good early childhood practice in general, but these elements are critical to the success of programs serving linguistically diverse children.

## Multilingual classrooms

Despite positive research outcomes from programs such as the Carpinteria preschool program, primary-language instruction, bilingual education, or dual-language programs are not possible everywhere due to practical barriers. The primary barrier is the lack of qualified staff. Unfortunately, the availability of language-minority staff members is a serious problem; the need for speakers of the various different languages spoken by young children in this country is far greater than available resources. The challenge is to develop these resources and pursue a variety of means to bring minority languages into the classrooms. A second barrier is the degree of diversity among language-minority children in many areas of the country. In situations where several minority languages are represented in one classroom, primary-language instruction or bilingual education is difficult. The question be-

*LEARNING THAT TAKES PLACE IN THE CHILD'S PRIMARY LANGUAGE DOES NOT SLOW DOWN THE CHILD'S ACQUISITION OF ENGLISH; RATHER, INSTRUCTION BY MEANS OF THE PRIMARY LANGUAGE IN PRESCHOOL THROUGH THE EARLY GRADES PROMOTES AND DEVELOPS THE DEEPER COGNITIVE AND ACADEMIC SKILLS THAT PREDICT FUTURE SUCCESS IN THE MAINSTREAM.*

comes one of how best to provide instruction and opportunities for interaction to children who are in the very early stages of acquiring a second language. To provide effective, linguistically appropriate instruction, teachers must understand the process of second-language acquisition, just as to be developmentally appropriate they must understand child development. Programs for second-language learners should reflect principles of high-quality, developmentally appropriate curriculum and teaching for young children (Soto, 1991). Such programs must meet guidelines for developmentally appropriate practice (Bredekamp, 1987) as well as the Curriculum and Assessment Guidelines described in this book.

Recent research on second-language acquisition has greatly expanded our understanding of how a second language is acquired and how this acquisition is best promoted in a classroom. Research described by Krashen (1981) and Terrell (1981) notes several similarities between the acquisition of a second language and the development of a first language. The process of acquiring a second language is developmental and can be augmented by appropriate activities based on the meaningful communication of messages.

The natural approach to second-language acquisition (Terrell, 1981) is based on the understanding of these developmental stages. In the earliest stage of language acquisition, the preproduction stage, second-language learners have minimal comprehension and almost no verbal skills. At this stage children concentrate on listening and deciphering clues and input from teachers and peers. Educators must focus on building receptive vocabulary for these children. Comprehension increases through total physical response activities, a "natural approach" method to enhance listening comprehension, in which children respond to verbal commands and instructions ("Get your snack," "Wash your hands," "Put the toys away") without having to speak. Communication is aided by gestures, actions, pictures, manipulatives, and other hands-on, real objects. Teachers assess children's comprehension by asking them to perform nonverbal actions such as pointing, nodding, matching, acting, and drawing. This stage of language acquisition may last from a few weeks to three or four months depending on the child's self-esteem and the amount of anxiety he experiences in the program.

At the second stage of language acquisition, the early-production stage, children have internalized and can understand some basic vocabulary. They begin to use responses consisting of one or two words, such as "yes" or "no"; respond to who, what, and where questions; answer either/or questions; and list simple nouns. Children may be motivated and given the opportunity to speak and use the words they have heard and understood. Educators must refrain from pushing for verbal production, however, and must resist correcting errors. As in the first stage, children are still concentrating on listening, and comprehension is still limited. Children need to be surrounded by contextual clues to aid in negotiation of meaning. This stage may last for an additional two to three months.

The third stage of language acquisition, speech emergence, is the stage in which children begin to connect language to meaning. Children become more comfortable with their learning environment, and the need to communicate motivates them to use more language. They begin to use short sentences and phrases and to carry on dialogues. Their speech has frequent mistakes in pronunciation and grammar, but they are better able to communicate messages. Educators should be sensitive to these children's newfound sense of accomplishment with their new language. Direct correction of pronunciation and grammatical errors will hinder the children's future communication efforts. Modeling the correct form and continuing to encourage the children to communicate will increase the children's proficiency in their new language. Continued interaction with concrete manipulatives and real objects is essential for language acquisition and construction of knowledge. Children may operate in this stage for up to two years.

At the intermediate-fluency stage of language acquisition, children are fluent in survival language and are able to communicate in face-to-face conversational speech with few errors. They have excellent comprehension in everyday, conversational language but are still developing comprehension in the academic or content-area language. Often educators are confused by children who are at this stage. These children seem to be doing very well in oral-language development but are unable to understand or participate well in the content areas. This is the stage in which comprehensible input, the meaningful communication of messages in the content areas, is most crucial to the children's development of the academic language and concept attainment necessary to participate in the mainstream. Children at this stage need continued support in their primary language and in comprehensible subject-matter instruction if they are to make the bridge to native-like mainstream proficiency. Most children need this continued programmatic support for three to four more years.

Effective multilingual programs should reflect understanding of the process of second-language acquisition but should also reflect ethical and legal considerations. Coupled with the research on second-language acquisition is the 1974 Lau v. Nichols U.S. Supreme Court decision, in which the Supreme Court ruled that "there is no equality of treatment merely by providing students with the same facilities, textbooks, teachers, and curriculum; [because] **students who do not understand English are effectively foreclosed from any meaningful education**" (Teutelbaum & Hiller in Hakuta, 1986, p. 200). This court decision means that second-language learners need to be identified and given appropriate curriculum and instruction, preferably learning experiences that build on and support the primary language of the children. When minority-language diversity and lack of qualified minority-language speakers make this impractical, our challenge is to provide in the classroom the "comprehensible input" that second-language learners require to participate in "meaningful education." An effective way to achieve this goal is through collaboration with parents and the community.

# Collaboration with parents and the community

One of the elements in developing successful programs for linguistically diverse children is communication and collaboration with families. "The healthy development of young children begins in a relationship with another human being, the parent-child relationship being the primary example of social interaction through which very young children develop and learn" (NAEYC & NAECS/SDE, 1991; p. 15, this volume). Parents and family members must be convinced that interacting and working with children at home in their native language will pay off for their children at school. Teachers must be convinced that this is true as well.

Educators tend to assume that language-minority children do not do well in school because they lack the linguistic background that is perceived as essential to school success. This assumption causes teachers to ask parents of second-language learners to "practice more English at home." More harm than good can come of this advice. The quality of interaction in the home between parents and children is fundamental to children's self-esteem and social competence. By asking parents to communicate with their children in an unfamiliar language, we effectively limit the quality of their interactions.

Full use of family resources must be part of an ongoing parent and community involvement component of the schools (Legaretta-Marcaida, 1981). Bilingual staff members must visit homes early in the year and regularly thereafter to explain the program's goals and advantages for children and to stress to parents and other family members the value of maintaining and strengthening the child's native language at home. After an initial home visit, a link between home and school can be forged in numerous ways:

• Parents, other family members, and members of the community who are literate in their primary language may read stories aloud to the children in the classroom and at home, or make audiotapes for children to hear at school or take home. Reading aloud to young children is the single most effective key to later success in reading.

• Children and parents may be encouraged to participate in a home/school library program. Children may bring home primary-language stories, magazines, and books to share with their families. Parents may have access to books that are reflective of the culture instead of books that are just translations of culturally inappropriate texts.

• Parents and older family members may be encouraged to visit the school to tell stories, folktales, sayings, and riddles, and to share other oral traditions from their culture with the children.

• Parents may be encouraged to bring records, folk art, photos, and artifacts from their home cultures into the classroom to share and discuss.

• Parents and relatives may share their knowledge of traditional celebrations, music, poetry, dance, and costumes with the school through classroom visits, through setting up displays, by planning multicultural activities, or in other ways (these experiences reflect the children's own culture and therefore are not comparable to the "tourist" curriculum of visiting the superficial artifacts of other people's culture, referred to by Derman-Sparks in Chapter 8).

• The program may provide opportunities for parents—in their primary languages—to learn how to help their children at home, discipline, and other areas in which parents express needs and interests. Opportunities for parents may be provided in various formats, such as home visits or meetings at school, community centers, and other centrally located sites.

Parent and community involvement are key to ensuring cultural continuity for children. When a child's language is not incorporated into the school environ-

" ... THE ROOTS OF THE TERM EDUCATION IMPLY DRAWING OUT CHILDREN'S POTENTIAL, MAKING THEM MORE THAN THEY WERE; HOWEVER, WHEN CHILDREN COME TO SCHOOL FLUENT IN THEIR PRIMARY LANGUAGE AND THEY LEAVE SCHOOL ESSENTIALLY MONOLINGUAL IN ENGLISH, THEN OUR SCHOOLS HAVE NEGATED THE MEANING OF THE TERM EDUCATION BECAUSE THEY HAVE MADE THE CHILDREN LESS THAN THEY WERE."

ment, the message that is sent is that his language and culture are of low status. This message is then transferred to the home environment, and low self-esteem, cultural denial, and the disruption of familial relationships may ensue. If we are not careful, parents and children may lose the ability to communicate about the deep and critical experiences of growing up. What the parent is able to teach the child and what the child is able to express to his parents are irretrievably lost when their means of communication are lost (Wong Fillmore, 1991b).

# Assessment

One of the biggest challenges facing programs that serve linguistically diverse children is the area of assessment. The complexities of assessing young children in general and assessing children from culturally diverse backgrounds are discussed in Chapters 4 and 9, respectively. NAEYC (1988) has taken the position that for "non-native English speakers or speakers of some dialects of English, any test administered in English is primarily a language or literacy test" (p. 46). This caution applies to all of the various uses of assessment for decisions affecting young children.

An area of particular concern relevant to assessment of linguistically diverse children is the identification and diagnosis of special needs (Santos de Barona & Barona, 1991). Two kinds of errors must be prevented. Some children are misidentified as developmentally delayed or even disabled on the basis of their level of English-language proficiency. At the same time some children who *are* developmentally delayed or have a disability go without needed services because accurate assessments that are in their primary language and are sensitive to their culture are not available or are not used. In either case, a gross injustice is done.

The assessment guidelines succinctly state the issue and hold assessment of linguistically diverse children to a high standard: "Assessment recognizes individual diversity of learners and allows for differences in styles and rates of learning. Assessment takes into consideration children's ability in English, their stage of language acquisition, and whether they have been given the time and opportunity to develop proficiency in their native language as well as in English" (NAEYC & NAECS/SDE, 1991; p. 23, this volume).

# Summary

As educators, we must look closely at the choices we make for the children we teach. Underlying choices for curriculum and assessment procedures are the beliefs, attitudes, and expectations that we hold for each child. Implicit in the Curriculum and Assessment Guidelines are goals for the kind of children we want to produce (a sample goal statement appears on p. 18, this volume). In applying these goals to children who speak languages other than English, consider the following:

• If we want each child to develop "a positive self-concept and attitude toward learning, self-control, and a sense of belonging," we need to integrate the language and culture of each child into our classrooms.

• If we want each child to "use language to communicate effectively and to facilitate thinking and learning," we need to make appropriate determinations about primary-language instruction and integration and have a better understanding about the process of second-language development.

• If we believe that each child has the right to equal access to the curriculum, we need to look for curriculum developed in the primary language of each child.

• If we believe that each child has the capability to reach high levels of academic performance, we need to provide curriculum and instruction in the primary language of each child as he acquires English.

• If we want to reverse the pattern of widespread minority-group educational failure, we must redefine our roles within the classroom to empower children rather than disable them (Cummins, 1986).

The potential is there. As Cummins states, ". . . the roots of the term *education* imply drawing out children's potential, making them *more* than they were; however, when children come to school fluent in their primary language and they leave school essentially monolingual in English, then our schools have negated the meaning of the term *education* because they have made the children *less* than they were" (Cummins, 1989, p. vii).

# Reaching Potentials in a Multilingual Classroom: Opportunities and Challenges

*Teresa Rosegrant*

Having taught in a multilingual elementary school near a major metropolitan area for the past several years—in addition to years of previous experience in other states with large populations of linguistically diverse children, including Native American children—I agree with many of Wolfe's points about how best to serve them. The research on bilingual education, especially the work of Wong Fillmore (1991) and her colleagues, raises serious questions about our practices. The first rule of early childhood education should always be "do no harm." If programs for language-minority preschoolers are damaging their self-esteem, creating stress, and interfering with their relationships with parents, then we should all be deeply concerned; but several points must be considered as we proceed with caution toward achieving our best intentions for children. I do not have answers to these questions; I simply raise the issues in hopes of furthering the debate.

1. More research is needed on what educational strategies work best with which children and at what age. Although a growing body of research supports the effectiveness of bilingual education programs at the elementary and secondary levels, the amount of research specifically directed to preschool and primary grade children is still slim (Kagan & Garcia, 1991).

2. Consideration of the values and desires of parents is of primary importance in making decisions about second-language instruction. In my classroom the parents I serve represent the entire range of opinion on the question. Some families are members of groups that strongly value bilingualism, speak only the native language at home, and insist that the school reinforce their child's own language; others, usually recent immigrants to this country, are so deeply concerned about their children's future that they insist on only English at school and attempt to speak to their children in the very limited English that they possess, which undermines the child's native-language ability. I agree with Wolfe that our responsibility as educators is to help parents resist this temptation and encourage them to support the native language at home.

3. Among the more difficult questions raised by Wolfe is, *What is appropriate for language-minority preschoolers?* It seems abundantly clear, not only from research on second-language acquisition but also from knowledge of child development in general, that submersing 3- or 4-year-old children in programs in which they have no knowledge of the language is stressful, even cruel and potentially abusive. Does that mean that unless the preschool program offers at least some primary-language instruction, language-minority children should not participate? Not necessarily. What it does mean is that school districts should abandon any plans for introducing preschool programs for the *sole* purpose of teaching English. Preschool programs, like all early childhood activities, should be designed to serve the whole child. Children should be given many opportunities to play and interact with materials and with other children. A natural approach to second-language acquisition, as described by Wolfe, makes the best sense. Most importantly, parents or community members need to assist in the child's transition into the program, which literally requires translation.

© Francis Wardle

**4.** In my classroom I strive to create a culturally safe environment for all children. I equate the importance of cultural safety with physical and psychological safety as essential to children's sense of security and belonging—necessary prerequisites for learning. One example of how I build a culturally safe classroom is that I survey parents at the beginning of the year to get to know the family backgrounds and experiences of the children. (I use this opportunity to emphasize the importance of parents' speaking the primary language at home.) I find out which countries the children have lived in, and I seek literature from those cultures; we determine what holidays the children celebrate in their homes, and those are the only holidays we celebrate in our classroom regardless of what the district curriculum guide suggests. I don't read just one book from a given culture, but as many as I can find. I create a take-home library of children's books in primary languages to encourage parents to reinforce the native language as well as to read to their children. Then I listen and observe the children carefully to see what experiences seem to connect with them. One little girl from Africa had listened to many African stories before one in particular connected to her experience. The story was *Bringing the Rain to Kapiti Plain*, and in it a shepherd is depicted standing on one leg—"like a stork." The child brightened immediately and yelled out, "That's how people stand in my country!" Her enthusiasm communicated to me that she feels culturally safe in our classroom. I strongly support the other suggestions offered by Wolfe for involving parents and community members in the school experience of linguistically and culturally diverse children.

**5.** The two-way bilingual, or dual-language, approach, in which all the children are expected to become bilingual and biliterate, has not been discussed in detail here but is a promising strategy for situations in which there is one dominant language in addition to English. In fact, some school districts have adopted a goal for all graduates to become bilingual and biliterate. I have seen the dual-language approach used in classrooms in which for half the day, all communication is in Spanish, and for the other half, only English is spoken. This strategy is consistent with the additive principle of education that Wolfe describes. In addition, a dual-language approach ensures that the linguistic-minority children are the more competent communicators for significant periods of time, thus strengthening their sense of self-esteem and confidence as learners.

Our ability to help all children reach their potentials in early childhood programs depends on consideration of all of the above points as well as many others that will arise as the debates continue. In summary, Kuster (in press) offers five key points to consider as part of the expanding knowledge base of all early childhood educators, knowing that language-minority children will be in our classrooms—if not now, certainly in the future:

**1.** Teachers (or other adult role models) need to be fluent in children's languages. This will require infusing language instruction in teacher preparation programs as well as recruiting bilingual individuals to the teaching profession. (Perhaps this goal may not be achieved until the present generation is successfully educated in bilingual programs and enticed into the teaching profession, but the goal of providing adult role models in children's languages should be achievable now in places where the school serves one language minority group (for example, Spanish/English; Navajo/English).

**2.** We must adopt a nondeficit perspective in relation to linguistic diversity. The curriculum guidelines themselves use the pejorative term, *limited English proficiency*. This language denies children's strength: proficient Spanish and some English proficiency.

**3.** Teachers need the knowledge and the ability to preserve and enhance the best of a family's culture—not just the artifacts, but the deep structural rules that define and identify a group of people.

**4.** Teachers need a commitment to and strategies for multiage grouping as a method of maintaining family bonding, a strong value in the Latino community and among other non–European American groups. (Multiage grouping also holds the potential for providing additional linguistic role models for children; if teachers do not speak the dialect and parents are unavailable, perhaps an older sibling or other older child in the school can translate.)

**5.** All of us must examine our own racial attitudes and develop strategies to overcome the fears (including the fear of feeling stupid because one does not speak the language) that underlie negative attitudes toward cultural and linguistic diversity.

At its core, education is the process of making meaning together. Nothing is more central to making meaning than language. If our goal is for all children to reach their potentials, then schooling must be a meaningful experience for all children.

## References

Bredekamp, S. (Ed.). (1987). *Developmentally appropriate practice in early childhood programs serving children from birth through age 8* (exp. ed.). Washington, DC: NAEYC.

Cummins, J. (1981a). Empirical and theoretical underpinnings of bilingual education. *Journal of Education, 163*(1), 16–29.

Cummins, J. (1981b). The role of primary language development in promoting educational success for language minority students. In California State Department of Education, Office of Bilingual Bicultural Education, *Schooling and language minority students: A theoretical framework* (pp. 3–49). Sacramento: California State Department of Education.

Cummins, J. (1986). Empowering minority students: A framework for intervention. *Harvard Educational Review, 56*(1), 18–36.

Cummins, J. (1989). *Empowering minority students.* Sacramento: California Association of Bilingual Education.

Hakuta, K. (1986). *Mirror of language: The debate on bilingualism.* New York: Basic Books.

Hakuta, K., & Gould, L. (1987). Synthesis of research on bilingual education. *Educational Leadership, 44*(6), 38–45.

Kagan, S.L., & Garcia, E. (Eds.). (1991). Special issue: Educating linguistically and culturally diverse preschoolers. *Early Childhood Research Quarterly, 6*(3).

Krashen, S. (1981). Bilingual education and second language acquisition theory. In California State Department of Education, Office of Bilingual Bicultural Education, *Schooling and language minority students: A theoretical framework* (pp. 51–79). Sacramento: California State Department of Education.

Krashen, S., & Biber, D. (1988). *On course: Bilingual education's success in California.* Sacramento: California Association for Bilingual Education.

Kuster, C.A. (in press). Core content: What every early childhood professional should know. In J. Johnson (Ed.), *The early childhood profession coming together: Proceedings of the first annual meeting of the National Institute for Early Childhood Professional Development.* Washington, DC: NAEYC.

Legarreta-Marcaida, D. (1981). Effective use of primary language in the classroom. In California State Department of Education, Office of Bilingual Bicultural Education, *Schooling and language minority students: A theoretical framework* (pp. 83–116). Sacramento: California State Department of Education.

National Association for the Education of Young Children. (1988). Position statement on standardized testing of young children 3 through 8 years of age. *Young Children, 43*(3), 42–47.

Santos de Barona, M., & Barona, A. (1991). The assessment of culturally and linguistically different preschoolers. *Early Childhood Research Quarterly, 6*(3), 363–376.

Soto, L.D. (1991). Understanding bilingual/bicultural young children. *Young Children, 46*(2), 30–36.

Terrell, T. (1981). The natural approach in bilingual education. In California State Department of Education, Office of Bilingual Bicultural Education, *Schooling and language minority students: A theoretical framework* (pp. 117–146). Sacramento: California State Department of Education.

U.S. Bureau of the Census. (1990). Unpublished data from the 1990 Census of the Population.

Vobejda, B. (1992, April 14). America's many tongues: Immigration changing how the nation speaks. *Washington Post*, pp. 1, 14.

Wong Fillmore, L. (1991a). Language and cultural issues in the early education of language minority children. In S.L. Kagan (Ed.), *The care and education of America's young children: Obstacles and opportunities* (pp. 30–49). Chicago: University of Chicago Press.

Wong Fillmore, L. (1991b). When learning a second language means losing the first. *Early Childhood Research Quarterly, 6*(3), 323–346.

# SECTION

# IV

# Reaching Potentials
of
Teachers and Administrators

*I*mplementation of the Guidelines for Appropriate Curriculum Content and Assessment (NAEYC & NAECS/SDE, 1991) depends on committed, knowledgeable teachers and supportive administrators. The teacher's perspective on appropriate curriculum and assessment is presented in Chapter 11 by David Burchfield and Bonnie Burchfield, primary grade teachers in Albemarle County, Virginia. The larger administrative picture is painted by Linda Espinosa in Chapter 12. She relates the firsthand experiences of teachers and administrators in the Redwood City School District in California as they worked through curriculum and assessment reform in their preschool/primary program.

# Two Primary Teachers
# Learn and Discover
# Through a Process of Change

11

*David W. Burchfield and Bonnie C. Burchfield*

The Curriculum and Assessment Guidelines described in this book (pp. 9–27) and the guidelines for developmentally appropriate practice (Bredekamp, 1987) outline a vision for educating all young children. If that vision is to be achieved, teachers, administrators, school district personnel, teacher educators, parents, and legislators need a concrete description of how appropriate curriculum and teaching practices will work in the early grades. Practitioners, those of us who work with children day-to-day, must describe what a successful developmentally appropriate primary classroom looks like, how it operates, what children do, how they learn, what the teacher's role is, and how developmentally appropriate teaching practices allow children to learn more successfully than do traditional teaching methods.

For several years we have taught in a school and school district that encourage us to implement developmentally appropriate practice as best we know how. Our principal trusts and supports us as professionals to experiment, to take risks, and to struggle to find ways to make our classrooms places where children are respected, happy, and challenged to learn in ways that are appropriate to their age and to their individual rates of learning and development.

What we have discovered through our own experience and process of change is that we need not reinvent

the wheel in order to implement appropriate curriculum and practice with young children in the primary grades. Many sound instructional methods and strategies are highly consistent with the principles of developmentally appropriate practice and the Curriculum and Assessment Guidelines—the use of multiage and/or heterogeneously grouped classrooms, authentic and child-centered assessment and evaluation, timely and appropriate intervention and interaction, whole language arts (including the writing process and literature-based reading), manipulative-based math and discovery science, and a meaning-centered project approach to teaching and learning. *These approaches to teaching young children are developmentally appropriate practices.* Indeed, in light of the demand for school reform and improvement in the primary grades (NASBE, 1988), the early childhood profession's efforts to change teaching and curriculum will be more effective in influencing practice in the primary grades (and beyond) if their views are more explicitly aligned with these instructional practices.

A strong alliance of the concept of developmentally appropriate practice with sound instructional methods, based on recent research and recommendations of major professional organizations, may make developmentally appropriate practice more attractive for those who come from a more traditional approach and are exploring the idea, or for those who are already involved in a process of change and are committed to a child-centered way of teaching young children. Such a conceptual link adds credibility and provides concrete instructional techniques for those who may think in a naive or simplistic way that "developmentally appropriate" means putting children of certain developmental ages together or watering down the curriculum, or that children will magically learn how to read, for example.

In this chapter, we describe how we discovered that the principles of developmentally appropriate practice are a natural match with certain instructional practices through our own exciting and, at times, arduous process of change as teachers of young children, ages 4 to 8 (Grades K–2). We first briefly describe our theoretical base, our vision of how children learn, because our theory or vision is fundamental to life in our classroom communities and to our teaching. Second, we describe our school and the process of change we went through as we moved toward a more developmentally appropriate philosophy and approach that resulted in the formation of our two multiage primary classrooms. Finally, relying on examples from our experience with children, we present the instructional practices and strategies that we have found to be the most effective and the most developmentally appropriate.

# Our theoretical principles: Why we do what we do

As educators, we all have a theoretical framework, explicit or implicit, for what we do with the children in our classrooms. Our own theory or vision of the way children learn and develop, certainly influenced by experience and by others, deeply affects the community, the children we teach, and our role as teachers. Our theoretical principles tell us *why* we do what we do.

Our theoretical framework is fluid and changing. We readjust and fine-tune our theoretical lens from time to time, just as the children in our classrooms adjust their understandings about the world. In addition to our experiences as teachers and students ourselves, we draw on the work of many noted psychologists and educators for our own theoretical understandings, including, but not limited to, Dewey, Vygotsky, Bruner, Piaget, Walsh, DeVries, Katz, and Hatano. Following are the basic tenets from which we operate. The implications of these principles are illustrated later in this chapter in the description of our classrooms and the discussion of the instructional strategies we use. We also note that the theory underlying our practice is highly consistent with the Guidelines for Appropriate Curriculum Content and Assessment (NAEYC & NAECS/SDE, 1991; pp. 9–27, this volume).

## *Theoretical principles that underlie our practice*

**1.** Children learn best when their physiological needs are met and when they feel physically and psychologically safe and secure.

**2.** Children construct knowledge and want to make meaning and sense out of their world.

**3.** Children learn best and more naturally in diverse social contexts. Learning is a social process. Heterogeneity facilitates learning and better reflects the world that our children will inherit.

**4.** Children learn best when they are actively involved and when the content and context of learning are meaningful and relevant.

**5.** Children learn best when they initiate, evaluate, and, to an extent, direct their own work and play. Play is the work of young children and is a natural avenue for learning.

**6.** Children learn and develop expertise in different domains at very different rates. Learning leads development. Children do not develop in a lock-step or linear progression.

**7.** Children learn best when the curriculum is integrated and when all areas of a child's development are brought to the learning process (physical, social, emotional, moral, and cognitive).

---

*MANY SOUND INSTRUCTIONAL METHODS AND STRATEGIES ARE HIGHLY CONSISTENT WITH THE PRINCIPLES OF DEVELOPMENTALLY APPROPRIATE PRACTICE AND THE CURRICULUM AND ASSESSMENT GUIDELINES—THE USE OF MULTIAGE AND/OR HETEROGENEOUSLY GROUPED CLASSROOMS, AUTHENTIC AND CHILD-CENTERED ASSESSMENT AND EVALUATION, TIMELY AND APPROPRIATE INTERVENTION AND INTERACTION, WHOLE LANGUAGE ARTS (INCLUDING THE WRITING PROCESS AND LITERATURE-BASED READING), MANIPULATIVE-BASED MATH AND DISCOVERY SCIENCE, AND A MEANING-CENTERED PROJECT APPROACH TO TEACHING AND LEARNING.*

---

**8.** Children are unique and learn best when their individual needs, interests, and learning styles are known and respected and inform teaching.

**9.** Children learn how to be life-long learners when they focus on the processes of learning rather than on isolated skills, memorization, and rote recall.

**10.** Children learn best when they are challenged on the margin of their development in a given domain. Building on what children know and can do is essential to appropriate teaching practice.

Identifying and articulating our theoretical base was an important step in our developmental process as teachers. In conversations with other teachers, we find that one's root beliefs about children, learning, and teaching are much more influential than is often imagined or acknowledged.

# Our school

With this vision in mind of the way children learn, come with us as we take you on a journey to our school and our classrooms in rural central Virginia, at the foot of the Blue Ridge Mountains. Our school, Brownsville Elementary, in the Albemarle County public school system, serves about 260 children from kindergarten through fifth grade, including about 10% who are eligible for special education services. The children are from diverse socioeconomic levels. About one-third of the children are considered to be at-risk for school failure, from low socioeconomic homes, or from families that did not find success in school. Many children come from families with two employed parents. Some are children of rural, blue collar workers, and some, of professionals or university or college professors.

## *Our process of change*

The staff at Brownsville, individually and corporately, and many practitioners at other Albemarle County schools have experienced an extensive process of change over the past several years. One part of the change took place in early childhood classrooms—a change toward more child-centered and developmentally appropriate practice.

Much of the rigid structure and pressure of more traditional programs has been eliminated; for example, our school no longer uses basals as the primary source of our reading program, and a few years ago the workbooks were abandoned, freeing funds to purchase manipulatives, such as blocks, and materials, such as trade books. Classrooms are formed heterogeneously, and children with special needs are included in regular classrooms. The special education staff consults with the regular classroom teacher and comes into the classroom to assist the children with their learning. Inflexible, permanent grouping has been abandoned.

The locus of control in most classrooms has shifted and is now shared with children. As a result the children have developed a sense of ownership and pride. They have more control over their learning; they feel more successful and demonstrate improved self-esteem.

In a sense, developmentally appropriate practice has begun to "trickle up" the grades: children are being accepted for who they are as people and as learners and are being challenged to move forward from where they are. No longer are they being asked to fit THE curriculum or the basal reader. The objectives are still there; age- and grade-level benchmark goals in various curricular areas have been developed, but the needs and interests of the children and our community—instead of the curriculum—now drive what we do.

Our school community has chosen to corporately and individually examine what we believe about how children learn and then to attempt to design a comprehensive, developmentally appropriate program for all ages and grade levels in our school. Fundamentally we attempt to do three things:

**1.** Teach and promote learning in a child-centered, developmentally appropriate manner (respecting the individuality and age of the learner). In essence, this means challenging each child to learn up to his or her potential.

**2.** Allow children to learn and progress on a more flexible time schedule by rejecting retention as a solution. As a result, especially in the area of reading, we discover that children—frequently boys—who might have been retained in kindergarten or first grade are often (but not always), making remarkable progress in second and third grade.

**3.** Provide timely and appropriate intervention for children through a multifaceted effort; identify and adapt for those children who are not making adequate progress.

Treating children as individuals called for new instructional methods, more appropriate and authentic

---

*IDENTIFYING AND ARTICULATING OUR THEORETICAL BASE WAS AN IMPORTANT STEP IN OUR DEVELOPMENTAL PROCESS AS TEACHERS. IN CONVERSATIONS WITH OTHER TEACHERS, WE FIND THAT ONE'S ROOT BELIEFS ABOUT CHILDREN, LEARNING, AND TEACHING ARE MUCH MORE INFLUENTIAL THAN IS OFTEN IMAGINED OR ACKNOWLEDGED.*

---

© Francis Wardle

assessment strategies, and more child-centered ways of evaluating and reporting learning and progress. The means of reporting to parents had to change; descriptive narrative reports were developed. Parent-teacher conferences began, in which parents were involved in sharing assessment data and setting goals for their child's progress and learning. Parents had to be seen as allies in education, not adversaries.

At the same time that we, as teachers of young children ages 4 to 8 (grades K–2), attempted to develop more child-centered, developmentally appropriate classrooms, our county initiated programs to support teachers throughout the grades to implement cutting-edge instructional methods. These strategies, previously mentioned and discussed below, are based on classroom research done in the last 15 to 20 years. These instructional practices are child centered and developmentally appropriate in that they are responsive to the individual student, and they allow children to learn in age-appropriate ways; they build on what the child can do, and they involve the child in meaningful, relevant, active learning.

# Developmentally appropriate instructional strategies

## Multiage/heterogenous classrooms

We discovered that multiage and/or heterogenous grade-level classrooms are a natural extension of a child-centered and developmentally appropriate philosophy. Once we accepted the premise that children should be respected as individuals and that they should learn in age-appropriate ways, we agreed to purposely form diverse classroom communities. Our K–1 (ages

4 to 7) and 1–2 (ages 5 to 8) classrooms are mixed, with children of different ages, abilities, socioeconomic levels, races, and cultures. We concur with the research on multiage classrooms (Katz, Evangelou, & Hartman, 1990) and nongradedness (Goodlad, 1987) that there are many benefits for children socially, emotionally, and cognitively.

Our classroom communities have become places where individuality is honored and a child's accomplishments are celebrated. A sense of family and a cooperative, helpful spirit pervade the environment; competition and comparisons are not emphasized. For example, in the K–1 class a young 6-year-old, Jonathon, was spontaneously helped one day by a few of his more capable peers to write a simple message to narrate a drawing. Afterward, Jonathon felt quite proud and successful. He consequently remarked, "I really like this classroom because we have a lot of helpers." This example illustrates the cognitive benefits of creating a classroom environment where children of mixed ages and abilities can work together. More importantly, it demonstrates that Jonathon felt emotionally and socially supported to take risks.

Jonathon's response is typical of the helpfulness and cooperation that can develop in a multiage community of learners and shows how a child's self-esteem can be elevated. Time after time we observe children teaching and working with each other. We discover that children can often express an understanding or articulate a strategy for writing, for example, more clearly and effectively than we can.

## Authentic and child-centered assessment and evaluation

A commitment to teaching and caring for the individual child implies getting to know the child in useful, informative ways. The goal of assessment in our classrooms is twofold: to be able to "paint a picture" of how the child is progressing in different areas of development and to inform our instructional practice.

Teachers in our county developed assessment procedures that are used at the beginning of the year and then on an ongoing basis that allow us to get to know the child as a learner. This information—largely qualitative and gathered, as much as possible, informally in the context of the child's work and play—informs our practice.

The child and her parents benefit from authentic assessment. Children can view their progress concretely by looking back at their portfolios and records and can be involved in evaluating their own learning. At any time, but especially at conferences, parents can view samples of work and hear anecdotes about the progress their child has made. The parent is asked to participate in a "negotiated" conference, where they

*IN A SENSE, DEVELOPMENTALLY APPROPRIATE PRACTICE HAS BEGUN TO "TRICKLE UP" THE GRADES: CHILDREN ARE BEING ACCEPTED FOR WHO THEY ARE AS PEOPLE AND AS LEARNERS AND ARE BEING CHALLENGED TO MOVE FORWARD FROM WHERE THEY ARE. NO LONGER ARE THEY BEING ASKED TO FIT THE CURRICULUM OR THE BASAL READER.*

share their view of their child's progress, along with the teacher's ideas, and then the parent and teacher set goals for the child's learning and development for a specified period of time.

Much of the work on assessment and evaluation in our school system has been done in the area of literacy development. A literacy assessment package that challenges teachers to be "kidwatchers" is used beginning in kindergarten. Teachers and children work together to develop a portfolio that follows the child through school and documents progress in literacy development. Literacy knowledge is measured—alphabet; sense of word; concepts of print (Clay, 1979); spelling stages; holistic scoring of writing samples; sight vocabulary; samples of books read; strategies used when reading; and a qualitative, descriptive rating of the attitude, experience, and independence of the child in reading and writing (to name a few areas).

One of the useful assessment tools that we use is the Informal Spelling Inventory. This instrument, drawing on research about the development of children's word knowledge, spelling development, and "invented spelling," is a qualitative way to measure a child's spelling development and is extremely useful as a diagnostic procedure. Three or four times a year, each child is asked to try to spell 20 words that are grade-level designated or that are in lists that get gradually more difficult based on within-word patterns. For example, a first grader or 6-year-old might progress in spelling the word SLIDE through the following stages:

S >>>>> SD >>>>> SID >>>>> SLIED >>>>> SLIDE

Last year 6-year-old Alicia and her parents witnessed this kind of progress in spelling development. In the fall she spelled BLACK as "BK," and by spring she was closely approximating the correct spelling as "BLAK." This reflected an increase not only in her spelling knowledge but also in her reading and writing ability.

This type of assessment tool, used in conjunction with authentic spelling observed in writing samples, is

useful to the teacher in that it monitors the progress the child is making and informs practice. It also allows the child and his parents to be a part of the ongoing process of monitoring literacy development. All involved can celebrate the child's achievement.

## Timely and appropriate intervention/ interaction

Intervention has become a key word in our vocabulary as teachers. We use the term *intervention* in two ways. First, in a broad sense, it refers to moments during the school day when we intervene—also called *scaffolding*—in a learning situation and interact with an individual child or a small group of children. Through our process of change toward a more developmentally appropriate learning environment, we have not taken the verb "to teach" out of the classroom, but we have redefined what it means "to teach" young children in a child-centered manner. We believe that there is more teaching going on in our classrooms than in more traditional, curriculum-driven schools; it just looks different! "To teach" a child becomes "to facilitate" a learning situation or "to respond to" a child within the context of a particular task.

When a child is ready, the teacher intervenes (mediates or scaffolds) and coaches her to develop more efficient problem-solving strategies. For example, Laura was trying to solve a series of addition problems, a self-initiated activity during the free-choice worktime at the beginning of the day. When she came to the algorithm 2+7=_, she went to her number line, started at the number 2, and then proceeded to add 7 on top. She came up with the correct answer and she clearly understood the procedure; she has had lots of experience adding two numbers up to 10 using unifix cubes (concrete materials). On this day, though, it was clear that she was ready to learn that it's easier to add a small number to a bigger number. So I showed her the strategy of looking for the bigger number first and adding on the smaller number (essentially that 7+2 is the same problem as 2+7). With some practice she understood, and she now performs simple addition algorithms with much greater efficiency. In the general sense, intervention is knowing what the child is ready for, building on what he can do, and taking advantage of "teachable moments" throughout the daily life of the developmentally appropriate classroom.

Intervention is also the term we use to describe the extra staff resources that we provide for children who for one reason or another are not making adequate progress. This extra attention most often targets literacy development in children from homes where literacy is not practiced or emphasized or children who score in the low quartile on a variety of mostly informal qualitative measures. This intervention ranges from special education assistance to Chapter I services in the classrooms to extra time focusing on literacy with the classroom teacher.

Perhaps the most useful strategies we have found come from the work of the New Zealander, Marie Clay, whose research and techniques ask the teacher to identify the child's literacy strengths and then build on those strengths through intervention and instruction. Clay, like other current researchers in reading and writing, no longer debates the old question, Is it phonics or sight words or whole language? She offers the teacher a variety of ways to help the child develop a repertoire of strategies and cuing systems (semantic, syntactic, grapho-phonemic, and configuration clues) to decode and gain meaning from text. Children are challenged to develop a wide range of strategies and to learn to articulate those strategies so that they become automatic or habitual.

## Whole language arts: The writing process and literature-based reading

The teaching and learning of literacy—reading and writing—is a cornerstone of primary school. In traditional, basal-driven schools, reading is paramount. When children are "below grade level" in reading, they are seen as deficient and are often retained. In reality, even though such programs are filled with "reading" activities, research shows that most children read very little in or out of school (National Academy of Education, National Institute of Education, & Center for the Study of Reading, 1985). In many classrooms children spend months or even years getting "ready" to read—filling out worksheets, copying from the board, and learning their "sounds" in meaningless, isolated drills.

In our opinion the most significant educational trend to come along in decades, and the practice that is possibly the most "developmentally appropriate," is the whole language movement. Whole language helps children acquire literacy knowledge and skills in more meaningful and natural ways. Children are viewed as competent and able to learn written language in much the same way they learned to speak—by focusing on meaning and communication, both receptive and expressive.

The language arts permeate our classroom communities. During early morning worktime, children and teachers often choose to write and read for a variety of purposes, and we speak and listen to each other throughout the day. Productive talk is encouraged at a level of noise that allows others to think and work. Often we read aloud to the children from a variety of genres twice or even three times a day. Nonfiction books related to our units of study have a special place in the classroom. Poetry and songs on charts and in individual music and poetry collections play an important part in our day. Our classroom libraries, which the children may use at any time, are filled with a selection of trade books, organized in general order of difficulty and by theme, author, or genre.

Perhaps the richest time of the day is "Reader's and Writer's Workshop," an hour that is devoted to literacy development. During this workshop we implement many of the ideas of authors and researchers such as Calkins, Graves, Harste, and Hansen. After a brief minilesson or "huddle," drawing from the work of the children, from good-quality children's literature, or from the objectives we are asked to teach, the children write and read about topics of their choice and for a variety of purposes. The children read books of different genres at their instructional level chosen from our library. Author and reader talk fills the classroom. A time for celebration and sharing is reserved daily at the end of the workshop to highlight children's successes. The goal is to develop reading and writing ability while at the same time developing the idea that "I am one who writes and reads" (Calkins, 1986).

Skills in reading and writing are taught mostly in context. Children are challenged to spell as best they can (in invented spellings); however, the understood goal is that we all strive to become more correct spellers. Children are challenged to hear letters in new words and to master beginning-level spelling words. Around the age of 8, varying with the individual, children begin more structured word-study activities

© Jean-Claude Lejeune

that help them to discover and master the within-word patterns of conventional spelling.

One highly useful technique for teaching skills in a more meaningful way involves small groups or the whole class in "sentence problem solving." We write two or three sentences with skill errors (often taken from familiar songs, poems, books, or the children's writing). Then the group tries to solve the problems by describing and correcting what we see wrong in the sentence. The children work cooperatively to find problems with conventions of print, such as spacing, letter formation, use of upper- and lower-case letters, spelling, and punctuation.

Just as children more effectively learn to steer, pedal, and brake while actually riding a bike, children best learn to refine their abilities in the actual context of meaningful reading and writing. The goals of our language arts curriculum are to facilitate the development of skilled and strategic readers, writers, listeners, and speakers who understand why, when, and how to meaningfully apply skills to the processes of language.

## Manipulative-based math and discovery science

The "subjects" of math and science are often separated in the curriculum, taught at different times during the day, and driven by grade-level texts and curriculum developed in places far removed from the learners. When this occurs children's natural constructive thinking and interest in the scientific process is thwarted; children quickly learn that science and math are not so much a way of thinking and looking at the world, but a series of facts and ideas to be memorized and displayed for the teacher to fulfill a list of isolated objectives.

Children are naturally inquisitive about their world and discover the patterns in their world and in their environment through active experimentation. Children often come to school as young scientists, ready to apply what they already know and to test more hypotheses about the scientific world and their mathematical understandings. Kamii's research with children in the area of mathematics (1985, 1989) demonstrates that young children invent (construct) their own understandings and strategies to solve meaningful problems. Our job as teachers and facilitators is to replicate real-world problems in the classroom for children to solve and to take advantage of children's inquisitive nature.

Although we often teach and learn using an integrated approach, identifying large umbrella themes from the areas of science, social studies, language, and health, we also do minifocus units on ideas that bridge the often-separated areas of math and science. We

discovered that many of the objectives in these two areas are related and similar and can be woven into the classroom experience during thematic work and play.

While we are involved in a health and social studies unit about ourselves and our place in our family, school, and community, for example, we study the mathematical concept of measurement. The children measure themselves in a variety of ways, using non-standard units (unifix cubes and hands, for example), and then begin to explore the use of inches and centimeters. The children also identify objects in the classroom to measure in length, and then go about measuring, writing down their data, and reporting back to the group. Pairs or small groups (heterogeneously formed) work well because a more capable child can share her strategies and methods with the other children.

In addition to challenging children to become involved in this type of integrated, meaningful science and math activity, we have found it necessary to build in opportunities for children to become competent with written algorithms in beginning addition and subtraction. They progress from concrete, hands-on ways of representing addition and subtraction (beans, counting chips, unifix cubes), to a semiconcrete experience with a number line, and then finally to more abstract number operations. All the while we are challenging them to articulate their strategies, asking them, "How did you solve that problem?" or "Tell us how you thought about that." Errors are seen as opportunities for learning, and the community of learners benefits when children share their strategies and the results of their thinking.

## A thematic/unit/project approach to teaching/ learning

Each year we ask ourselves how we can cluster the objectives we are asked to teach in meaningful ways for our children while at the same time allowing the children's voices—their needs, interests, and abilities—to influence our curriculum planning. We sketch out units of study—taking into account input from the children—that we believe would provide meaningful context and content for children in rural central Virginia.

We have found Katz and Chard's (1989) "project approach" very useful for the purpose of "engaging children's minds." We believe that children must be guided to be engaged in meaningful, challenging learning activities, and that learning cannot be left up to haphazard, random, or completely child-initiated work and play. We ask children to "plug into" themes and involve them in creating challenging learning activities and projects that allow them to dwell on a topic, to come at the larger umbrella theme we are studying from their own meaningful angle.

For example, during the winter months we often spend three to four weeks or so involved in a unit of study about "Healthy Habits." This theme is drawn primarily from the areas of health and science, although it integrates other areas of the curriculum, such as language arts, math, social studies, and drama. This unit provides the children an opportunity to explore the concepts of health and "wellness" and to develop their understandings of what they can do to take care of themselves. The teachers and children plan a variety of activities that help us learn to eat well, get plenty of exercise, take care of ourselves, and develop positive self-images.

At the beginning of our study, we discuss as a team what objectives in the curriculum could be covered by the unit. We brainstorm resources, activities, and materials that might assist us in implementation. Then we begin the unit by brainstorming with the children what they know about the topic and what they understand to be the difference between "good" and "bad" habits, citing examples from home, the neighborhood, and school. Once we understand the difference and have explored each person's personal meaning, we search for ways that we can practice being happy and healthy individuals (create "healthy habits").

What kinds of activities and projects have we negotiated with our children? The children enjoy measuring each other in nonstandard units (one of our objectives that the school district asks us to cover). The children measure each other's height with unifix cubes, for example, and then cooperatively construct a chart to record the data. After the chart is complete, the children report to the class what they have found, and we discuss who is tallest, who is shortest, which numbers are more common, and so forth. Many children also enjoy drawing and writing books that reflect what they are learning. When we are done with our study, they have a piece of writing to share with others about what they've learned.

As another project, the children keep a journal (with their parent's assistance) of the foods they eat at home for a few days, and then we sort and classify the foods into the four basic food groups. We write books together, read quality literature about nutrition, and allow children to angle off with a particular idea that will allow them to become meaningfully engaged.

Throughout the unit of study we daily fix a "healthy snack" in small groups during the morning free-choice work time. Heterogeneous small groups of children plan the snacks, negotiate the recipes, sometimes go to the store to shop for the ingredients, fix the food, serve it to the other children, and then explain why they believe that the food is healthy. This type of activity clearly reflects all curricular areas and involves the children in active, relevant ways. The

*CHILDREN SEE TEACHING AND LEARNING EXPERIENCES AS MEANING-MAKING ADVENTURES, IN WHICH THEY DEVELOP OWNERSHIP, PRIDE, AND THE KNOWLEDGE THAT LEARNING IS NOT SOMETHING WE DO ONLY AT SCHOOL BUT A CHOICE THAT CAN LAST A LIFETIME.*

children interact socially as they plan, negotiate, cook, serve, and articulate their reasons for choosing certain foods. The teacher guides, coaches, negotiates, and facilitates.

Daily, and at the end of the unit of study, we check in with one another, share and celebrate what we are learning, and compare our new knowledge to what we shared at the beginning of the unit.

What we have learned is that every year the units we teach are different, depending on what the children bring to them, the stories they have to tell, and how much interest they show. A unit of study that we think might last four to six weeks might last only two or three if the children do not seem to be interested, or it might last eight weeks if they begin to dwell in their explorations and projects.

We have also discovered that it is important to strike a balance between teacher-directed activities and child-initiated projects, both work and play. Children can often design and carry out valuable "learning choices" (as we call them). We continually ask ourselves whether or not the project the child or we have designed is a challenging activity, and this, of course, is a question that has to be asked for each individual child. If the learning choice is not challenging, we negotiate with the child to find something else that we can both agree is challenging. Children quickly appreciate that we are together in school to learn, and with practice and guidance they develop the ability to challenge themselves as learners.

The success of all of these practices is based on getting to know the child, becoming "kidwatchers" (Goodman, Goodman, & Hood, 1989). When we assess, observe, and get to know the strengths, interests, needs, and passions of the children we teach, then we can design and negotiate useful and challenging learning experiences that both help the child move along the learning continuum related to the objectives of the curriculum and identify and carry out activities that are important to the child. Children then see teaching and learning experiences as meaning-making adventures, in which they develop ownership, pride, and the knowledge that learning is not something we do only at school but a choice that can last a lifetime.

# Summary

What have we learned and discovered as we and our children have attempted to implement developmentally appropriate curriculum, teaching, and assessment practices? Here is a summary of our major discoveries:

• The concept of developmentally appropriate practice reflects the crystallization of much research and theory on how young children best learn; however, it is important to remember that this body of knowledge changes over time and should always be thought of as fluid and formative. Each person, school, and school system should examine their own theoretical perspective through which they view children. Only then will their practice be profoundly influenced and the lives of children in school be affected at a broader level.

• Each person, and each school staff, must go through their own process of change, learning, and discovery to determine what developmentally appropriate practice means to them and how it can be implemented in their classroom and community. Parents are an important part of the process and must be involved if they are to buy into this new vision of the way schooling should look. Mistakes are learning opportunities for adults, just as they can be for children. Risk taking must be encouraged, and results should not be judged too quickly. The results of change take time to be effective, profound, and long lasting.

• The role of the teacher must be examined and re-thought. Some descriptors that we use are listener, kidwatcher, facilitator, researcher, decision maker, guide, coach, and, yes, teacher. We believe that the verb "to teach" should not be taken out of the picture; after all, we are the ones who have been trained to do all of the things it takes to help children learn. We should never see our role as finite or fixed. Teaching in child-centered ways is much more challenging, thoughtful, creative, and even fun.

• Teachers who come from more traditional models can discover that sound instructional strategies and practices (some of which are described in this chapter) are based on research and are developmentally appropriate. Teachers cannot be expected to invent the curriculum every day, nor can they be expected to construct a new method of teaching without assistance. Teachers need and deserve staff development that is responsive (developmentally appropriate) to their needs; the materials to implement more experience-based education; and support from administrators, who are often in decision-making positions to influence the way classrooms look.

• Finally, developmentally appropriate practice, curriculum, and assessment are about trusting and challenging children—trusting children who naturally are scientists, language learners and users, thinkers, mathematicians, and people who take joy and pride in learning and accomplishment; and challenging children—and ourselves—to reach our many potentials.

## References

Bredekamp, S. (Ed.). (1987). *Developmentally appropriate practice in early childhood programs serving children from birth through age 8* (rev. ed.). Washington, DC: NAEYC.

Calkins, L.M. (1986). *The art of teaching writing.* Portsmouth, NH: Heinemann.

Clay, M. (1979). *The early detection of reading difficulties.* Portsmouth, NH: Heinemann.

Goodlad, J.R. (1987). *The non-graded elementary school* (2nd ed.). New York: Teachers College Press.

Goodman, K., Goodman, Y., & Hood, W. (1989). *The whole language evaluation book.* Portsmouth, NH: Heinemann.

Kamii, C. (1985). *Young children reinvent arithmetic: Implications of Piaget's theory.* New York: Teachers College Press.

Kamii, C. (1989). *Young children continue to reinvent arithmetic: 2nd grade.* New York: Teachers College Press.

Katz, L., & Chard, S.C. (1989). *Engaging children's minds: The project approach.* Norwood, NJ: Ablex.

National Academy of Education, National Institute of Education, & Center for the Study of Reading. (1985). *Becoming a nation of readers: The report of the Commission on Reading.* Washington, DC: National Institute of Education.

National Association for the Education of Young Children & National Association of Early Childhood Specialists in State Departments of Education. (1991). Position statement on guidelines for appropriate curriculum content and assessment of children ages 3 through 8. *Young Children, 46*(3), 21–37.

National Association of State Boards of Education. (1988). *Right from the start: The report of the NASBE Task Force on Early Childhood Education.* Alexandria, VA: NASBE.

# The Process of Change: 12
# The Redwood City Story

*Linda Espinosa*

This book presents a new vision of early education and schooling that requires a fundamental shift in our thinking about the role of school in the lives of young children. The Curriculum and Assessment Guidelines of NAEYC and NAECS/SDE (pp. 9–27, this volume) clearly advocate a constructivist approach, "a model that emphasizes that learners need to be actively involved, to reflect on their learning and make inferences, and to experience cognitive conflict" (Fosnot, 1989). This approach cannot supplement but must replace the traditional model of education in which teachers tell, children listen, and knowledge is defined as an accumulation of facts. I am convinced that transforming primary education in this country from a transmission model to a model of constructivist, developmentally appropriate practices will be one of the most difficult and challenging education reforms to date. But I am equally convinced that such a transformation is essential if we wish to keep our young children's minds alive and ensure that our schools develop the productive, thinking citizens this nation needs.

Successfully changing educational practices is not a simple process, particularly when the nature of the change requires a new way of thinking. Implementing the Curriculum and Assessment Guidelines requires not only knowledge of the content of the guidelines but an understanding of the change process, *how* educational institutions change. In this chapter I will describe the events that occurred during a major reform of preschool and primary education in Redwood City School District, California. I will then discuss some of the general principles of effective educational change and relate them to our experiences in Redwood City.

Before outlining the details of our experience in Redwood City, it is important to reiterate that change is a developmental process; therefore, the concept of "developmental appropriateness" (Bredekamp, 1987) applies to the process of change in schools and programs, as well as to the development of children. As institutions move toward successful integration of new practices, they experience predictable stages of change. Just as age-referenced, normative expectations for children's development provide a general framework for understanding children's growth and learning, the predictable stages of institutional change also provide a normative perspective for understanding the developmental process of change. Just as age-appropriate practices must be adapted to what is known about each individual child, however, the unique individual characteristics of each local situation must be considered if institutional change is to be successful. As a result, planning and implementing major curriculum reform must not only apply general principles of effective educational change but also adapt to the specifics of the individual situation, such as the history, availability of resources, political realities, characteristics of personnel, and values of the community. Other districts and schools have attempted to implement such reforms (Goffin & Stegelin, 1992). Each individual situation has uniquenesses as well as generalizable aspects related to the principles of change. This balance is well expressed by Fullan (1982):

> . . . successful educational change involves two components: a theory of education relating to what should change, and a theory of change concerning how to bring about change. The problem of meaning is one of how those involved in change can come to understand what it is that should change and how that can be best accomplished. Of course, the additional problem is that the what and how interact and influence each other. (p. 4)

## The Redwood City story

Redwood City is a medium-size school district with about 8,000 students from prekindergarten through eighth grade, located midway between San Francisco and San Jose, California. The student population is 65% minority, of which 93% are Hispanic. Socioeconomically the school population is heterogeneous, with some very wealthy families and many recent immigrants from Mexico; 40% of the children are eligible for free or reduced lunch. In 1987 the Redwood City School Board, the superintendent, and other top administrative staff agreed after several years of study that the primary grades should become more "developmentally oriented" and that the knowledge of best early childhood practices should be extended into kindergarten and first grade (Hill, 1987). This decision resulted from several converging factors: the state-subsidized child development program that provides all-day child care for low-income families was in jeopardy due to financial difficulty; the district drop-out rate for minority youths was increasing; the school achievement of economically disadvantaged children was not improving; and top administrators were influenced by their review of current information about the long-term benefits of early education. A debate that began with the question of whether to continue the preschool program actually concluded with a decision to strengthen the district's commitment to the preschool program and incorporate more child-centered teaching practices in the primary grades. During the summer of 1987, I was hired as the director of primary education and child development services to manage and guide the reform.

The school board and the superintendent had devoted considerable time to discussion, debate, and review of the research before coming to this important decision. Unfortunately the site administrators, teachers, and parents who would be directly affected were not included in these discussions; therefore, the first year of implementation, 1987–88, turned out to be more difficult, divisive, and emotionally painful than anyone had anticipated. Our motto became, *You can kill a good idea with poor implementation.* In fact, I remember long discussions with the superintendent, during which we kept asking ourselves, "Why is everyone resisting this wonderful change?" Fortunately we learned from our mistakes and revised our original plans and timelines. We found it necessary to build in more time for collegial team building, parent education, and teacher support. We also requested additional funds to purchase books, manipulatives, and equipment. Grant funds provided release time for teachers to plan and develop curriculum. The surprising lesson we learned from the first year of implementation was that strong support from the top administration, combined with a clear vision, adequate resources, and a research base, are *not* guarantees that teaching practices will change. We learned that we could not overlook the need to develop ownership and foster the participation of everyone who was affected by the change.

During the first year of implementation, we tried to accomplish significant classroom change too quickly with staff who were not ready. Issues that seemed trivial to me became major points of contention, such as how to label the materials on the shelves, whether or not each child must have an individual crayon box, and where to store the unused textbooks. We realized that our probability of succeeding required a new game plan that demonstrated respect for and attention to the teachers' and parents' state of "readiness" to change.

The new two-year plan included the following:

**1.** creating a model center—the Primary Education Center—that reflects developmentally appropriate practices for children ages 3 to 7;

**2.** assigning the daily administration of the model center to the director of primary education to guarantee that the supervision and evaluation of the staff is consistent with our stated values and goals;

**3.** using the model center for training and dissemination;

**4.** acquiring additional resources to purchase materials and release time for staff for training and curriculum development;

*IMPLEMENTING THE CURRICULUM AND ASSESSMENT GUIDELINES REQUIRES NOT ONLY KNOWLEDGE OF THE CONTENT OF THE GUIDELINES BUT AN UNDERSTANDING OF THE CHANGE PROCESS, HOW EDUCATIONAL INSTITUTIONS CHANGE.*

**5.** focusing on our training and coaching support at the model center for at least two years;

**6.** developing a model curriculum guide to replace the scope-and-sequence binders previously used in the district;

**7.** developing appropriate assessment procedures to document each child's progress along the curriculum continuum; and

**8.** developing an evaluation plan to document the success of the program.

As we approached the second year, we had a clearer idea of the challenges ahead. We carefully organized small teams of teachers—preschool, kindergarten, and first grade—to develop curriculum expectations, thematic units, assessment procedures, and resource lists. We also intensified our communication efforts with parents. Most importantly the tone of the second year shifted from our "telling" the staff about how and why they should change to our stressing shared responsibility and mutual interdependence.

During this time we realized that even under the best of circumstances, when an education change is viewed as critical to the organization's central mission and is adequately supported, *change is difficult,* and that the personal and psychological dimensions of professional growth cannot be ignored. Our revised plan incorporated more time for staff team building, more

support for teachers in the classroom, and more shared decision making with all staff about the direction of the program. We also realized that we needed at least one successful example of a developmentally appropriate primary program. As a result it was necessary to reduce the amount of training and support districtwide in order to focus our resources and attention on the model site. In retrospect, this was one of our most important decisions. By concentrating on creating a successful example of what we were advocating, we demonstrated that it is possible to achieve our vision in a real school setting. We demonstrated that without relying on extraordinary outside resources or experts, we could overcome the many obstacles to change inherent in any large institution (Espinosa, 1990). At about this time our case for proceeding forward was strengthened by the publication of supportive documents at state and national levels (Bredekamp, 1987; California State Department of Education, 1988; National Association of State Boards of Education, 1988).

During the second year of implementation, it became clear that some of the teachers were not well suited to the new curriculum. From my work with other diverse groups of teachers, I am convinced that not all teachers can become competent in implementing a developmentally appropriate program (although this statement could easily apply to any teaching innovation, I believe that it is especially true of devel-

*EVEN UNDER THE BEST OF CIRCUMSTANCES, WHEN AN EDUCATION CHANGE IS VIEWED AS CRITICAL TO THE ORGANIZATION'S CENTRAL MISSION AND IS ADEQUATELY SUPPORTED, CHANGE IS DIFFICULT, AND THE PERSONAL AND PSYCHOLOGICAL DIMENSIONS OF PROFESSIONAL GROWTH CANNOT BE IGNORED.*

opmentally appropriate practices). A small percentage of teachers do not have the temperament—essential understanding of child development—or willingness to examine and reflect on their own teaching practices. Adults who have a strong need to be in control at all times and who use a fairly rigid authoritarian approach to children will not be able to accept and implement the practices we are advocating. With this realization came the need to make a few crucial staff changes. Making these tough personnel decisions made a tremendous difference in our ability to achieve schoolwide consensus and foster the competencies and creativity of teachers who were willing to work together. Deciding that some staff or even one teacher cannot continue in the program is never easy but is sometimes necessary. The procedures for making such critical changes depend on the specific conditions and policies governing personnel decisions in a program or district.

During the third year all of the elements of the program—curriculum, assessment procedures, collegial spirit, and discipline practices—came together with an energy and vitality that surprised even me. It seemed as though the prior difficulties provided the necessary disequilibrium to lead us to a higher level of understanding and a high level of mutual trust and belief in the mission of the Primary Education Center (PEC). At this point all teachers were actively developing their own integrated units, engaging the children in the performing arts, incorporating field trips, encouraging parent involvement, and designing multicultural activities to expand the program. A sense of ownership and pride developed. Several teachers have since become local "experts" and are frequently asked to provide training and workshops for other programs.

After the third year of implementation, the visionary superintendent who had been largely responsible for initiating the changes resigned, most of the central office administrators took other positions, and about half of the principals in the district changed. Obviously we needed to reaffirm the district's commitment

to and understanding of our program. One way to establish our credibility was to clearly demonstrate the effectiveness of the program with outcomes that are important to the district as a whole. Fortunately the results of a preliminary evaluation of our program are very positive.

The preliminary evaluation compared the achievement test scores at the end of second grade for the first wave of children who completed the Primary Education Center program with the scores of a comparable group of children who had received a more traditional primary program. We also analyzed the scores of children who attended the PEC for three years (preschool, kindergarten, and first grade) with those who attended for only two years (no preschool). The standardized achievement measures used were the math and language arts scores on the California Test of Basic Skills (CTBS). The results demonstrated that the PEC group's academic achievement was equal to or higher than the comparison group of children. Two of our preliminary findings were striking. While the PEC groups' basic skills—such as math computation, word attack, and phonics—were comparable to those of the comparison group, their scores on mathematical concepts and applications subtests were considerably higher. Also the achievement test scores of those children who had participated in the preschool program in addition to the kindergarten and first grade at PEC were one-half grade higher in mathematics, reading, and language arts than were the scores of the children who had not participated in the preschool. It must be emphasized that these are preliminary evaluation results of the PEC, which should be interpreted with caution. We will continue to monitor the school performance of children attending the PEC; nevertheless, these positive preliminary evaluation results are encouraging. The goals of the PEC are congruent with the development of both basic and higher order skills, as demonstrated by the scores achieved on relatively traditional achievement tests. The results might be even more favorable if more authentic, performance-based assessment measures were used, such as those advocated in the Curriculum and Assessment Guidelines.

In Redwood City School District, our current goal is to develop a dissemination plan to guide our efforts as we work with other schools and teachers in implementing developmentally appropriate practices. The real test will be if, five years from now, the PEC is still flourishing and other schools have transformed their primary classes into "worlds of wonder." Achieving this goal will depend in large part on our ability to individualize and adapt the general principles of educational change. The remainder of this chapter describes these principles of change with recommendations for implementation in specific situations.

# The process of change

Institutional change is a complex process that can only be addressed briefly here. The major dimensions to be considered in planning and implementing large-scale change are the need to create personal meaning, the types of change required, and the stages of the change process. Each of these aspects of the change process is addressed below.

## Personal meaning and change

Planning for systematic change in an early childhood program must be guided by a clear understanding of the goals and values of the institution. If we set goals for change, we must be able to articulate how these changes are central to our educational mission and how they will increase our chances of accomplishing our mission. The people responsible for implementing or advocating for the change must understand why the change is necessary, what the change "looks like," and how they can become proficient in these new practices. Real educational change occurs—or fails to occur—at the level of the individual teacher; this is especially true for the types of complex practices we are recommending that require considerable teacher knowledge and judgment.

Developmentally appropriate practices are not teacher-proof. In fact, teachers must have a deep understanding of how children learn, as well as what is important for children to learn. Teachers must therefore be encouraged in their efforts to bring personal meaning, personal values, and personal interpretation to how the change process will be implemented. Teachers must understand the need for change, agree with the philosophy and assumptions of developmentally appropriate practice, and participate in creating their own solutions.

## Types of change

A more complete discussion of types of change is available from other sources (Fullan, 1981; Fullan & Park, 1981). For our purposes, it is sufficient to emphasize that at least three dimensions of change exist in any educational reform that occurs at the level of the teacher: use of new or revised materials; use of new teaching strategies or activities; and the possible alteration of beliefs or values.

From my experience, I conclude that it is not possible for teachers to successfully implement developmentally appropriate practices without understanding and believing in the underlying pedagogical and theoretical assumptions. It may be possible, for instance, to arrange many interesting materials and allow children to make choices, but it is not possible to respond appropriately to children's questions, requests, and demands unless the teacher understands and agrees with children's need to actively experience the world and construct their own meaning from the information they obtain. At the same time, as teachers gain experience using appropriate materials and teaching strategies, their underlying beliefs about how children learn are also likely to change. In short, it is necessary to address all three types of changes—materials, strategies, and belief systems—whether simultaneously or one at a time.

## Stages of change

Educational researchers have identified three broad stages of the change process (Fullan, 1982):

1. initiation or mobilization—the process leading to the decision to select a particular educational reform;

2. implementation—the first few years of experience with a new program; and

3. institutionalization—possible incorporation of the change into the daily, ongoing life of the institution.

*Initiation.* During stage 1, initiation, an important management principle to remember is that "top-down" initiatives don't work. This aphorism became a truism in our experience in Redwood City. It is also true, however, that "bottom-up" initiatives frequently fail. To achieve fundamental change in the role of the teacher and in pedagogical practices in preschool and primary education, broad political support from the top *and* the bottom is essential during the initiation stage. Everyone who has a stake in the educational system and its outcomes must understand the nature of the change and agree with the need to initiate the change process.

---

*DEVELOPMENTALLY APPROPRIATE PRACTICES ARE NOT TEACHER-PROOF. IN FACT, TEACHERS MUST HAVE A DEEP UNDERSTANDING OF HOW CHILDREN LEARN, AS WELL AS WHAT IS IMPORTANT FOR CHILDREN TO LEARN. TEACHERS MUST THEREFORE BE ENCOURAGED IN THEIR EFFORTS TO BRING PERSONAL MEANING, PERSONAL VALUES, AND PERSONAL INTERPRETATION TO HOW THE CHANGE PROCESS WILL BE IMPLEMENTED.*

---

## CHARACTERISTICS OF EFFECTIVE STAFF DEVELOPMENT

1. Staff development is viewed as continuous and cumulative, adding up to a comprehensive whole.

2. A variety of methods are used—hands-on activities, lectures, and time for reflection.

3. Learning new skills is combined with learning the conceptual underpinnings necessary for sustained use.

4. Staff development is continually adapted to the unique needs and abilities of the participants.

5. Follow-up and ongoing support is provided in many forms, such as expert coaching, peer coaching, collegial meetings, "rap" sessions, visits to model programs, or demonstrations.

6. The staff are involved in decisions about staff development and implementation of new ideas.

7. Staff development is not "done to" anyone, but rather emerges from the perceived needs of the staff through a consensus process.

**Implementation.** Stage 2, implementation, is the technically and socially difficult task of transforming the paper plan into practice. Not surprisingly, researchers conclude that the vast majority of curricular reforms that are initiated or adopted are never, in fact, implemented in classrooms (Silberman, 1970; Fullan & Pomfret, 1977). Lack of successful implementation at the classroom level is probably due in part to the reformers' failure to see change as a developmental process. In Redwood City we were reminded that "as you do unto teachers, so they will do unto children." In trying to implement developmentally appropriate practices, we must realize that teachers are engaged in *adult* learning that will change the way they approach *children's* learning. The vision of learning articulated in the Curriculum and Assessment Guidelines, therefore, is also applicable to the adults. Teachers need to become aware of more appropriate practices (through seeing models and reading the literature), explore using more appropriate practices in their own classroom without fear of being wrong, and determine how their practice compares to the widely accepted views of the profession through experiencing mentoring and coaching and by attending professional development

activities. Only after this thorough process, in which individual teachers are allowed to construct their own understanding of the concept, can they be expected to fully utilize the new practices and make them a part of each teachers' repertoire. Successful implementation depends on never losing sight of the developmental perspective and the unique individual characteristics of the people involved.

Other factors that influence whether an educational change is successfully implemented are (1) the nature of the change—its perceived need, clarity, complexity, and practicality; (2) centralized support—the extent to which the central administration advocates for and supports the change with sufficient staff development and meaningful evaluation procedures; and (3) the unique characteristics of the local program, such as the role of the principal or administrator, relationships among teachers, and characteristics of teachers. Each of these factors is described more thoroughly elsewhere (Fullan, 1982); here I briefly address issues related to the nature of the change and discuss in more detail issues related to support and unique characteristics.

### Nature of the change

As mentioned above, the well-established educational practice of teachers telling and children passively responding is difficult to change. The concept of developmentally appropriate, constructivist education may be easier to understand theoretically than to translate into practice. Implementing developmentally appropriate practice requires adequate materials, a high degree of professionalism and commitment, and understanding of the complex process of how children learn. Obviously this is more difficult than showing everyone how to use programmed learning devices, organizing five reading groups, or implementing assertive discipline (all practices that I believe are inappropriate for young children). Understanding the deeper meaning of developmentally appropriate practices takes more time and requires that teachers internalize the values and beliefs. In short, the nature of the change we are advocating is complex. Does that mean that it is too difficult? No. Our experience in Redwood City, as well as the experience of numerous teachers and administrators throughout the country, demonstrates that the change to more developmentally appropriate practice is doable, but those educators contemplating such a reform should not underestimate what it will take to be successful.

### Centralized support

Central administrative support is critical to any successful change effort. This support must be reflected in action, as well as in rhetoric, funding priorities, and visible follow-up. Most essential are adequate staff development and teacher support as teachers learn new ways of thinking and doing.

The Developmental Studies Center (1990) in San Ramon, California, and the High/Scope Educational Research Foundation (1991) in Ypsilanti, Michigan, are two organizations that have considerable knowledge and experience about the effectiveness of various approaches to staff development. Their conclusions regarding the characteristics of effective staff development are summarized in the box on p. 164.

Obviously, successful implementation of educational reform requires resources and time—the resources to hire and train staff developers and the time to release teachers for training, planning, and interacting; for example, from our experience in Redwood City, attempting to implement developmentally appropriate practice and cooperative learning, we learned that it took two to five years to realize lasting educational change. Just as we cannot hurry children's development along by condensing their experiences, we cannot rush people and systems into premature, hasty, externally imposed changes in practice.

All educational systems are increasingly being held accountable—to their funding source, to state officials, and to the public at large. To be judged successful an educational reform must be linked to some kind of child outcome. Meaningful evaluation data that

relate to the central mission and goals of a school or program must be collected and reported. Although early childhood professionals have articulated strong opinions about appropriate assessment practices and the need to prevent abuses of testing (see assessment guidelines, pp. 22–26, this volume; Chapter 4, this volume; NAEYC, 1988), it is incumbent on us to develop appropriate, meaningful assessment and accountability procedures. Again I turn to my experience in Redwood City to support this point. When the top administrators who had initiated the change to more developmentally appropriate practices left, it was not our theories and our good intentions that protected the primary program, it was the positive results of our evaluation study.

### Characteristics of the local program

Consideration of the unique characteristics of the local program—such as the quality of staff relationships, the role of the administrator, and the strengths and weaknesses of individual teachers—is essential to successful implementation. The extent to which a school or program supports and nurtures collegiality, open communication, and mutual trust will greatly influence teachers' willingness to risk trying new teaching strategies. To create school- or program-level capacity to change from one teaching model to another, teachers and support staff must be given time to work together, to observe each other, to communally reflect on their practice, and to adapt or create local curriculum that reflects developmentally appropriate practice. Widespread use of the Curriculum and Assessment Guidelines will—it is hoped—lead to the development of better, more appropriate curriculum so that each new generation or group of teachers does not have to recreate their own curriculum, but only to adapt a curriculum appropriate to their specific group of children.

As the new ideas and practices are described and modeled, sensitivity to each teacher's personal background, existing beliefs, and need for support must be maintained. Just as we continually adapt our daily curriculum and expectations based on individual children's abilities and interests, we need to individualize our expectations for each teacher's capacity to internalize and implement new practices. All teachers need to feel successful and competent. The need to feel competent during a stressful period of learning new beliefs and behaviors is further compounded by the complexity of the change: to fully implement developmentally appropriate curriculum, a teacher must have a deep understanding of how children learn, a thorough grounding in the curricular expectations of the school and the community, sensitivity to the diverse cultures and abilities of the children, and the

self-confidence and flexibility to constantly make decisions about how to respond to the emerging dynamics of a very busy classroom. No small task!

In my work with preschool and primary teachers, I am often painfully reminded of the need to respect teachers' need for understanding and support as they struggle with the demands of changing what they do before they have had the time to internalize the beliefs underlying the approach. My failure to give teachers adequate time to come to their own understanding of what is developmentally appropriate, combined with my haste for all teachers to enthusiastically embrace my ideas, resulted in several emotionally charged sessions. I learned that I cannot impose my beliefs and desires on other teachers, but I can provide the conditions and access to knowledge that allow teachers to come to their own conclusions about the need for change and the strength to struggle with personal change.

*Institutionalization of developmentally appropriate practice.* Stage 3 of the change process is institutionalization. This is the point at which the educational reform is either continued and becomes an ongoing aspect of the institution or is discontinued or replaced by another initiative. The probability of developmentally appropriate, constructivist early education becoming institutionalized nationwide depends on our ability to influence or revise several key structural features of our educational systems. Major barriers that must be addressed are

• clinging to the practice of assigning children to grades based on age;

• the insidious school bells that divide the day into arbitrary blocks of time;

• large class sizes at the primary level, with only one teacher;

• inappropriate paper-and-pencil testing to identify children who might be gifted or in need of special services;

• large elementary schools with inadequate administrative support;

• little, if any, planning or preparation time for teachers;

• practices that isolate teachers and interfere with the development of collegial support;

• overreliance on standardized test scores as the only measure of accountability; and

• a hierarchical governance structure that provides upward mobility only by leaving the classroom.

While these institutional barriers are real, they are not insurmountable, as our work in Redwood City demonstrates. Currently it is possible to achieve significant progress when the necessary conditions exist, and certainly, individual teachers and some schools have developed exemplary programs, but the widespread implementation of developmentally appropriate practice for *all* young children will not be realized until the barriers listed above are systematically addressed on a large scale. My personal experience in one school district demonstrates that developmentally appropriate practice can be successfully integrated into a school culture and that teachers can become powerful advocates for maintaining new practices. This accomplishment took considerable time and required resources, a strong commitment from the total educational community, and the willingness of those of us who were implementing the program to be flexible, take risks, and learn from our mistakes. It is likely that there will always be isolated teachers, schools, and even school districts that will successfully institutionalize appropriate practices; however, the goal of NAEYC and NAECS/SDE is not simply to influence a few highly motivated individuals, but to bring about systemic educational change throughout the nation. Transforming schools into centers of learning for children and adults is a challenge, but it is well worth the effort.

## References

Bredekamp, S. (Ed.). (1987). *Developmentally appropriate practice in early childhood programs serving children from birth through age 8* (rev. ed.). Washington, DC: NAEYC.

California State Department of Education. (1988). *Here they come: Ready or not.* Sacramento, CA: Author.

Developmental Studies Center. (1990). *Cooperative learning implementation project staff development manual.* San Ramon, CA: Author.

Espinosa, L. (1990). One school, one program. *Educational Leadership, 20*(2), 28–30.

Fosnot, C. (1989). *Enquiring teachers, enquiring learners: A constructivist approach for teaching.* New York: Teachers College Press.

Fullan, M. (1981). School district and school personnel in knowledge utilization. In R. Lehming & M. Kane (Eds.), *Improving schools* (pp. 212–252). Beverly Hills, CA: Sage.

Fullan, M. (1982). *The meaning of educational change.* Toronto: The Ontario Institute for Studies in Education Press. (Reference for the second and current edition of this book is: Fullan, M., with Stiegelbauer, S. [1991]. *The new meaning of educational change.* New York: Teachers College Press.)

Fullan, M., & Park, P. (1981). *Curriculum implementation: A resource booklet.* Toronto: Ontario Ministry of Education.

Fullan, M., & Pomfret, A. (1977). Research on curriculum and instruction implementation. *Review of Educational Research, 47*(1), 335–397.

Goffin, S., & Stegelin, D. (Eds.). (1992). *Changing kindergartens.* Washington, DC: NAEYC.

High/Scope Educational Research Foundation. (1991, Winter). *High/ Scope Resource.* Ypsilanti, MI: Author.

Hill, K. (1987). *Intensifying early childhood education in the Redwood City School District.* Redwood City, CA: Redwood City School District. (ERIC Document Reproduction Service No. PS 017 527)

National Association for the Education of Young Children. (1988). Position statement on standardized testing of young children 3 through 8 years of age. *Young Children, 43*(3), 42–47.

National Association of State Boards of Education. (1988). *Right from the start.* Alexandria, VA: Author.

Silberman, C. (1970). *Crisis in the classroom.* New York: Vintage Books.

# Recommended Resources

*Following are resources, in addition to the references cited in each chapter, that were recommended by various contributors to this volume as helpful in developing and implementing the Curriculum and Assessment Guidelines. Harriet Egertson and Tynette Hills assisted in the compilation of this bibliography.*

American Association of School Administrators. (1989). *Testing: Where we stand.* Arlington, VA: Author. (ASA No. 021–00253)

American Association of School Administrators. (1991). *Transforming primary schools to improve student learning: Philosophy and strategies for developmentally appropriate education* (Audio Workshop Professional Development Series). Arlington, VA: Author.

Bank Street College. (in press). *Explorations with young children: A curriculum guide from Bank Street College.* New York: Author.

Beaty, J. (1990). *Observing development of the young child* (2nd ed.). Columbus, OH: Merrill.

Belanoff, P., & Dickson, M. (Eds.). (1991). *Portfolios: Process and product.* Portsmouth, NH: Boynton-Cook.

Bertrand, A., & Cebula, J. (1980). *Tests, measurement, and evaluation: A developmental approach.* Reading, MA: Addison-Wesley.

Blackwell, F., & Hohmann, C. (1991). *High/Scope K–3 curriculum series: Science.* Ypsilanti, MI: The High/Scope Press.

Brandt, R.S. (1988). *The content of the curriculum. 1988 ASCD Yearbook.* Alexandria, VA: Association for Supervision and Curriculum Development.

British Columbia Ministry of Education. (1990). *Primary program foundation document.* Victoria, BC: Author.

British Columbia Ministry of Education. (1990). *Primary program resource document.* Victoria, BC: Author.

British Columbia Ministry of Education. (1991). *Supporting learning: Understanding and assessing the progress of children in the primary grades. A resource for parents and teachers.* Victoria, BC: Author.

Burton, L. (1991). *Joy in learning: Making it happen in early childhood classes.* Washington, DC: National Education Association.

Calkins, L.M. (1991). *Living between the lines.* Portsmouth, NH: Heinemann.

Clay, M.M. (1982). *Observing young readers.* Exeter, NH: Heinemann.

Connecticut State Department of Education. (1990). *The teacher's ongoing role in creating a developmentally appropriate early childhood program: A self-study process for teachers of children ages 5–8.* Hartford, CT: Author.

Cowles, M., & Aldridge, J. (1992). *Activity-oriented classrooms.* Washington, DC: National Education Association.

Derman-Sparks, L., & the A.B.C. Task Force. (1989). *Anti-bias curriculum: Tools for empowering young children.* Washington, DC: NAEYC.

DeVries, R., & Kohlberg, L. (1990). *Constructivist early education: Overview and comparison with other programs.* Washington, DC: NAEYC.

Dewey, J. (1938). *Experience and education.* New York: Macmillan.

Dodge, D.T., & Colker, L.J. (1992). *The creative curriculum for early childhood* (3rd ed.). Washington, DC: Teaching Strategies.

Driscoll, J., & Confrey, J. (Eds.). (1986). *Teaching mathematics: Strategies that work.* Portsmouth, NH: Heinemann.

Faddis, B. (1991). *Alternative program evaluation ideas for early childhood education programs.* Portland, OR: Northwest Regional Educational Laboratory.

Fogarty, R. (1991). *How to integrate the curriculum.* Palatine, IL: Skylight.

Forman, G.E., & Kuschner, D.S. (1983). *The child's construction of knowledge: Piaget for teaching children.* Washington, DC: NAEYC.

Fromberg, D.P. (1989). Kindergarten: Current circumstances affecting curriculum. In F.O. Rust & L.R. Williams (Eds.), *The care and education of young children* (pp. 56–67). New York: Teachers College Press.

Gamberg, R., Kwak, W., Hutchings, M., Altheim, J., & Edwards, G. (1988). *Learning and loving it: Theme studies in the classroom.* Portsmouth, NH: Heinemann.

Gentry, J.R. (1987). *SPEL is a four-letter word.* Portsmouth, NH: Heinemann.

Gnezda, M.T., Garduque, L., & Schultz, T. (Eds.). (1991). *Improving instruction and assessment in early childhood education: Summary of a workshop series.* National Forum on the Future of Children and Families. Washington, DC: National Academy Press.

Goffin, S.G., & Stegelin, D.A. (Eds.). (1992). *Changing kindergartens: Four success stories.* Washington, DC: NAEYC.

Goodman, K. (1986). *What's the whole in whole language?* Portsmouth, NH: Heinemann.

Goodman, K., Bird, L., & Goodman, Y. (1992). *The whole language catalog: Supplement on authentic assessment.* New York: Macmillan/McGraw-Hill.

Gordon, A., & Browne, K. (1985). *Beginnings and beyond: Foundations in early childhood education.* Albany, NY: Delmar.

Grace, C., & Shores, E.F. (1991). *The portfolio and its use: Developmentally appropriate assessment of young children.* Little Rock, AR: Southern Association on Children Under Six.

Graves, D. (1982). *Writing: Teachers and children at work.* Portsmouth, NH: Heinemann.

Graves, D. (1991). *Build a literate classroom.* Portsmouth, NH: Heinemann.

Gredler, G.R. (1992). *School readiness: Assessment and educational issues.* Brandon, VT: Clinical Psychology Publishing Co.

Gullo, D.F. (1992). *Developmentally appropriate teaching in early childhood.* Washington, DC: National Education Association.

Hancock, J., & Hill, S. (Eds.). (1988). *Literature-based reading programs at work.* Portsmouth, NH: Heinemann.

Hansen, J. (1987). *When writers read.* Portsmouth, NH: Heinemann.

Harste, J.C. (1988). *Creating classrooms for authors: The reading-writing connection.* Portsmouth, NH: Heinemann.

Hatano, G., & Inagaki, K. (1983). *Two courses of expertise.* Paper reprinted from the annual report of the Research and Clinical Center for Child Development, Hokkaido University, Sapporo, Japan.

Haugland, S., & Shade, D. (1990). *Developmental evaluations of software for young children.* New York: Delmar.

Hendrick, J. (1986). *Total learning: Curriculum for the young child.* Columbus, OH: Merrill.

Hidi, S. (1990). Interest and its contribution as a mental resource for learning. *Review of Educational Research, 60*(4), 549–571.

Hildebrand, V. (1986). *Introduction to early childhood education.* New York: Macmillan.

Hildebrand, V. (1990). *Guiding young children.* New York: Macmillan.

Hohmann, C. (1991). *High/Scope K–3 curriculum series: Mathematics.* Ypsilanti, MI: The High/Scope Press.

Jacobs, H.H. (1989). *Interdisciplinary curriculum: Design and implementation.* Alexandria, VA: Association for Supervision and Curriculum Development.

Jaggar, A., & Smith-Burke, M.T. (1985). *Observing the language learner.* Newark, DE: International Reading Association.

Jardine, D.W. (1990). "To dwell with a boundless heart": On the integrated curriculum and the recovery of the earth. *Journal of Curriculum and Supervision, 5*(2), 107–119.

Jervis, K., & Montag, C. (Eds.). (1991). *Progressive education for the 1990s: Transforming practice.* New York: Teachers College Press.

Kamii, C. (1985). Leading primary education toward excellence: Beyond worksheets and drill. *Young Children, 40*(6), 3–9.

Kamii, C., Manning, M., & Manning, G. (Eds.). (1991). *Early literacy: A constructivist foundation for whole language.* Washington, DC: National Education Association.

Katz, L., Evangelou, D., & Hartman, J.A. (1990). *The case for mixed-age grouping in early education.* Washington, DC: NAEYC.

Kostelnik, M.J. (1992). Myths associated with developmentally appropriate programs. *Young Children, 47*(4), 17–23.

Kostelnik, M., Soderman, A.K., & Whiren, A.P. (in press). *A practical guide to developmentally appropriate practice in early childhood programs serving children ages three to eight.* Columbus, OH: Charles Merrill.

Krechevsky, M. (1991). Project Spectrum: An innovative assessment alternative. *Educational Leadership, 48*(5), 43–48.

Krogh, S. (1990). *The integrated early childhood curriculum.* Highstown, NJ: McGraw-Hill.

Labinowicz, E. (1985). *Learning from children: New beginnings for teaching mathematical thinking—A Piagetian approach.* Menlo Park, CA: Addison-Wesley.

Langhorst, B.H. (1989). *Assessment in early childhood education: A consumer's guide.* Portland, OR: Northwest Regional Educational Laboratory.

Leigh, C., et al. (1990). *Primary guide for instructional planning.* Jackson, MS: Early Childhood Leadership Institute, Mississippi University.

Maehr, J. (1991). *High/Scope K–3 Curriculum Series: Language and literacy.* Ypsilanti, MI: The High/Scope Press.

Meisels, S., & Steele, D. (1991). *The early childhood portfolio collection process.* Ann Arbor, MI: University of Michigan Center for Human Growth and Development.

Minnesota Department of Education. (1990). *Model learner outcomes for early childhood education programs, birth to 9 years.* St. Paul, MN: Author.

Murphy, D., & Goffin, S. (Eds.). (1992). *Understanding the possibilities: A curriculum guide for Project Construct.* Columbia, MO: Center for Educational Assessment, University of Missouri–Columbia.

National Association for the Education of Young Children & National Association of Early Childhood Specialists in State Departments of Education. (1991). Position statement on guidelines for appropriate curriculum content and assessment of children ages 3 through 8. *Young Children, 46*(3), 21–37.

National Association of State Boards of Education. (1991). Caring communities: Report of the National Task Force on School Readiness. Alexandria, VA: Author.

New, R. (1990). *Projects and provocations: Curriculum ideas from Reggio Emilia, Italy.* Unpublished paper.

North Central Regional Educational Laboratory & The PBS Elementary/Secondary Service. (1992). *Schools that work: The research advantage—Meeting children's needs* (fifth of an eight-part video conference series, with guidebook available). Oakbrook, IL: NCREL. (This program features David Burchfield's classroom [see Chapter 11] and the Primary Education Center in Redwood City, California [see Chapter 12].)

Nunnelley, J.C. (1990). Beyond turkeys, Santas, snowmen, and hearts: How to plan innovative curriculum themes. *Young Children, 46*(1), 24–29.

Pattillo, J., & Vaughan, E. (1992). *Learning centers for child-centered classrooms.* Washington, DC: National Education Association.

Perrone, V. (1991). On standardized testing: A position paper of the Association for Childhood Education International. *Childhood Education, 67*(3), 131–142.

Piaget, J. (1954). *The construction of reality in the child.* New York: Ballantine Books.

Raines, S.C., & Canady, R.J. (1989). *Story s-t-r-e-t-c-h-e-r-s: Activities to expand children's favorite books.* Mt. Rainier, MD: Gryphon House.

Resnick, L.B., & Klopfer, L.E. (Eds.). *Toward the thinking curriculum: Current cognitive research. 1989 ASCD yearbook.* Alexandria, VA: Association for Supervision and Curriculum Development.

Richardson, K. (1984). *Developing number concepts using unifix cubes.* Menlo Park, CA: Addison-Wesley.

Schickedanz, J. (1986). *More than the ABCs: The early stages of reading and writing.* Washington, DC: NAEYC.

Schweinhart, L.J. (1987, Spring/Summer). Child-initiated activity: How important it is in early childhood education. *High/Scope Resource, 1*, 6–10.

Schweinhart, L.J. (1988). *A school administrator's guide to early childhood programs.* Ypsilanti, MI: The High/Scope Press.

Schweinhart, L.J., & McNair, S. (1991). *The new child observation record.* Ypsilanti, MI: High/Scope Educational Research Foundation.

Schweinhart, L.J., & Weikart, D.P. (1988). Education for young children living in poverty: Child-initiated learning or teacher-directed instruction? *The Elementary School Journal, 89*(2), 213–225.

Schweinhart, L.J., Weikart, D.P., & Larner, M.B. (1986). Consequences of three preschool curriculum models through age 15. *Early Childhood Research Quarterly, 1*(1), 15-45.

Seefeldt, C. (Ed.). (1992). *The early childhood curriculum: A review of current research* (rev. ed.). New York: Teachers College Press.

Seefeldt, C., & Barbour, N. (1990). *Early childhood education: An introduction.* Columbus, OH: Merrill.

Shepard, L.A. (1989). Why we need better assessments. *Educational Leadership, 46*(7), 4–9.

Shepard, L.A., & Smith, M.L. (1989). *Flunking grades: Research and policies on retention.* London: The Falmer Press.

Sherwood, E.A., Williams, R.A., & Rockwell, R.E. (1990). *More mudpies to magnets: Science for young children.* Mt. Rainier, MD: Gryphon House.

Shores, E. (1992). *Explorers' classrooms: Good practice for kindergarten and the primary grades.* Little Rock, AR: Southern Association on Children Under Six.

Southern Association on Children Under Six. (1991). *The portfolio and its use: Developmentally appropriate assessment of young children.* Little Rock, AR: Author.

Spodek, B. (Ed.). (1991). *Educationally appropriate kindergarten practices.* Washington, DC: National Education Association.

Spodek, B., & Saracho, O. (Eds.). (1991). *Issues in early childhood curriculum.* New York: Teachers College Press.

Strickland, D.S., & Morrow, L.M. (Eds.). (1989). *Emerging literacy: Young children learn to read and write.* Newark, DE: International Reading Association.

Tann, S. (1988). *Developing project work in the primary school.* New York: Taylor & Francis.

Tchudi, S. (1991). *Planning and assessing the curriculum in English language arts.* Alexandria, VA: Association for Supervision and Curriculum Development.

Tegano, D., Moran, J., & Sawyers, J. (1991). *Creativity in early childhood classrooms.* Washington, DC: National Education Association.

Tierney, R.J., Carter, M.A., & Desai, L.E. (1991). *Portfolio assessment in the reading-writing classroom.* Norwood, MA: Christopher-Gordon.

Vold, E. (Ed.). (1992). *Multicultural education in early childhood classrooms.* Washington, DC: National Education Association.

Vygotsky, L. (1978). *Mind in society: The development of higher psychological processes.* Cambridge, MA: Harvard University Press.

Vygotsky, L. (1986). *Thought and language* (rev. ed.). Cambridge, MA: MIT Press.

Walsh, D. (1991). How children learn. *Virginia Journal of Education, 84*, 7–11.

Wasserman, S. (1990). *Serious players in the primary grades.* New York: Teachers College Press.

Williams, R.A., Rockwell, R.E., & Sherwood, E.A. (1987). *Mudpies to magnets: A preschool science curriculum.* Mt. Rainier, MD: Gryphon House.

Wilson, J. (1989). *Equal opportunity in the primary school: New dimensions in topic work.* East Brunswick, NJ: Nichols.

Wortham, S.C. (1990). *Tests and measurement in early childhood education.* Columbus, OH: Merrill.

Young, R. (1991). *Risk-taking in learning, K–3.* Washington, DC: National Education Association.

# Information about NAEYC

## NAEYC is . . .

. . . a membership-supported organization of people committed to fostering the growth and development of children from birth through age eight. Membership is open to all who share a desire to serve and act on behalf of the needs and rights of young children.

## NAEYC provides . . .

. . . educational services and resources to adults who work with and for children, including

• *Young Children, the* journal for early childhood educators

• **Books, posters, brochures,** and **videos** to expand your knowledge and commitment to young children, with topics including infants, curriculum, research, discipline, teacher education, and parent involvement

• An **Annual Conference** that brings people from all over the country to share their expertise and advocate on behalf of children and families

• **Week of the Young Child** celebrations sponsored by NAEYC Affiliate Groups across the nation to call public attention to the needs and rights of children and families

• **Insurance plans** for individuals and programs

• **Public affairs** information for knowledgeable advocacy efforts at all levels of government and through the media

• The **National Academy of Early Childhood Programs,** a voluntary accreditation system for high-quality programs for children

• The **National Institute for Early Childhood Professional Development,** providing resources and services to improve professional preparation and development of early childhood educators

• The **Information Service,** a centralized source of information sharing, distribution, and collaboration

*For free information about membership, publications, or other NAEYC services . . .*

. . . call NAEYC at 202–232–8777 or 800–424–2460, or write to . . .

**National Association for the Education
  of Young Children
1509 16th Street, N.W.
Washington, DC 20036–1426**